"Assuredly, I say unto you, whosoever does not receive the Kingdom of God as a little child will by no means enter therein."

The Teachings of Jesus Christ

In His Own Words

Wallace M. Thomas

First Edition for Worldwide Distribution

Camino, California

Steven LeRoy Publishing
ISBN-13: 978-0615964720
ISBN-10: 0615964729

"I say unto you, he who hears my word and believes in Him who sent me has everlasting life."

"I am the way, the Truth and the Life. No one comes to the Father except through me."

The Teachings

Of

Jesus Christ

In His Own Words

Wallace M. Thomas

The words from Jesus are from God to you. Jesus came unto the world to give them to you and to all of God's children of which we are. His teachings are for all people; here on earth and in heaven, so we may grow in light, in truth, in belief and the love of Christ Jesus; for we belong to him and to God who gave us to Jesus.

Jesus claims everyone of us as his own. He blesses us to have ears to hear and eyes to read so we may know and understand his words from God, and that we will learn to love one another and love God and Jesus. Thereby we receive God's promise of oneness with them in life everlasting.

Through his grace and atoning sacrifice Christ Jesus has made this possible for each of us.

May our beliefs be strengthened and learn from Jesus and take into our lives and souls His Light of Life and cherish his teachings forever.

With God our Heavenly Father's Blessings,

Our love always,

Wally and Marilyn Thomas

Acknowledgements

I began studying the words of Christ 25 years ago when my son, Kenny, encouraged me to maintain the Sabbath day as a day of rest and study of the Gospel. As a result of that study and over a period of more than two years, I was able to complete this compilation of Christ's words and derive from His words key lessons and principles that we can apply in our own lives. It is my hope that by applying Christ's teachings to our own lives, we can draw closer to Him and learn of His and our Heavenly Father's love for us.

In putting together this work I had considerable help from others who I would like to acknowledge. First, my thanks go to my wife Marilyn, for her support and for her tireless efforts in helping create the first typewritten copy of the Words of Christ. Without her help, this work never would have come to pass and I owe much to her efforts. This new edition is a reformatted version of the original volume that Marilyn helped to create.

I would also like to thank my brother, George, for his contribution in providing the duplication service for the first edition. Through his company, Validity, George made available his copying machines and paper that resulted in more than 50 sets of ring-bound volumes that I previously provided to many family members.

Thanks also go to Amanda Petersen for her work in formatting this new edition so it could be printed in book form for the first time. Amanda's computer skills, editing abilities and professional formatting have made this work more readable and much easier to reference.*

Wally Thomas

* The preceding acknowledgements were included with the original printed and bound version of this manuscript which was presented, over the years, privately to friends and family members.

The author wishes to also acknowledge, Steven L. Monroe, grandson of the late Frank Hartwick, neighbor and friend, for his participation in editing, formatting and the publishing of this first edition for worldwide public distribution.

What Marilyn and I do is we set a day aside to read, study and learn from one chapter a week.

At the end of each chapter is a page to write your own thoughts about Jesus' teachings in that chapter. This then may become ones own spiritual journal.

By the end of the year one will have completed all fifty chapters. Then what we do is start over the next year. Each time we study his teachings they seem to be needed and very fitting at the time.

God Bless you in your path!

Our love and prayers,

Wally and Marilyn

The Teachings of Jesus Christ
In His Own Words

The Teachings, Doctrines & Commandments of
Jesus the Christ: The Christ of God

TABLE OF CONTENTS
(With Biblical Reference)

Table of Contents with Biblical Reference

Table of Contents with Biblical Reference

Table of Contents with Biblical Reference

Table of Contents with Biblical Reference

Table of Contents with Biblical Reference

Table of Contents with Biblical Reference

PART VI: FROM THE THIRD PASSOVER TO THE BEGINNING OF THE LAST PASSOVER WEEK

Table of Contents with Biblical Reference

Table of Contents with Biblical Reference

Table of Contents with Biblical Reference

Table of Contents with Biblical Reference

Table of Contents with Biblical Reference

Table of Contents with Biblical Reference

Table of Contents with Biblical Reference

Table of Contents with Biblical Reference

Table of Contents with Biblical Reference

Table of Contents with Biblical Reference

Table of Contents with Biblical Reference

Table of Contents with Biblical Reference

Table of Contents with Biblical Reference

PART IX: JESUS THE CHRIST CONTINUES HIS MISSION AFTER HIS RESURRECTION AND ASCENSION

Table of Contents with Biblical Reference

PART X: THE REVELATION

Table of Contents with Biblical Reference

NOTES

Part I - Introduction

Introduction

J esus Christ is known to most of us, and he is known among practically every land and peoples. At Christmas and Easter celebrations and observances they certainly highlight his birth, crucifixion, resurrection, and ascension.

Since historical times many scribes, teachers, and prophets have indicated or have foretold of the Christ, the Messiah. Even pre-historic peoples tell of a Creator and his son.

To know more about Christ Jesus, one must study and know his words and teachings from God, which is so important for all of God's children to know and to live them in their daily lives. Only then do we know more about Jesus the Christ because in his doctrines and teachings, he testifies of himself.

Our Heavenly Father has blessed the world with the birth, life, crucifixion, and resurrection and ascension of Jesus the Christ, our Redeemer.

"For God so loved the world that he gave his only begotten son, that whosoever believeth in him should not perish, but have everlasting life." **(John 3:16)**

"For God sent not his Son into the world to condemn the world; but that the world, through him, might be saved." **(John 3:17)**

The Teachings, Doctrines and Commandments of Jesus Christ: The Christ of God (In His own words), is written from the New Testament, King James Version, which is translated out of the original Greek, and with the former translation diligently compared and revised (words of Christ in red) in the Bible.

The book is a chronological order of events, words and teachings from his first recorded words, when about the age of twelve, and ends with his last words after his resurrection and ascension.

Part I - Introduction

In the contents, one may observe that the book contains fifty chapters separated into ten parts.

The public ministry of Jesus' life starts in Part IV and the events in each chapter are in fairly close order as they took place from one Passover to the next one, a year later. The words of Jesus are designated by italic type letters.

Great care has been given to make sure that all of Jesus' words, in each topic and event, have been diligently compared and taken from all of the gospels in the New Testament, which are Christ's words.

At the end of each chapter, every topic is listed and referenced with the book, chapter and verse to find it. Also, the doctrines in each chapter are listed.

"The Lessons We Should Learn" from each chapter, are to be studied, pondered and considered; and there is a journal page for your notes, ideas, impressions and inspirations.

A suggested study plan is to take a chapter a week and take about a year to complete the fifty chapters for there are over five hundred doctrines and commandments.

Upon your heartfelt study of Christ Jesus' life and teachings you will know more of Him and who He is. In each chapter and topic you may know Him as your: spiritual teacher, personal counselor, friend, healer, and guide to show the way to God. You may see: His grace and atoning sacrifice as your redeemer; and one who shares his glory with you as you are one with him and God. In his words, one will learn that Jesus came to teach God's children about the words of God, about being the light of the world and about everlasting life with Him and God.

Jesus says, *"He that believeth on me, believeth not on me, but on him that sent me."* **(John 12:44)**

"My doctrine is not mine, but his that sent me." **(John 7:16)**

"I am the light of the world; he that followeth me shall not walk in darkness, but shall have the light of life." **(John 8:12)**

Part I - Introduction

About his words, Jesus says, *"For I have not spoken of myself; but the Father which sent me, he gave me a commandment, which I should say and what I should speak."*

"And I know that his commandment is life everlasting; whatsoever I speak therefore, even as the father said unto me, so I speak." (John 12:49,50)

To know God and Jesus is to be blessed with their love which is one of Jesus' greatest commandments.

"A new commandment I give unto you, That ye love one another, as I have loved you, That ye also love one another."
(John 13:34)

Jesus proclaims his love of God, saying, *"But that the world may know that I love the Father; and as the Father gave me commandment, even so I do."* (John 14:31)

The words of Christ Jesus are so profoundly important in one's life today on earth and forever in everlasting life, for Jesus says, *"Heaven and Earth shall pass away, but my words shall not pass away."* (Matt 24:35)

May your quest to learn and know Jesus Christ's words bring you God's blessings of light, understanding of life, peace and love forever.

Part II – The Boy of Nazareth

1

Jesus at the Temple when
Twelve Years of Age

Jesus' mother and father saw him among the doctors and they were amazed and said to him, Son, why have you thus dealt with us?

Jesus said, *"How is it that ye sought me? wist ye not that I must be about my Father's business?"*

NOTES: Scriptures of the Topics   <u>Luke</u>

- Jesus at the Temple when
Years of Age   2:49

Doctrines and Commandments

1. I must know what my Father's work is (Luke 2:49)
2. I must do my father's work (Luke 2:49)
3. Doing my Father's work is the most important (Luke 2:49)

The Lessons We Should Learn

1. As parents or young children we should learn what our Father's work is for us and we should teach our children how to find out. (We must be as babes if we would receive Divine Light).
2. It is our daily duty to do those things that seem good in God's sight.

Part II – The Boy of Nazareth

My Thoughts About the Lessons

_____

_____

_____

_____

_____

_____

_____

_____

_____

_____

_____

_____

_____

_____

_____

_____

_____

_____

_____

_____

_____

_____

_____

_____

_____

_____

Part III – Inauguration of Christ's Public Ministry

2

Christ's Baptism in the Jordan River at Perean Bethany

Christ's Baptism in the Jordan River

Jesus came to Jordan unto John from Galilee, to be baptized of him. But John forbad him, saying, "I have need to be baptized of thee, and comest then to me?"

Jesus answered, *"Suffer it to be so now: for thus it becometh us to fulfill all righteousness."*

And Jesus, when he was baptized, went up straightway out of the water: and lo, the heavens were opened unto him, and he saw the Spirit of God descending like a dove, and lighting upon him.

And lo a voice from heaven, saying, This is my beloved Son, in whom I am well pleased.

The spirit leads Him to the Desert of Judea; Satan first tempts Him

After the baptism Jesus was lead up of the spirit unto the wilderness to be tempted of the devil. And when the tempter came to him, he said "If thou be the Son of God, command that these stones be bread."

Christ answered and said, *"It is written, Man shall not live by bread alone, but by every word that proceedeth out of the mouth of God."*

Second Temptation

Then the devil took him up into the holy city and set him on a pinnacle of the temple, and said unto him, "If thou be the Son of God, cast thyself down: for it is written, He shall give his angels charge concerning thee; and in their hands they shall bear thee up, lest at any time thou dash thy foot against a stone."

Jesus answered and said, *"It is written again, thou shalt not tempt the Lord thy God."*

Part III – Inauguration of Christ's Public Ministry

Third Temptation

Again the devil took him up into an exceeding high mountain, and sheweth him all the kingdoms of the world, and the glory of them; and saith unto him, "All these things will I give thee; if thou will fall down and worship me."

Jesus saith unto him (the devil), *"Get thee hence, Satan: for it is written, Thou shalt worship the Lord thy God, and Him only shalt thou serve."* Then the devil left him and behold, angels came and ministered unto him.

Jesus Chooses His First Disciples

John the Baptist stood with two of his disciples, and looking upon Jesus as he walked, he said, "Behold the Lamb of God!" And the two disciples heard him speak, and they followed Jesus.

Jesus saw them following and said to them, *"What seek ye?"* They said unto Jesus, "Rabbi, where dwellest thou?"

Jesus said unto them, *"Come and see."* One of the two which heard John speak, and followed him, was Andrew, Simon Peter's brother. He first finds his own brother Simon and said to him, we have found the Messias which is, being interpreted, the Christ. And he brought him to Jesus.

And when Jesus beheld him, he said, *"Thou art Simon the son of Jona: thou shalt be called Ce'-phas"* which is by interpretation a stone."

The following day Jesus went to Galilee, and findeth Philip and Jesus said to Philip, *"Follow me."* Philip findeth Nathanael.

Jesus saw Nathanael coming to him, and said to him, *"Behold an Israelite indeed, in whom is no guile!"* Nathanael saith unto him, "whence knowest thou me?"

Jesus answered him, *"Before that Philip called thee, when thou wast under the fig tree, I saw thee."* Nathanael answered and saith unto him, "Rabbi thou art the Son of God; thou art the King of Israel."

Jesus answered him, *"Because I said unto thee, I saw thee under the fig tree, believest thou? Thou shalt see greater things than these."*

Part III – Inauguration of Christ's Public Ministry

And Jesus said unto him, *"Verily, verily, I say unto you, Hereafter ye shall see heaven open, and the angels of God ascending and descending upon the Son of man."*

First Miracle at Cana, and Visit to Capernaum

Jesus and his disciples were called to a marriage in Cana of Galilee and the mother of Jesus was there.

And when they wanted wine, the mother of Jesus said to him, they have no wine.

Jesus saith unto her, *"Woman, what have I to do with thee? mine hour is not yet come."* His mother said to the servants, "Whatsoever he saith unto you, do it."

Jesus said unto them, *"Fill the waterpots with water."* And they filled them up.

And he said unto them, *"Draw out now, and bear unto the governor of the feast."*

And the ruler tasted the water that was made wine.

This beginning of miracles did Jesus in Cana of Galilee, and manifested forth his glory; and his disciples believed on him.

NOTES: Scriptures of the Topics:	Matt.	Luke	John
- Christ's Baptism in the Jordan River	3:15-17		
- The Spirit leads Jesus to Desert of Judea Where Satan tempts Him	4:4,7,10	4:4,12,8	
- Jesus chooses His first disciples			1:38,39,42,43,48,50,51
- First miracle at Cana, and visit to Capernaum			2:4,7,8

Part III – Inauguration of Christ's Public Ministry

Doctrines and Commandments

4. Jesus came to fulfill all righteousness.

5. Jesus was baptized with water by John the Baptist.

6. Satan will tempt us fervently and try to turn us away from God.

7. Man shall not live by bread alone, but by every word that proceedeth out of the mouth of God.

8. We are to worship the Lord thy God, and Him only shalt thou serve.

9. Jesus chooses his disciples. His disciples do not choose him.

10. Jesus knows us and may foretell what is in our heart.

11. God has angels in heaven.

12. Angels ascend and descend upon Jesus.

13. Jesus is the Son of Man.

The Lessons We Should Learn

1. We should recognize that Jesus is the Son of Man and that he came to fulfill all righteousness.

2. We should be baptized, giving ourselves to serve God.

3. Individually each of us must realize when we are being tempted by Satan. Christ was tempted three times while in the desert and rebuked the evil one each time. Each of us should be on guard and rebuke Satan when he tries to lead us astray.

4. We should look for every word of God and live by those words.

5. We should pray only to God and worship only him. We should not influence our prayer to God with our own personal wants and desires, but our prayer should be for healing and good health, protection from dangers and Satan's influences; also, for faith and trust in Christ Jesus knowing that he has everything known and under control with our Heavenly Father's blessings. Then, be repentant and patient to receive and manifest God's blessings.

6. When one realizes the time that Jesus spent in the desert of Judea (40 days) while he was fasting, praying and communing with God, after his baptism, the devil himself appears and tempts Jesus, three different times. How often then must Satan continually be tempting each of us and, most likely, we are unaware of it happening, since we are not in continual prayer and oneness with God and Jesus. One can certainly see how one is doing unessential things that crowd out the time that we could be doing what God has for each of us to do… doing his will.

Part III – Inauguration of Christ's Public Ministry

My Thoughts About the Lessons

_____

_____

_____

_____

_____

_____

_____

_____

_____

_____

_____

_____

_____

_____

_____

_____

_____

_____

_____

_____

_____

_____

_____

NOTES

Part IV – Public Ministry From the First Passover to the Second

3

Jesus Goes to Jerusalem for the Passover

Jesus Expells Sellers and Money Changers from Temple

The Jews' Passover was at hand, and Jesus went up to Jerusalem, and found in the temple those that sold oxen and sheep and doves and the changers of money. When he made a scourge of small cords, he drove them from the temple.

To them that sold doves, he said, *"Take these things hence; make not my Father's house an house of merchandise."*

Jesus Foretells his Resurrection Within Three Days after Death

After Jesus had cleared the temple of sellers and money chargers, the Jews asked him, What sign shewest thou unto us seeing that thou doest these things?"
Jesus answered, *"Destroy this temple, and in three days I will raise it up."*

The Jews then said, "Forty and six years was this temple in building, and wilt thou rear it up in three days?"

But he spake of the temple of his body.

When therefore he was risen from the dead, his disciples remembered that he had said this unto them.

When he was in Jerusalem at the Passover, in the feast days many believed in his name, when they saw the miracles which he did.

Part IV – Public Ministry From the First Passover to the Second

Nicodemus Interviews with Jesus at Night

While in Jerusalem a man of the Pharisees named Nicodemus came to Jesus by night.

Nicodemus said unto Jesus, "Rabbi we know that thou art a teacher come from God: for no man can do these miracles that thou doest, except God be with him.

Jesus answered, *"Verily, verily, I say unto thee, except a man be born again, he cannot see the kingdom of God."* Nicodemus asked Jesus, "How can a man be born again when he is old? Can he enter the second time into his mother's womb and be born?"

Jesus answered, *"Verily, verily, I say unto thee, Except a man be born of water and of the Spirit, he cannot enter into the kingdom of God.*

"That which is of the flesh is flesh; and that which is born of the Spirit is spirit.

"Marvel not that I said unto thee, Ye must be born again. "The wind bloweth where it listeth, and thou hearest the sound thereof, but canst not tell whence it cometh, and whither it goeth: so is everyone that is born of the Spirit."

Nicodemus answered and said unto him, "How can these things be?"

Jesus answered and said unto him, *"Art thou a master of Israel, and knowest not these things?"*

Verily, verily, I say unto thee, we speak that we do know, and testify that we have seen; and ye receive not our witness.

"If I have told you earthly things, and ye believe not, how shall ye believe, if I tell you of heavenly things?

"And no man hath ascended up to heaven, but he that came down from heaven, even the Son of man which is in heaven.

Part IV – Public Ministry From the First Passover to the Second

"And as Moses lifted up the serpent in the wilderness, even so must the Son of man be lifted up: That whosoever believeth in him should not perish, but have eternal life.

"For God so loved the world that he gave his only begotten Son, that whosoever believeth in him should not perish, but have everlasting life.

"For God sent not this Son into the world to condemn the world; but that the world through him might be saved.

"He that believeth in him is not condemned: but he that believeth not is condemned already, because he hath not believed in the name of the only begotten Son of God.

"And this is the condemnation, that light is come into the world, and men loved darkness rather than light, because their deeds were evil.

For every one that doeth evil hateth the light, neither cometh to the light, lest his deeds should be reproved.

"But he that doeth truth cometh to the light, that his deeds may be made manifest, that they are wrought in God."

Part IV – Public Ministry From the First Passover to the Second

NOTES: Scriptures on the Topics	<u>John</u>
- Jesus expels sellers and money chargers from the temple	2:16
- Jesus foretells his resurrection within three days after death	2:19
- Nicodemus interviews with Jesus at night (Jesus' testimony and discourses of Heavenly and earthly things)	3:3,5-8, 10-21
- How to see and enter the kingdom of God	3:3
- Being born again, born of the flesh and of the Spirit	3:5-8,10-12
- Ascension to heaven and everlasting life	3:12-15
- God so loved the world that he sent His son	3:16,17
- The condemnation and saving the world	3:18-21

Doctrines and Commandments

14.   Churches and Temples should be used for the word of God and to glorify God, not to serve other gods as money and merchandising.

15.   Jesus declares he can resurrect his body.

16. To enter the kingdom of God, one must be baptized of water and of the Spirit.

17.   That which is born of flesh is flesh.

18.   That which is born of Spirit is spirit.

19. For those born in the Spirit, one cannot tell when they come or where they go.

20. Christ's words are his testimony of truth and he testifies to all of us things he has seen and what he sees is the truth.

21.   No man has ascended to heaven, but he that came down from heaven.

Part IV – Public Ministry From the First Passover to the Second

22.   Whosoever believes in Christ Jesus should not perish, but have eternal life.

23.   God so loved the world that He gave His only begotten Son, that whosoever believes in him should not perish but have everlasting life.

24.   Jesus was sent into the world to save it, not to condemn it.

25.   Those who are already condemned are those who do not or have not believed in the name of Christ Jesus the Light, and have not loved the Light, but love darkness, which is their evil deeds, and their evil deeds are not destroyed.

26.   Who comes into the light is he who doeth truth, that his deeds may be made manifest, that they are wrought in God.

The Lessons We Should Learn

1.   We should see that the church we attend is glorifying God and not worldly things and beliefs.

2.   Jesus is Lord over death and has power from God to resurrect his body.

3.   If one is serious about being a member of God's kingdom, one must be baptized of water and of the Spirit.

4.   If one is confused about interpretation of the scriptures one needs to realize that every word of Jesus the Christ is his testimony and truth for He is the Light.

5.   Our deeds are our testimony of the truth and the Light or the evil deeds are our testimony of darkness and Satan.

6.   Our evil deeds should be reproved and he or she that does the truth and God's will shall come to the Light.

7.   God so loved the world that he gave his only begotten Son, so that anyone who believes in Christ Jesus should not perish but have everlasting life.

Part IV - Public Ministry From the First Passover to the Second

My Thoughts About the Lessons

_____

_____

_____

_____

_____

_____

_____

_____

_____

_____

_____

_____

_____

_____

_____

_____

_____

_____

_____

_____

_____

_____

_____

Part IV - Public Ministry From the First Passover to the Second

4

The Woman of Sychar in Samaria is Converted and Many Others

Upon leaving Jerusalem Jesus and his disciples tarried with the people in Judae and baptized them. But when the Pharisees had heard that Jesus made and baptized more disciples than John, he left Judae and departed toward Galilee.

Passing through Samaria in a town called Sychar and while sitting on the local well, a woman came to the well for water.

Jesus spoke to her, saying, *"Give me to drink."*

Then the woman inquired unto him, "how is it that thou, being a Jew, askest drink of me?"

Jesus answered, *"If thou knewest the gift of God, and who it is that saith to thee, Give me to drink, thou wouldest have asked of him, and he would have given thee living water."*

The woman asked Jesus if he was greater than Jacob who gave them the well.

Jesus answered, *"Whosoever drinketh of this water shall thirst again; But whosoever drinketh of the water that I shall give him shall never thirst; but the water that I shall give him shall be in him a well of water springing up into everlasing life."*

The woman asked Jesus for this water.

Jesus said to her, *"Go call thy husband, and come hither."* The woman answered and said, "I have no husband."

Jesus said, *"Thou hast well said, I have no husband: For thou hast had five husbands; and he whom thou now hast is not thy husband: in that saidst thou truly."*

Part IV - Public Ministry From the First Passover to the Second

The woman said to him, "Sir, I perceive that thou art a prophet."

Jesus said to her, *"Woman, believe me, the hour cometh, when ye shall neither in this mountain, nor yet at Jerusalem, worship the Father.*

"Ye worship ye know not what: we know what we worship: for salvation is of the Jews."

"But the hour cometh, and now is, when the true worshippers shall worship the Father in Spirit, and in truth; for the Father seeketh such to worship him.

"God is a spirit: and they that worship Him must worship Him in spirit and in truth."

The woman said to Jesus, "I know that Messias cometh which is called Christ: When he comes, he will tell us all things."

Jesus said unto her, *"I that speak unto thee am he."*

The woman left the well and went into the city and told others about Jesus.

Upon him came his disciples and asked Jesus to eat.

But he said to them, *"I have meat to eat that ye know not of."* His disciples asked if someone brought him food.

Jesus said unto them, *"My meat is to do the will of him that sent me, and to finish his work.*

"Say not ye that there are yet four months, and then cometh harvest? Behold I say unto you, lift up your eyes and look on the fields: for they are white already to harvest.

"And he that reapeth receiveth wages, and gathereth fruit unto life eternal: that both he that soweth and he that reapeth may rejoice together.

Part IV - Public Ministry From the First Passover to the Second

"And herein is that saying true, One soweth, and another reapeth.

"I sent you to reap that whereon ye bestowed no labour: other men laboured, and ye are entered into their labours."

Jesus stayed with them two days and many believed that He is indeed the Christ, the Saviour of the world.

NOTES: Scriptures of the Topics	John
- Gifts of God; living water and everlasting life	4:7,10.13,14
- Jesus tells woman about five husbands	4:16,18
- How to worship the Father	4:21,22
- God is a Spirit and must worship Him in Spirit and in truth	4:23,24
- Jesus declares that he is the Christ, the Messias	4:26
- Jesus instructs his disciples to convert the people	4:32,34-38

Doctrines and Commandments

27.   Christ Jesus is the way to everlasting life. Those who drink the water he gives us shall never thirst and there shall be in them a well of water springing up into everlasting life.

28.   Jesus knows the truth about us and he knows our secrets.

29.   God is a Spirit.

30.   They that worship God must worship him in spirit and in truth.

31.   There are many to be harvested and missionaries are needed.

32.   Missionaries and teachers are needed to sow and to reap.

The Lessons We Should Learn

1.   When we have problems to solve, we must place them in His hands and partake of that which He gives us.

2.   We shouldn't be tempted to do things that we wouldn't do if Christ was present. For he knows all things and our secrets.

3.   We must know that God is Spirit and must worship him in Spirit and keep his spirit in our hearts.

4.   Christ may call us to be sowers or reapers or both.

Part IV – Public Ministry from the First Passover to the Second

My Thoughts About the Lessons

_____

_____

_____

_____

_____

_____

_____

_____

_____

_____

_____

_____

_____

_____

_____

_____

_____

_____

_____

_____

_____

_____

_____

Part IV – Public Ministry from the First Passover to the Second

5

Commencement of His Public Ministry in Galilee

When Jesus had heard that John was cast into prison, He departed into Galilee; and leaving Nazareth he came and dwelt in Capernaum, which is upon the sea coast in the borders of Zabulon and Nephtalim:

That it might be fulfilled which was spoken by Esaias the prophet saying, the land of Zabulon, and the land of Nephthalim by the way of the sea, beyond Jordan, Galilee of the Gentiles; the people which sat in darkness saw great light, and to them which sat in the region and shadow of death light is sprung up.

From that time Jesus began to preach and to say,

"Repent: For the kingdom of heaven is at hand. The time is fulfilled, and the kingdom of God is at hand: repent ye, and believe the gospel."

Visiting Cana again, He heals a Noble Man's Son at Capernaum

Then when he was come into Galilee, the Galileans received him, having seen all the things that he did at Jerusalem at the feast: for they also went unto the feast.

So Jesus came again into Cana of Galilee, where he made the water wine. And there was a certain nobleman, whose son was sick at Capernaum.

When he heard that Jesus was come out of Judaea into Galilee, he went unto him and he sought him that he would come down, and heal his son; for he was at the point of death.

Then said Jesus unto him, *"Except ye see signs and wonders, ye will not believe."*

The nobleman saith unto him, sir, come down ere my child die. Jesus saith unto him, *"Go thy way: thy son liveth."*

And the man believed the word that Jesus had spoken unto him, and he went his way.

Part IV – Public Ministry from the First Passover to the Second

NOTES: Scriptures of the Topics	Matt.	Mark	John
- Commencement of His Public Ministry in Galilee	4:17	1:15	
- Healing a Noble Man's Son at Capernaum			4:48,50,53

Doctrines and Commandments

33.   The Kingdom of Heaven and God is at hand and the time is fulfilled with Christ doing the work of his Heavenly Father. (Matt. 4:17, Mk. 1:15)

34.   One must repent and believe the gospel for the Kingdom of

God and Heaven is at hand. (Matt. 4:17, Mk. 1:15)

35.   Many of us doubt unless we see signs and wonders. (Jn. 4:48)

36.   Christ heals those who believe and the healing happens at the time that the healing is done. (Jn. 4:52,53)

Lessons We Should Learn

1.   One must realize with Christ's work he has fulfilled God's plan and His Kingdom is at hand.

2.   We should analyze our thoughts, words, and deeds each day and repent our wrongdoing and we should study and believe the gospel, the word of God.

3.   With Christ's words (the truth) written in the scriptures we can trust the gospels to know they are the truth and that they are the true word of God and that God has preserved his word for us to know. Man need not to seek after signs and miracles.

4.   Man should believe that he can be healed by God as Jesus has done.

5.   Jesus tells the world and all of God's children that the Kingdom of Heaven is at hand. All born into the earth are entering this Kingdom. To manifest this kingdom, each must repent each day and believe the gospel doctrines.

Part IV – Public Ministry From the First Passover to the Second

My Thoughts About the Lessons

_____

_____

_____

_____

_____

_____

_____

_____

_____

_____

_____

_____

_____

_____

_____

_____

_____

_____

_____

_____

_____

_____

_____

NOTES

Part V – Events of Christ Jesus From His Second to His Third Passover
(His Main Galilean Ministry)

6

Jesus Does His Father's Work On the Sabbath

Jesus went to Jerusalem by a pool which is called Bethesda. There lay a great multitude of impotent folk, of blind, halt, withered, waiting for the moving of the water.

For an angel went down at a certain season into the pool, and troubled the water; whosoever then first after the troubling of the water stepped in was made whole of whatsoever disease he had.

And a certain man was there which had an infirmity for thirty-eight years.

When Jesus saw him and knew that he had been now a long time in that case, He saith unto him, *"Wilt thou be made whole?"*

The impotent man told Jesus he had trouble getting into the pool.

Jesus said to him, *"Rise, take up thy bed, and walk."* And immediately the man was made whole, and took up his bed, and walked: and it was on the Sabbath day.

The Jews therefore said unto him that was cured, "It is the Sabbath day: it is not lawful for thee to carry thy bed."

He answered them, "He that made me whole, the same said unto me, *Take up thy bed, and walk.*"

Then the Jews asked him, "What man is that which said unto thee *Take up thy bed and walk?*"

The man that was healed knew not who it was: for Jesus had conveyed himself away, a multitude being in that place.

Part V – Events of Christ Jesus From His Second to His Third Passover
(His Main Galilean Ministry)

Afterward Jesus findeth him in the temple, and said unto him, *"Behold thou art made whole: sin no more, lest a worse thing come unto thee."*

The man departed, and told the Jews that it was Jesus which had made him whole. And therefore did the Jews persecute Jesus, and sought to slay him, because he had done these things on the Sabbath day.

NOTES: Scriptures of the Topic   <u>John</u>

- Jesus does his work on the Sabbath   5: 6,8,10-14

Doctrines and Commandments

36. God can heal man through Christ Jesus and with our faith.

37. After one is healed and touched by God, the person should sin no more, or a worse affliction could develop.

Lessons We Should Learn

1. One must realize that a healing is a blessing from God.

Every attempt to seek knowledge about what caused it— improper food, lack of exercise, over eating, harboring stress, wrongdoings of any type, and actions that are counter to good health practices should be stopped—"Sin no more." If one's faith in God's blessing fades away and if there is no change in an individual's efforts towards his or her wellness, then the condition could return and worse afflictions may result.

Part V – Events of Christ Jesus From His Second to His Third Passover
(His Main Galilean Ministry)

My Thoughts About the Lessons

_____

_____

_____

_____

_____

_____

_____

_____

_____

_____

_____

_____

_____

_____

_____

_____

_____

_____

_____

_____

_____

_____

_____

NOTES

Part V – Events of Christ Jesus From His Second To His Third Passover
(His Main Galilean Ministry)

7

The Father and the Son's Relationship Told to the Jews

Jesus had healed an infirm man at the Bethesda Pool, therefore did the Jews persecute Jesus, and sought to slay him, because he had done these things on the Sabbath day.

But Jesus answered them, *"My Father worketh hitherto, and I work."*

Therefore the Jews sought the more to kill him, because he not only had broken the Sabbath, but said also that God was his father, making himself equal to God.

Then answered Jesus and said unto them,

"Verily, verily, I say unto you, The Son can do nothing of himself, but what he seeth the Father do: for what things soever he doeth, these also doeth the Son likewise.

"For the Father loveth the Son, and sheweth him all things that himself doeth: and he will shew him greater works than these, that ye may marvel.

"For as the Father raiseth up the dead, and quickeneth them; even so the Son quickeneth whom he will.

"For the Father judgeth no man, but hath committed all judgement unto the Son:

"That all men should honour the Son, even as they honour the Father. He that honoureth not the Son honoureth not the Father which hath sent him.

"Verily, verily, I say unto you, He that heareth my word, and believeth on him that sent me, hath everlasting life, and shall not come into condemnation, but is passed from death unto life.

Part V – Events of Christ Jesus From His Second To His Third Passover
(His Main Galilean Ministry)

"Verily, verily, I say unto you, the hour is coming, and now is, when the dead shall hear the voice of the Son of God: and they that hear shall live.

"For as the Father hath life in Himself; so hath he given to the Son to have life in himself;

"And hath given him authority to execute judgment also, because he is the Son of man.

"Marvel not at this: for the hour is coming, in the which all that are in the graves shall hear his voice,

"And shall come forth; they that have done good, unto the resurrection of life; and they that have done evil, unto the resurrection of damnation.

"I can of mine own self do nothing; as I hear, I judge: and my judgment is just; because I seek not mine own will, but the will of the Father which hath sent me.

"If I bear witness of myself, my witness is not true. "There is another that beareth witness of me; and I know that the witness which he witnesseth of me is true.

"Ye sent unto John, and he bare witness unto the truth. "But I receive not testimony from man: but these things I say, that ye might be saved.

"He was a burning and shining light: and ye were willing for a season to rejoice in his light.

"But I have greater witness than that of John: for the works which the Father hath given me to finish, the same works that I do, bear witness of me, that the Father hath sent me.

"And the Father himself, which hath sent me, hath borne witness of me. Ye have neither heard his voice at anytime, nor seen his shape.

"And ye have not his word abiding in you: for whom he hath sent, him ye believe not.

Part V – Events of Christ Jesus From His Second To His Third Passover
(His Main Galilean Ministry)

"Search the scriptures; for in them ye think ye have eternal life: and they are they which testify of me.

"And ye will not come to me, that ye might have life. "I receive not honour from men.

"But I know you, that ye have not the love of God in you. "I am come in my Father's name, and ye receive me not: if another shall come in his own name, him ye will receive. "How can ye believe, which receive honour one of another, and seek not the honour that cometh from God only?

"Do not think that I will accuse you to the Father: there is one that accuseth you, even Moses, in whom ye trust.

"For had ye believed Moses, ye would have believed me: for he wrote of me.

"But if ye believe not his writings, how shall ye believe my words?"

NOTES: Scriptures of the Topic   John

- The Father and the Son's relationship   5:17,19-47

Doctrines and Commandments

38.   My father and I work.

39.   Christ Jesus can do nothing by himself.

40.   Christ Jesus can do only what he sees his Father do.

41.   Whatever God the Father does, the Son does likewise.

42.   Heavenly Father loves the Son and shows him all things that he does.

43.   God the Father raises the dead and Christ Jesus raises the dead whom he will.

44.   God the Father judges no man.

45.   God commits all judgment to Christ Jesus (the Son).

46.   All men should honor the Son, as they honor God the Father.

47.   Those who have everlasting life are those that hear Christ's word and believe God the Father that sent Christ Jesus to us.

Part V – Events of Christ Jesus From His Second To His Third Passover
(His Main Galilean Ministry)

48.   Those who will not come unto damnation are those that hear Christ's words and believe God the Father that sent Christ Jesus to us.

49.   Those who pass from death unto life are those that hear Christ's words and believe God the Father that sent Christ Jesus to us.

50.   Dead shall live; they shall hear the voice of the Son of God.

51.   God the Father has life in himself.

52.   God the Father has given the Son to have life in himself.

53.   Authority is given to Christ to execute judgment.

54.   All that are in the graves shall hear His voice, for the hour is coming.

55.   Resurrection of life—those who have died and have done good.

56.   Resurrection of damnation—those who have died and done evil.

57.   Christ doesn't seek his own will, but the will of his Father who sent him.

58.   Just judgment by Christ, for he seeks the will of his Father.

59.   Witness of Christ—he can't bear witness of himself. His works of his father bear witness of Christ.

60.   If you had Christ's word abiding in you, you would believe in him.

61.   God's word is not abiding in us if we don't believe that God did sent his Son to us.

62.   Eternal life is not attained by searching scriptures: we must come unto Christ.

63.   Seek honor from God only—we have honor with other men, but not with God.

64.   Believe in Christ: for if we would believe in the prophets, as Moses, we would believe in Christ.

Lessons We Should Learn

1.   Jesus knows what his Father's work is and that his Father does work and continues to work. Therefore Jesus works. Jesus can know only what he sees the Father do and then he sets his goal to do the same. For of himself he can do nothing. Therefore, since we have the words of God and Christ and have the ability to read the scriptures, we should strive to do, to work, to put into action those thoughts, words and actions (deeds) that Christ Jesus says for us to do. As Jesus did the will of his Father, we also should strive to do His will.

2.   God the Father loves his Son and He has shown him all the things that He does. Therefore, Jesus has achieved all knowledge from His Father; His Father has shared that with him. There is not one thing not revealed to Christ Jesus. Therefore, it is all revealed to us through Christ Jesus. Christ's words reveal that knowledge to us, for he loves us.

Part V – Events of Christ Jesus From His Second To His Third Passover
(His Main Galilean Ministry)

3.   God the Father raises the dead; He gives us life after life.

Jesus the Christ raises the dead and he gives us all life after life, as his Father does. God judges no man, but commits all judgment to Christ Jesus. We may have everlasting life if we honor Christ Jesus as we honor God, search for and hear Christ's words and believe God the Father that sent Christ Jesus to us.

4.   We each have a choice before we die and experience death.

That choice is life after death or damnation. Those that hear Christ's words and believe God the Father that sent Christ Jesus to us and have done good, shall pass from death unto life and will not come into damnation and may have everlasting life. Those who have done evil will experience the resurrection of damnation rather than life everlasting.

5.   Christ Jesus cannot bear witness of himself and his works of his Father are verification of His witness. Our work likewise is verification of our witness that we believe in God the Father and in His Son Christ Jesus.

6.   There should be no doubt in us that we do the will of God, believe in Christ Jesus, and his words abide in us. If we would take the equal time given to our mortal pleasure and study the words of Christ and put them into practice in our own lives each day, his words would abide in us, and we would truly believe in him, Christ Jesus.

Part V – Events of Christ Jesus From His Second To His Third Passover
(His Main Galilean Ministry)

My Thoughts About the Lessons

_____

_____

_____

_____

_____

_____

_____

_____

_____

_____

_____

_____

_____

_____

_____

_____

_____

_____

_____

_____

_____

_____

_____

_____

Part V – Events of Christ Jesus From His Second To His Third Passover
(His Main Galilean Ministry)

8

Christ Preaches in the Synagogue at Nazareth;
Upon Returning to Galilee

And Jesus returned in the power of the Spirit into Galilee: and there went out a fame of him through all the region round about. And he taught in their synagogues being glorified of all. And he came to Nazareth, where he had been brought up: and as his custom was he went into the synagogue on the Sabbath day and stood up for to read.

And there was delivered unto him the book of the prophet Esaias. And when he had opened the book, he found the place where it was written,

"The Spirit of the Lord is upon me, because he hath anointed me to preach the gospel to the poor; he hath sent me to heal the brokenhearted, to preach deliverance to the captives, and recovering of sight to the blind, to set at liberty them that are bruised, "To preach the acceptable year of the Lord."

And he closed the book, and he gave it again to the minister, and sat down. And the eyes of all them that were in the synagogue were fastened on him.

And he began to say unto them, *"This day is this scripture fulfilled in your ears."*

And all bare him witness, and wondered at the gracious words which proceeded out of his mouth. And they said, Is this not Joseph's son?

And he said unto them, *"Ye will surely say unto me this proverb, Physician, heal thyself: whatsoever we have heard done in Capernaum. do also here in thy country."*

And he said, *"Verily I say unto you, No prophet is accepted in his own country.*

Part V – Events of Christ Jesus From His Second To His Third Passover
(His Main Galilean Ministry)

"But I tell you of a truth, many widows were in Israel in the days of Elias, when the heaven was shut up three years and six months, when great famine was throughout all the land;

"But unto none of them was Elias sent, save unto Sarepta city of Sidon, unto a woman that was a widow.

"And many lepers were in Israel in the time of Eliseus the prophet; and none of them was cleansed, saving Naaman the Syrian."

And all they in the synagogue when they heard these

things, were filled with wrath. And rose up, and thrust him out of the city.

NOTES: Scriptures of the Topics   <u>Luke</u>

- Christ preaches in the Synagogue   4:18,19,21,23-27
at Nazareth

Doctrines and Commandments

65.   The Spirit of the Lord is upon Christ and anoints him to preach the gospel to the poor, to heal the broken hearted, to preach deliverance to the captives, to recover the sight to the blind, and to set at liberty those that are bruised.

66.   No prophet is accepted in his own country.

Lessons We Should Learn

1.   The spirit of the Lord will come upon us as it did Christ Jesus when we are chosen by God to do His work and we may be anointed with great gifts as Christ Jesus was.

2.   As one strives to do the will of God and live a Christ-like life with a new birth of the Spirit, few see the new child off God but the old person.

3.   One can apply Jesus' words and teachings daily, as Jesus has come and does come each day, as we each invite him into our life to teach us his gospel, to heal us, to deliver us from the world and Satan's harm, and to set us, that are bruised, at liberty. We each need this as much today as when Jesus gave this lesson to the children of Israel during his mission on Earth. How often do we dismiss him and thrust him out of our lives, as the people did in Israel?

Part V – Events of Christ Jesus From His Second To His Third Passover
(His Main Galilean Ministry)

My Thoughts About the Lessons

_____

_____

_____

_____

_____

_____

_____

_____

_____

_____

_____

_____

_____

_____

_____

_____

_____

_____

_____

_____

_____

_____

_____

_____

_____

NOTES

Part V – Events of Christ Jesus From His Second To His Third Passover
(His Main Galilean Ministry)

9

Christ Goes to Many Cities Where The Father Sends Him; After He Chooses Several Disciples

Jesus stood by the lake at Gennesaret as the people pressed upon Him to have the word of God, and saw two ships standing by the lake: but the fishermen were gone out of them and were washing their nets. And he entered into one of the ships which was Simon's, and prayed him that he would thrust out a little from the land. And he sat down, and taught the people out of the ship.

Now when he had left speaking, he said unto Simon,

"Launch out into the deep, and let down your nets for a draught."
And Simon answering said unto him, Master, we have toiled all the night, and have taken nothing: Never the less, at thy word I will let down the net. And when they had this done, they inclosed a great multitude of fishes: and their net brake.

When Simon Peter saw it, he fell down at Jesus' knees, saying, Depart from me; for I am a sinful man, O Lord.

And so was also James, and John and the sons of Zebedee, which were partners with Simon.

And Jesus said unto Simon, *"Fear not; from henceforth thou shalt catch men."* And Jesus said unto Simon and Andrew, his brother, *"Come ye after me, and I will make you to become fishers of men."* And they straightway left their nets and followed him.

Jesus also, called James, the son of Zebedee, and John, his brother, and they immediately left the ship and their father and followed him.

And they went into Capernaum; and on the Sabbath day he went into the Synagogue, and taught. And they were astonished at his doctrine: for he taught them as one that had authority, and not as the scribes.

Part V – Events of Christ Jesus From His Second To His Third Passover
(His Main Galilean Ministry)

Jesus Heals a Man of an Unclean Spirit

And there was in their synagogue a man with an unclean spirit; and he cried out. Saying, Let us alone; what have we to do with thee, thou Jesus of Nazareth? Art thou come to destroy us? I know thee who thou art, the Holy One of God.

And Jesus rebuked him saying, *"Hold thy peace, and come out of him."*

And the unclean spirit cried out with a loud voice and he came out of him.

And they were all amazed, in so much they questioned among themselves, saying, what new doctrine is this? For with his authority that he commandeth even the unclean spirits do obey him.

Jesus healed Simon's wife's Mother of a fever, and all the city was gathered and he healed many that were sick of divers diseases and cast out many devils.

And in the morning, rising up a great while before day, he went out, and departed into a solitary place, and there prayed. His disciples followed him and said, all men seek for thee.

And he said unto them, *"Let us go into the next towns, that I may preach there also: for therefore came I forth."*

"I must preach the Kingdom of God to other cities also; for therefore am I sent."

And he preached in their synagogues throughout all Galilee, and cast out devils. And there came a leper to Him asking Jesus to make him clean.

Part V – Events of Christ Jesus From His Second To His Third Passover
(His Main Galilean Ministry)

He Heals a Leper

And Jesus, moved with compassion, put forth his hand and touched him, and said unto him, *"I will; be thou clean."*

And as soon as he had spoken, immediately the leprosy departed from him and he was cleansed.

And charged him to *"Tell no man; but go, and show thyself to the priest, and offer for thy cleansing, according as Moses commanded, for a testimony unto them."*

But so much the more went there a fame abroad of him; and great multitudes came together to hear, and to be healed by him of their infirmities. And he withdrew himself into the wilderness, and prayed.

And again he entered into Capernaum after some days: And it was noised that he was in the house.

And they came unto him, bringing one sick of the palsy. When they couldn't get near Jesus for the press, they uncovered the roof where he was, they let down the bed and the sick palsied one.

He Heals a Palsied Man

When Jesus saw their faith, he said unto the one sick of the palsy, *"Son, be of good cheer, thy sins be forgiven thee."* And behold, certain of the scribes said within themselves, this man blasphemeth.

And Jesus knowing their thoughts said, *"Wherefore think ye evil in your hearts?*
"For whether is easier, to say, thy sins be forgiven thee; or to say, Arise and walk?
"But that ye may know that the Son of man hath power on earth to forgive sins."

He said unto the sick one of the palsy, *"I say unto thee, Arise, and take up thy couch, and go into thine house."*

And immediately he rose up before them, and took up his bed and departed to his own house, glorifying God.

Part V – Events of Christ Jesus From His Second To His Third Passover
(His Main Galilean Ministry)

<u>Jesus calls Matthew</u>

And after these things he saw a publican, named Levi sitting at the receipt of custom, and he said unto him, *"Follow me."*

And he left all, rose up, and followed him.

And Levi made him a great feast in his own house; and there was a great company of publicans and of others that sat down with them.

But their scribes and Pharisees murmured against his disciples, saying, why do Ye eat and drink with publicans and sinners?

And Jesus answering said, *"They that are whole need not a physician; but they that are sick.*

"But go ye and learn what that meaneth, I will have mercy, and not sacrifice:

"I came not to call the righteous, but sinners to repentance."

<u>Jesus Gives His Reasons For Not Fasting</u>

And they said unto him, why do the disciple of John fast often, and make prayers and likewise the disciples of the Pharisees; but thine eat and drink?

And he said unto them, *"Can ye make the children of the bride chamber fast, while the bridegroom is with them?"*

"As long as they have the bridegroom with them, they cannot fast"

"But the days will come, when the bridegroom shall be taken away from them, and then shall they fast in those days,

"No man putteth a piece of new cloth unto an old garment, for that which is put in to fill it up taketh from the garment, and the piece that was taken out of the new agreeth not with the old and the rent is made worse.

Part V – Events of Christ Jesus From His Second To His Third Passover
(His Main Galilean Ministry)

"And no man putteth new wine into old bottles; else the new wine will burst the bottles, and be spilled, and the bottles will be marred and shall perish, "But new wine must be put into new bottles; and both are preserved.

"No man also having drunk old wine straight way desireth new: for he saith, the old is better."

Jesus is Lord of the Sabbath

And it came to pass on the second Sabbath after the first, that he went through the corn fields; and his disciples plucked the ears of corn, and did eat, rubbing them in their hands.

And certain of the Pharisees said unto them, why do ye that which is not lawful to do on the Sabbath days?

And Jesus answering them said, *"Have ye not read so much as this, what David did, when himself was an hungered, and they which were with him;*

"How he went into the house of God, and did take and eat the shewbread, which was not lawful for him to eat, neither for them which were with him, and gave also to them that were with him; which is not lawful to eat, but only for the priests alone?

"Or have ye not read the law, how that on the Sabbath days the priests alone?

"Or have ye not read the law, how that on the Sabbath says the priests in the temple profane the Sabbath, and are blameless?

"But I say unto you, That in this place is one greater than the temple.

"But if ye had known what this meaneth, I will have mercy, and not sacrifice, ye would not have condemned the guiltless.

"The Sabbath was made for man, and not man for the Sabbath:

"For the Son of man is Lord even of the Sabbath day."

Part V – Events of Christ Jesus From His Second To His Third Passover
(His Main Galilean Ministry)

Jesus Heals on the Sabbath

And it came to pass also on another Sabbath, that he entered into the synagogue and taught and there was a man whose right hand was withered. And they watched him, whether he would heal him on the Sabbath day; that they might accuse him.

And he said unto them, *"What man shall there be among you, that shall have one sheep, and if it fall into a pit on the Sabbath day, will he not lay hold on it, and lift it out?*

"How much then is a man better than a sheep? Wherefore it is lawful to do well on the Sabbath days."

Jesus knew their thoughts and said to the man with the withered hand, *"Rise up and stand forth in the midst"*

Then Jesus said, *"I will ask you one thing; is it lawful on the Sabbath days to do good, or do evil? To save life, or to destroy it? Or to kill?"*

And when he looked around about on them with anger, being grieved for the hardness of their hearts, he saith unto the man, *"Stretch forth thine hand."* And the man stretched it out; and his hand was restored whole as the other.

Then the Pharisees went out an held a council against him, how they might destroy him.

But Jesus withdrew himself with his disciples to the sea; and a great multitude from Galilee, Judaea, Jerusalem, Idumaea, beyond Jordan, Tyre and Sidon when they heard what great things he did came unto him. He rebuked many unclean spirit and healed many.

Part V – Events of Christ Jesus From His Second To His Third Passover
(His Main Galilean Ministry)

NOTES: Scriptures of the Topics	Matt.	Mark	Luke
- Jesus chooses several disciples	4:19	1:17	5:4,10
- Jesus heals a man of an unclean spirit		1:25	4:35
- Jesus goes to other cities		1:38	4:43
- He heals a leper	8:3,4	1:41,44	5:13,14
- Jesus heals a palsied man	9:2,3,5,6	2:5,8-11	5:20,22-24
- Jesus calls Matthew	9:9,12,13	2:14,17	5:27,31,32
- Jesus gives his reasons for not fasting	9:15-17	2:19-22	5:34-39
- Jesus is the Lord of the Sabbath	12:2-8	2:25-28	6:3-5
- Jesus heals on the Sabbath	12:11-13	3:3-5	6:8-10

Doctrines and Commandments

67. Jesus rebukes Satan, devils and unclean spirits.

68. Jesus came to preach the Kingdom of God to many cities and places.

69. Jesus does His Father's will by healing those afflicted of many types of diseases.

70. Jesus has power on earth to forgive sins.

71. Jesus came not to call the righteous, but sinners to repentance.

72. We must fast to be in the Spirit of the Lord, the disciples never fasted until he was crucified, for Christ the Lord was with them.

73. Christ Jesus is Lord of the Sabbath day. He will do the will of His Father; to save lives; to heal and to do good.

Lessons We Should Learn

1. We are continually tempted by Satan, and unclean spirits may be with us. We may learn to rebuke them and not follow temptations, but repent and do the will of God.

2. If we become ill we may bring about a blessing from God and attain a spiritual healing.

3. We must repent our wrong doings and sins for Christ Jesus has power to forgive sins.

Part V – Events of Christ Jesus From His Second To His Third Passover
(His Main Galilean Ministry)

4.   Fasting is helpful to obtain the Spirit of the Lord. To attain control of one's physical desires is strengthening to our inner spiritual self.

5.   We must strive to keep the Sabbath for spiritual work and to be in His word, but our deeds should be to help others, save lives, do good and do the will of our Heavenly Father.

6.   Before Jesus had chosen his disciples he was teaching the word of God to the people for they were hungry to hear and know the word of God. As Jesus taught from Simon Peter's fishing ship in the lake of Gennesaret and before he called Simon Peter to come after him to catch men, he had Peter learn to put his work and the world aside and to be prepared by being repentant before following Jesus. For Jesus had Peter set his net. After fishing all night and catching nothing Peter pulled in his net so full his net broke and had enough fish to fill two boats.

Peter, realizing the miracle of this from God, fell at Jesus' knees saying, "Depart from me; for I am a sinful man, O Lord."

This very miracle and lesson not only was for Peter but also for Andrew, Peter's brother, who was with Peter fishing, and also James and John, sons of Zebedee, who were partners with Simon. All that were with Simon were astonished with such a large catch that was sinking two boats.

When they brought the ship to land they forsook all and followed him, Jesus.

This lesson is for each of us to put down the things of the world—even when blessed with great material blessing and miracles—and follow him, Jesus. How often do we do this? Or don't do it? When did the disciples do it? Did they wait a day or two to think it over? What do the scriptures say? They immediately left their ship and father and followed him, Jesus (Matt. 4:22).

When should we do it? Are we called so that we shall catch men? Are we coming after Jesus, so he will make us to become fishers of men? Is he saying we are to be taught by Jesus to teach others his the teachings and words?

7.   How did Jesus teach? It says that when Jesus taught in the synagogue, they were astonished at His doctrine: for he taught them as one that had authority, and not as the scribes (Mk. 1:21,22)

Part V – Events of Christ Jesus From His Second To His Third Passover
(His Main Galilean Ministry)

My Thoughts About the Lessons

_____

_____

_____

_____

_____

_____

_____

_____

_____

_____

_____

_____

_____

_____

_____

_____

_____

_____

_____

_____

_____

NOTES

Part V – Events of Christ Jesus From His Second To His Third Passover
(His Main Galilean Ministry)

10

The Chosen Twelve Disciples:
Jesus Sends Them Forth Into Their Ministry

And Jesus went out into the mountain to pray, and continued all night in prayer to God. And when it was day he calleth unto him whom he would; and they came unto him.

And he ordained twelve, that they should be with him, that he might send them forth to preach, and to have power to heal sicknesses, and all manner of diseases and to cast out devils and he gave them power against unclean spirits, to cast them out.

The names of twelve apostles are these: the first (1) Simon who is called Peter; (2) Andrew, Peter's brother; (3) James the son of Zebedee; (4) John, James's brother; (5) Philip; (6) Bartholomew; (7) Thomas; (8) Matthew the publican; (9) James the son of Alphaeus, (10) Lebbaens whose surname was Thaddaeus; (11) Simon the Cananite; (12) Judas Iscariot who betrayed him.

These twelve Jesus sent forth, and commanded them, saying,

"Go not into the way of the Gentiles, and into any city of the Samaritans enter ye not:

"But go rather to the lost sheep of the house of Israel. "And as ye go, preach, saying, The kingdom of heaven is at hand.

"Heal the sick, cleanse the lepers, raise the dead, cast out devils: freely ye have received, freely give.

"Provide neither gold, nor silver, nor brass in your purses, "Nor scrip for your journey, neither two coats, neither shoes, nor yet staves: for the workman is worthy of his meat. "And into whatsoever city or town ye shall enter, enquire who in it is worthy; and there abide till ye go thence.

Part V – Events of Christ Jesus From His Second To His Third Passover
(His Main Galilean Ministry)

"And when ye come into an house, salute it.

"And if the house be worthy, let your peace come upon it: but if it be not worthy, let your peace return to you.

"And whosoever shall not receive you, nor hear your words, when ye depart out of that house or city, shake off the dust of your feet.

"Verily I say unto you, it shall be more tolerable for the land of Sodom and Gomorrha in the day of judgment, than for that city.

"Behold I send you forth as sheep in the midst of the wolves: be ye therefore wise as serpents, and harmless as doves.

"But beware of men: for they will deliver you up to the councils, and they will scourge you in their synagogues;

" And ye shall be brought before governors and kings for my sake, for a testimony against them and the Gentiles.

"But when they deliver you up, take no thought how or what ye shall speak: for it shall be given you in that same hour what ye shall speak.

"For it is not ye that speak, but the Spirit of your Father which speaketh in you.
"And the brother shall deliver up the brother to death, and the father the child: and the children shall rise up against their parents, and cause them to be put to death.

"And ye shall be hated of all men for my name's sake: but he that endureth to the end shall be saved.

"But when they persecute you in this city, flee ye into another: for verily I say unto you, Ye shall not have gone over the cities of Israel, till the Son of man be come.

"The disciple is not above his master, nor the servant above his lord.

Part V – Events of Christ Jesus From His Second To His Third Passover
(His Main Galilean Ministry)

"Is it enough for the disciple that he be as his master, and the servant as his lord. If they have called the master of the house Be-el'-ze-bub, how much more shall they call them of his household?

"Fear them not therefore: for there is nothing covered, that shall not be revealed; and hid, that shall not be known.

"What I tell you in darkness, that speak ye in light: and what ye hear in the ear, that preach ye upon the housetops.

"And fear not them which kill the body, but are not able to kill the soul: but rather fear him which is able to destroy both soul and body in hell.

"Are not two sparrows sold for a farthing? and one of them shall not fall on the ground without your Father.

"But the very hairs of your head are all numbered. "Fear ye not therefore, ye are of more value than many sparrows.

"Whosoever therefore shall confess me before men, him will I confess also before my Father which is in heaven.

"But whosoever shall deny me before men, him will I also deny before My Father which is in heaven.

"Think not that I am come to send peace on earth: I came not to send peace, but a sword.

"For I am come to set a man at variance against his father, and the daughter against her mother, and the daughter in law against her mother in law.

"And a man's foes shall be they of his own household. "He that loveth father or mother more than me is not worthy of me: and he that loveth son or daughter more than me is not worthy of me.

"And he that taketh not his cross, and followeth after me, is not worthy of me.
"He that findeth his life shall lose it: and he that loseth his life for my sake shall find it.

Part V – Events of Christ Jesus From His Second To His Third Passover
(His Main Galilean Ministry)

"He that receiveth you receiveth me, and he that receiveth me receiveth him that sent me.

"He that receiveth a prophet in the name of a prophet shall receive a prophet's reward; and he that receiveth a righteous man in the name of a righteous man shall receive a righteous man's reward.

"And whosoever shall give to drink unto one of these little ones a cup of cold water only in the name of a disciple, verily I say unto you, he shall in no wise lose his reward."

And it came to pass, when Jesus had made an end of commanding his twelve disciples, he departed thence to teach and to preach in their cities.

NOTES: Scriptures of the Topics   Matt.

- Jesus sends the 12 disciples into their ministry   10:5-42

Doctrines and Commandments

74.   Christ Jesus ordains His disciples to: preach His words, heal the sick, raise the dead, cast out devils, freely give.

75.   Jesus gives commandments to disciples going on their mission and should be used in their daily missions.

1) Take no money with you.

2) Take the bare necessities for your traveling and salute no man by the way.

3) Inquire about the worthy in each place you may go.

4) Salute the house you enter and if worthy bless it.

5) Whosoever does not receive you as you depart, shake off the dust of your feet for a testimony against them when you leave that city.

6) Jesus sends his disciples, followers and missionaries forth as sheep in the midst of wolves, but He tells us to be wise and harmless.

7) Beware of men who look to charge you falsely before courts and in their churches.

8) If you are taken before authorities or a court trust in the Lord to give you what to say. It will be from the Spirit of our Father which speaks in us.

Part V – Events of Christ Jesus From His Second To His Third Passover
(His Main Galilean Ministry)

9) You shall be hated of all men for Christ Jesus' name's sake: but he that endures to the end shall be saved.

10) If they persecute you in a city, flee to another: you shall not have gone over the cities of Israel till Christ will come.

11) The disciples are not above his master, nor the servant above his lord.

12) Fear not those who charge you and call you false names for all that is hid shall be known.

13) What Christ Jesus tells we will speak in the light and truth and preach it upon the housetops.

14) Fear not that which kills the body, but is not able to kill the soul.

15) Fear him that is able to destroy both soul and body in hell.

16) God knows of each hair upon your head, so we should fear not for God will take care of us.

17) Whosoever shall confess Christ Jesus before me, him will I confess also before my Father which is in heaven.

18) Whosoever shall deny Me before men him will I also deny before my Father.

19) Jesus came to send a sword, not peace.

20) Jesus came to set the children at variance against the parents.

21) Man's foes shall be they of his own household.

22) Those who love their parents more than Christ Jesus are not worthy of Christ, and parents that love their children more than Christ Jesus are not worthy of Christ.

23) Those who will not take their cross and follow Jesus are not worthy of Christ Jesus.

24) Those who find their life shall lose it: and those that lose their life for Jesus' sake shall find it.

25) Those that receive you receive Me, and those that receive Me receive God the Father, that sent Jesus.

26) Those that receive a prophet in the name of a prophet shall receive a prophet's reward: those that receive a righteous man in the name of a righteous man shall receive a righteous man's reward.

27) Whosoever shall give a drink or help to those on a mission or a disciple shall not lose his reward.

Part V – Events of Christ Jesus From His Second To His Third Passover
(His Main Galilean Ministry)

Lessons We Should Learn

1.   If one prepares to go on a mission or become a disciple of Christ, you should know that Jesus gives us specific commandments to follow daily and to do them and live by them.

2.   Our daily life is a mission in doing the will of our Heavenly Father. His son, Christ Jesus, fulfilled the will of God each day. And Christ in His words and doctrines teaches us how to do the same. Many of the commandments, listed above, that Christ gave to His disciples should be used in our own daily mission in life.

Part V – Events of Christ Jesus From His Second To His Third Passover
(His Main Galilean Ministry)

My Thoughts About the Lessons

_____

_____

_____

_____

_____

_____

_____

_____

_____

_____

_____

_____

_____

_____

_____

_____

_____

_____

_____

_____

_____

_____

_____

_____

Part V – Events of Christ Jesus From His Second To His Third Passover
(His Main Galilean Ministry)

11

The Sermon on the Mount

After Jesus had chosen his twelve apostles and had ordained them and gave them his commandments upon the mountain, he came down with them and stood in the plain and the company of his disciples and a great multitude of people out of all Judea, Jerusalem and from the sea coast or Tyre and Sidon which came to hear him and to be healed of their diseases: and they were vexed with unclean spirits: and they were healed.

And the whole multitude sought to touch him: for there went virtue out of him, and healed them all. And he lifted up his eyes on the disciples, and said,

"Blessed are the poor in spirit: for theirs is the kingdom of   heaven.

"Blessed are they that mourn: for they shall be comforted.

"Blessed are ye that weep now: for ye shall laugh.

"Blessed are the meek: for they shall inherit the earth.

"Blessed are they which do hunger and thirst after righteousness: for they shall be filled.

"Blessed are the merciful: for they shall obtain mercy.

"Blessed are the pure in heart: for they shall see God.

"Blessed are the peacemakers: for they shall be called the children of God.

"Blessed are they which are persecuted for righteousness sake: for theirs is the kingdom in heaven.

"Blessed are ye, when men shall revile you, and persecute you, and shall say all manner of evil against you falsely, for my sake.

Part V – Events of Christ Jesus From His Second To His Third Passover
(His Main Galilean Ministry)

"Rejoice, and be exceeding glad: for great is your reward in heaven: for so persecuted they the prophets which were before you.

"But woe unto you that are rich! For ye have received your consolation.

"Woe unto you that are full! for ye shall hunger. Woe unto you that laugh now! for ye shall mourn and weep.

"Ye are the salt of the earth: but if the salt have lost his savour, wherewith shall it be salted? it is thenceforth good for nothing, but to be cast out, and to be trodden under foot of men.

"Ye are the light of the world. A city that is set on an hill cannot be hid.

"Neither do men light a candle, and put it under a bushel, but on a candlestick; and it giveth light unto all that are in the house.

"Let your light so shine before men, that they may see your good works, and glorify your Father which is in heaven.

"Think not that I am come to destroy the law or the prophets: I am not come to destroy, but to fulfil.

"For verily I say unto you, Till heaven and earth pass, one jot or one tittle shall in no wise pass from the law, till all be fulfilled.

"Whosoever therefore shall break one of these least commandments, and shall teach men so, he shall be called the least in the kingdom of heaven: but whosoever shall do and teach them, the same shall be called great in the kingdom of heaven.

"For I say unto you, That except your righteousness shall exceed the righteousness of the scribes and Pharisees, ye shall in no case enter into the Kingdom of heaven.

"Ye have heard that it was said by them of old time, thou shalt not kill; and whosoever shall kill shall be in danger of the judgment:

Part V – Events of Christ Jesus From His Second To His Third Passover
(His Main Galilean Ministry)

But I say unto you, That whosoever is angry with his brother without a cause shall be in danger of the judgment: and whosoever shall say to his brother, Ra'-ca, shall be in danger of the council: but whosoever shall say, Thou fool, shall be in danger of hell fire.

"Therefore if thou bring thy gift to the altar, and there rememberest that thy brother hath ought against thee;

"Leave there thy gift before the altar, and go thy way; first be reconciled to thy brother, and then come and offer thy gift.

"Agree with thine adversary quickly, whiles thou art in the way with him; lest at any itme the adversary deliver thee to the judge, and the judge deliver thee to the officer, and thou be cast into prison.

"Verily I say unto thee, Thou shalt by no means come out thence, till thou hast paid the uttermost farthing.

"Woe unto you, when all men shall speak well of you! for so did their fathers to the false prophets.

"Ye have heard that it was said by them of old time, thou shall not commit adultery:

"But I say unto you, That whosoever looketh on a woman to lust after her heart hath committed adultery with her already in his heart.

"And if thy right eye offend thee, pluck it out, and cast it from thee: for it is profitable for thee that one of thy members should perish, and not that thy whole body should be cast into hell.

"And if thy right hand offend thee, cut it off, and cast it from thee: for it is profitable for thee that one of thy members should perish, and not that thy whole body should be cast into hell.

"It hath been said, Whosoever shall put away his wife, let him give her a writing of divorcement:

"But I say unto you, That whosoever shall put away his wife, saving for the cause of fornication, causeth her to commit adultery: and whosoever shall marry her that is divorced committeth adultery.

Part V – Events of Christ Jesus From His Second To His Third Passover
(His Main Galilean Ministry)

"Again, ye have heard that it hath been said by them of old time, thou shalt not forswear thyself, but shalt perform unto the Lord thine oaths:

"But I say unto you, Swear not at all; neither by heaven; for it is God's throne:

"Nor by the earth; for it is his foot stool: neither by Jerusalem; for it is the city of the great King.

"Neither shalt thou swear by thy head, because thou canst not make one hair white or black.

"But let your communication be, Yea, Yea; Nay, nay: for whatsoever is more than these cometh of evil.

"Ye have heard that it hath been said, An eye for and eye and a tooth for a tooth.

"But I say unto you, That ye resist not evil: but whosoever shall smite thee on thy right cheek, turn to him the other also.

"And if any man will sue thee at the law, and take away thy coat, let him have thy cloke also.

"And as ye would that men should do to you, do ye also to them likewise.

"And whosoever shall compel thee to go a mile, go with him twain.

"Give to him, and every man that asketh thee, and from
him that would borrow of thee turn not thou away and of him that taketh away thy goods ask them not again.

"Ye have heard that it hath been said, Thou shalt love thy neighbour, and hate thine enemy.

"But I say unto you, love your enemies, bless them that curse you, do good to them that hate you, and pray for them which despitefully use you, and persecute you;

Part V – Events of Christ Jesus From His Second To His Third Passover
(His Main Galilean Ministry)

"That ye may be the children of your Father which is in heaven: for he maketh his sun to rise on the evil and on the good, and sendeth rain on the just and on the unjust.

"For if ye love them which love you, what reward have ye? Do not even the publicans the same? for sinners also love those that love them.

"And if ye do good to them which do good to you, what thank have ye? for sinners also do even the same.

"And if ye lend to them of whom ye hope to receive, what thank have ye? for sinners also lend to sinners, to receive as much again,

"But love ye your enemies, and do good, and lend, hoping for nothing again; and your reward shall be great, and ye shall be the children of the Highest: for He is kind unto the unthankful and to the evil.

"Be ye therefore merciful, as your Father also is merciful.

"And if ye salute your brethren only, what do ye more than others? Do not even the publicans so?

"Be ye therefore perfect, even as your Father which is in heaven is perfect.

"Take heed that ye do not your alms before men, to be seen of them: otherwise ye have no reward of your Father which is in heaven.

"Therefore when thou doest thine alms, do not sound a trumpet before thee, as the hypocrites do in the synagogues and in the streets, that they may have glory of men. Verily I say unto you, They have their reward.

"But when thou doest alms, let not thy left hand know what thy right hand doeth:

"That thine alms may be in secret; and thy Father which seeth in secret himself shall reward thee openly.

Part V – Events of Christ Jesus From His Second To His Third Passover
(His Main Galilean Ministry)

"And when thou prayest, thou shalt not be as the hypocrites are: for they love to pray standing in the synagogues and in the corners of the streets, that they may be seen of men. Verily I say unto you, They have their reward.

"But thou, when thou prayest, enter into thy closet, and when thou hast shut thy door, pray to thy Father which is in secret; and thy Father which seeth in secret shall reward thee openly.

"But when ye pray, use not vain repetitions, as the heathen do: for they think that they shall be heard for their much speaking.

"Be not ye therefore like unto them: for your Father knoweth what things ye have need of, before ye ask him.

"After this manner therefore pray ye: Our Father which art in heaven, Hallowed be thy name.

"Thy Kingdom come, Thy will be done in earth, as it is in heaven.

"Give us this day our daily bread.

"And forgive us our debts, as we forgive our debtors.

"And lead us not into temptation, but deliver us from evil: For thine is the Kingdom, and the power, and the glory, for ever. Amen.

"For if ye forgive men their trespasses, your heavenly Father will also forgive you:

"For if ye forgive not men their trespasses, neither will your Father forgive your trespasses.

"Moreover when ye fast, be not, as the hypocrites, of a sad countenance: for they disfigure their faces, that they may appear unto men to fast. Verily I say unto you, They have their reward. "But thou, when thou fastest, anoint thine head, and wash thy face;

"That thou appear not unto men to fast, but unto thy Father which is in secret: and thy Father, which seeth in secret, shall reward thee openly."

● ● ●

Part V – Events of Christ Jesus From His Second To His Third Passover
(His Main Galilean Ministry)

"Lay not up for yourselves treasures upon earth, where moth and rust doth corrupt, and where thieves break through and steal:

"But lay up for yourselves treasures in heaven, where neither moth nor rust doth corrupt, and where thieves do not break through nor steal:

"For where your treasure is, there will your heart be also.

"The light of the body is the eye: if therefore thine eye be single, thy whole body shall be full of light.

"But if thine eye be evil, thy whole body shall be full of darkness. If therefore the light is in thee be darkness, how great is that darkness!

"No man can serve two masters; for either he will hate one, and love the other; or else he will hold to one, and despise the other. Ye cannot serve God and mammon.

"Therefore I say unto you, Take no thought for your life, what ye shall eat, or what ye shall drink; nor yet for your body, what ye shall put on. Is not the life more than meat, and the body than raiment?

"Behold the fowls of the air: for they sow not, neither do they reap, nor gather into barns; yet your Heavenly Father feedeth them. Are ye not much better than they?

"Which of you by taking thought can add one cubit unto his stature?

"And why take ye thought for raiment? Consider the lilies of the field, how they grow; they toil not; neither do they spin:

"And yet I say unto you, that even Solomon in all his glory was not arrayed like one of these.

"Wherefore, if God so clothe the grass of the field, how they grow; they toil not; neither do they spin:

Part V – Events of Christ Jesus From His Second To His Third Passover
(His Main Galilean Ministry)

"And yet I say unto you, that even Solomon in all his glory was not arrayed like one of these.

"Wherefore, if God so clothe the grass of the field, which to day is and to morrow is cast into the oven, shall he not much more clothe you, O ye of little faith?

"Therefore take no thought, saying, What shall we eat? or, What shall we drink? or, Wherewithal shall we be clothed? "(For after all these things do the Gentiles seek:) for your heavenly Father knoweth that ye have need of all these things.

"But seek ye first the kingdom of God, and his righteousness; and all these things shall be added unto you. "Take therefore no thought for the morrow: for the morrow shall take thought for the things of itself. Sufficient unto the day is the evil thereof.

"Judge not; that ye be not judged.

"For with what judgment ye judge, ye shall be judged: and with what measure ye mete, it shall be measured to you again."

"Judge not, and ye shall not be judged: Condemn not, and ye shall not be condemned: forgive and ye shall be forgiven:

"Give, and it shall be given unto you; good measure, pressed down, and shaken together and running over, shall men give into your bosom. For with the same measure that ye mete withal it shall be measured to you again.

"Can the blind lead the blind? shall they not both fall into the ditch?

"The disciple is not above his master: but every one that is perfect shall be as his master.

"And why beholdest thou the mote that is in thy brother's eye, but considerest not the beam that is in thine own eye?

"Or how wilt thou say to thy brother, Let me pull out the mote out of thine eye; and then shalt thou see clearly to cast out the mote out of thy brother's eye.

"Thou hypocrite, first cast out the beam out of thine own eye; and then shalt thou see clearly to cast out the mote out of thy brother's eye.

Part V – Events of Christ Jesus From His Second To His Third Passover
(His Main Galilean Ministry)

"Give not that which is holy unto the dogs, neither cast ye your pearls before the swine, lest they trample them under their feet, and turn again and rend you

"Ask, and it shall be given you; seek, and ye shall find; knock, and it shall be opened unto you:

"For every one that asketh receiveth; and he that seeketh findeth; and to him that knocketh it shall be opened.

"Or what man is there of you, whom if his son ask bread, will he give him a stone?
"Or if he ask a fish, will he give him a serpent?

"If ye then, being evil, know how to give good gifts unto your children, how much more shall your Father which is in heaven give good things to them that ask him?

"Therefore all things whatsoever ye would that men should do to you, do ye even so to them; for this is the law and the prophets.

"Enter ye in at the straight gate: for wide is the gate, and broad is the way, that leadeth to destruction, and many there be which go in thereat:

"Because straight is the gate, and narrow is the way, which leadeth unto life, and few there be that find it.

"Beware of false prophets, which come to you in sheep's clothing, but inwardly they are ravening wolves.

"Ye shall know them by their fruits. Do men gather grapes of thorns, or figs of thistles?

"Even so every good tree bringeth forth good fruit; but a corrupt tree bringeth forth evil fruit.

"A good tree cannot bring forth evil fruit, neither can a corrupt tree bring forth good fruit.

Part V – Events of Christ Jesus From His Second To His Third Passover
(His Main Galilean Ministry)

"Every tree that bringeth not forth good fruit is hewn down, and cast into the fire.

"For every tree is known by its own fruit. For of thorns men do not gather figs, nor of a bramble bush gather they grapes.

"A good man out of the good treasure of his heart bringeth forth that which is good; and an evil man out of the evil treasure of his heart bringeth forth that which is evil: for of the abundance of the heart his mouth speaketh.

"Wherefore by their fruits ye shall know them.

"Not every one that saith unto me, Lord, Lord, shall enter into the kingdom of heaven: but he that doeth the will of my Father which is in heaven.

"Many will say to me in that day, Lord, Lord, have we not prophesied in thy name? and in thy name have cast out devils? and in thy name done many wonderful works?

"And then will I profess unto them, I never knew you: depart from me, ye that work iniquity.

"And why call me Lord, Lord, and do not the things which I say?

"Therefore, whosoever heareth these sayings of mine, and doeth them, I will liken him unto a wise man, which built his house upon a rock:

"And the rain descended, and the floods came, and the winds blew, and beat upon that house; and it fell not: for it was founded upon a rock

"Whosoever cometh to me, and heareth my sayings, and doeth them, I will shew you to whom he is like:

"He is like a man which built an house, and digged deep, and laid the foundation on a rock: and when the flood arose, the stream beat vehemently upon that house, and could not shake it: for it was founded upon a rock.

"And everyone that heareth these sayings of mine, and doeth them not, shall be likened unto a foolish man, which built his house upon the sand:

Part V – Events of Christ Jesus From His Second To His Third Passover
(His Main Galilean Ministry)

"And the rain descended, and the floods came, and the winds blew, and beat upon that house; and it fell: and great was the fall of it."

When Jesus had ended these sayings, the people were astonished at his doctrine: for he taught them as one having authority, and not as scribes.

NOTES: Scriptures of the Topics	Matt	Luke
- Sermon on the Mount	5:3-7:27	6:20-49

Doctrines and Commandments

76.   Christ Jesus tells us how to become children of God, how to enter the Kingdom of God, how to see God, and how to do righteousness.

1)   Children of God—the peacemakers

2)   Kingdom of God—poor in spirit, those persecuted for righteousness

3)   To see God—the pure in heart.

77.   Jesus the Christ tells of those who are blessed:

1)   The poor in spirit

2)   They that mourn

3)   You that weep now

4)   The meek

5)   They which hunger and thirst after righteousness

6)   The merciful

7)   Pure in heart

8)   The peacemakers

9)   They which are persecuted for righteousness

10) You when men revile you, persecute you, and say all manner of evil against you falsely, for Jesus' sake.

Part V – Events of Christ Jesus From His Second To His Third Passover
(His Main Galilean Ministry)

78. You are the Light of the world. Let your light shine before men, that they may see your good works, and glorify your Father which is in heaven.

79. Jesus came not to destroy the law of the prophets but to fulfill.

80. Whosoever shall break one of these least commandments and shall teach men so, he shall be called the least in the Kingdom of Heaven.

81. To enter the Kingdom of Heaven, your righteousness shall exceed the righteousness of the Scribes and Pharisees.

82. Those in danger of the judgment: whosoever is angry with his brother without a cause.

83. Those in danger of the council: whosoever shall say to his brother Raca.

84. Those shall be in danger of hell fire: whosoever shall say thou fool.

85. Offer thy gift before the altar after you have reconciled with your brother.

86. Agree with your adversary quickly while you are dealing with him. Don't let things get out of hand and taken before judges and you may be cast into prison.

87. You shall by no means come out of prison until you have paid the uttermost farthing.

88. Those committing adultery—whosoever looks on a woman to lust after her has committed adultery with her already in his heart.

89. If you are looking at sinful and lustful things for sensuous pleasures, you have offended your being and it would be better to loose your sight and one member so that your whole body should not be cast into hell.

90. Whosoever shall put away his wife, let him give her a written divorcement.

91. Whosoever shall put away his wife, except for the cause of fornication, causing her to commit adultery: and whosoever shall marry her that is divorced is committing adultery.

92. We should not make false oaths to God or to ourselves, for we of ourselves cannot make one hair black or white. Jesus says, *"Swear not at all; neither by heaven; or by earth:"* But we should say yes or no for whatsoever is more than these comes of evil.

93. Whosoever shall hit you on your right cheek, turn to him the other also, so that you resist evil and temptation to strike back.

94. If any man sue you at the law and take away thy coat, let him have your cloke also.

95. Whosoever shall need you to go a mile, go with him two or three.

Part V – Events of Christ Jesus From His Second To His Third Passover
(His Main Galilean Ministry)

96.   Give to him that asks you to borrow something.

97.   Love your enemies, bless them that curse you, do good to them that hate you, and pray for them which despitefully use you and persecute you.

98.   You may be the children of your Father which is in heaven for he makes his sun to rise on the evil and on the good, and sends rain on the just and on the unjust. For if you love those who love you, what reward do you have? If you salute your brethren only, what do you do more than others? *"Be ye therefore perfect, even as your Father which is in heaven is perfect."*

99.   When you pay your alms and tithing, do it in secret and your Father knows, as he sees all things—even those in secret—and He shall reward you openly. Do not give alms before men as the hypocrites do in the synagogues and in the streets that they may have glory of men.

100.   When you pray to your Father in heaven, enter into your closet and after shutting the door, *"Pray to your Father which is in secret and your Father which sees in secret shall reward you openly."*

101.   Your Father knows your prayers and needs before you ask him: therefore avoid vain repetitions, as the heathens do.

102.   Our Father which art in heaven, hallowed be thy name. Thy kingdom come. Thy will be done in earth, as it is in heaven. Give us this day our daily bread. And forgive us our debts, as we forgive our debtors. And lead us not into temptation, but deliver us from evil; For thine is the Kingdom, and the power, and the glory, forever. Amen.

103.   If you forgive men their trespasses, your Heavenly Father will also forgive you. (Matt. 6:14) If you will not from your heart forgive everyone of their trespasses, God the Father shall likewise do unto you. (Matt 18:35)

104.   When you fast, fast unto your Father which is in secret;

anoint your head and wash your face, keep yourself up so that you don't appear to others to be fasting; and your Father which sees in secret shall reward you openly.

105.   Don't lay up treasures upon the earth for yourself, where it will deteriorate and corrupt and where thieves break through and steal.

106.   Lay up treasures in heaven for yourselves where it will not deteriorate and corrupt and where thieves do not break through or steal.

107.   Where your treasure is, there will your heart be also.

108.   The light of the body is the eye: if your eye is righteous, your whole body shall be full of light. But if your eye is evil, your whole body is full of darkness.

109.   No man can serve two masters: you cannot serve God and mammon: For either he will hate the one, and love the other; or else he will hold to the one and despise the other.

Part V – Events of Christ Jesus From His Second To His Third Passover
(His Main Galilean Ministry)

110. You must first seek the Kingdom of God and His righteousness, and then all things shall be added unto you.

"Therefore, take no thought saying what shall we eat? Or what shall we drink? or, where withal shall we be clothed?" For godless people worry about these things and strive to have them. Your Heavenly Father knows that you have need of all these things.

111. Take care of sufficient thought of the day. Give no thought for tomorrow, for tomorrow shall take the thought for the things of itself. *"Have faith" "O ye of little faith."*

112. *"Judge not that you be not judged"* For with what judgment you judge, you shall be judged.

113. *"First cast out the beam of your own eye, and then you shall see clearly to cast out the mote out of thy brother's eye."*

114. *"Give not that which is holy unto the dogs, neither cast you your pearls before swine, lest they trample them under their feet and turn again and rend you."*

115. For every one that asks receives; and he that seeks finds; and to him that knocks it shall be opened.

116. Your Father in Heaven gives good things to them that ask Him; for you, being evil, know how to give good gifts unto your children, how much more shall your Father give good things to them that ask Him.

117. All things whatsoever you would that men should do to you, do you so to them; for this is the law and the prophets.

118. You must enter in at the straight gate, because straight is the gate and narrow is the way which heads unto life and few there find it.

119. Wide is the gate and broad is the way that leads to destruction and many there go in thereat.

120. Beware of false prophets, which come to you in sheep's clothing, but inwardly they are ravening wolves. You will know them by their fruits.

121. *"Not every one saying, Lord, Lord, shall enter into the Kingdom of Heaven: but he that doeth the will of my Father which is in heaven."*

122. Christ Jesus will profess to them that work iniquity, that he never knew them and depart them from him. Many will say

to Jesus in that day, *"Lord, Lord, have we not prophesied in thy name? And in thy name have cast out devils? and in thy name done many wonderful works?"*

Part V – Events of Christ Jesus From His Second To His Third Passover
(His Main Galilean Ministry)

123. *"Therefore whosoever heareth these sayings of mine, and doeth them, I will liken him unto a wise man, which build his house upon a rock."*

124. *"And everyone that heareth these sayings of mine, and doeth them not, shall be likened unto a foolish man, which*

built his house upon the sand. And the rain descended, and the floods came, and the winds blew, and beat upon that house; and it fell: and great was the fall of it."

Lessons We Should Learn

1.   That everyone should strive to be a true child of God and strive to enter into the Kingdom of God, and strive to do the will of our Father which is in heaven—even when we may not know what our life is after our life in the world.

2.   Everyone should strive to read, to know, and to hear the sayings of Christ Jesus and his doctrines and commandments and do them. Live by them each day! Please read again doctrines and commandments 120, 121,122, and 123 and make your own judgment within yourself what Jesus Christ is telling you in these sayings.

Now reread all of His sayings and make your own judgment of how to apply them to your life daily.

Part V – Events of Christ Jesus From His Second To His Third Passover
(His Main Galilean Ministry)

My Thoughts About the Lessons

_____

_____

_____

_____

_____

_____

_____

_____

_____

_____

_____

_____

_____

_____

_____

_____

_____

_____

_____

_____

_____

_____

_____

Part V – Events of Christ Jesus From His Second To His Third Passover
(His Main Galilean Ministry)

12

Jesus Does His Father's Will As One Having Authority

Healing the Centurion's Servant

Jesus finished the Sermon on the Mount and when he had ended all his sayings in the audience of the people, he entered into Capernaum and there came a centurion, beseeching him.

And saying, Lord my servant is lying at home sick with palsy, grievously tormented.

And Jesus said unto him, *"I will come and heal him."* The centurion answered and said, "Lord, I am not worthy that thou shouldest come under my roof: but speak thy word only, and my servant shall be healed."

When Jesus heard it, he marveled and said unto them that followed, *"Verily I say unto you, I have not found so great faith, no, not in Israel.*

"And I say unto you, That many shall come from the east and west, and shall sit down with Abraham, and Isaac, and Jacob, in the kingdom of heaven.

"But the children of the kingdom shall be cast out into outer darkness: there shall be weeping and gnashing of teeth."

And Jesus said unto the centurion, *"Go thy way, and as thou has believed, so be it done unto thee."* And his servant was healed in the selfsame hour.

That same day in Capernaum when Jesus was come into Peter's house, he saw his wife's mother sick of fever.

And he touched her hand and the fever left her: and she arose, and ministered unto them.

Part V – Events of Christ Jesus From His Second To His Third Passover
(His Main Galilean Ministry)

When the even was come, they brought unto him many that were possessed with devils: and he cast out the spirits with his word, and healed all that were sick:

That it might be fulfilled which was spoken by Esaias the prophet, saying, Himself took our infirmities, and bare our sicknesses.

Raising of the Widow's Son at Nain

Jesus left Capernaum with many of his disciples and many people followed and he went into a city called Nain. Then he came to the gate of the city, there was a dead man being carried out, the only son of his mother; and she was a widow: and many people of the city were with her.

And when the Lord saw her, he had compassion on her, and said unto her, *"Weep not."*
And he came and touched the bier: and they that bare him stood still.

And he said, *"Young man, I say unto thee, Arise."*

And he that was dead sat up, and began to speak, and he delivered him to his mother.

And there came a fear on all: and they glorified God, saying, That a great prophet is risen up among us; and That God has visited his people.

And this rumour of him went forth throughout all Judaea, and throughout all the region round about.

John the Baptist's Mission of Inquiry from His Dungeon Machaerus

When John had heard in the prison the works of Christ, he sent two of his disciples. And they asked Jesus, "Art thou he that should come, or do we look for another?"

In that same hour Jesus cured many of their infirmities and plagues, and of evil spirits; and unto many that were blind he gave sight.

Part V – Events of Christ Jesus From His Second To His Third Passover
(His Main Galilean Ministry)

Then Jesus answering said unto them,

"Go your way, and tell John, and shew him again those things ye have seen and heard; how that the blind see, the lame walk, the lepers are cleansed, the deaf hear, the dead are raised up, to the poor the gospel is preached.

"And blessed is he, whosoever shall not be offended in me."

And when the messengers of John were departed, he began to speak unto the people concerning John, *"What went ye out into the wilderness for to see? A reed shaken with the wind?*

"But what went ye out for to see? A man clothed in soft raiment? Behold, they which are gorgeously apparelled that wear soft clothing, and live delicately, are in kings' houses and courts.

"But what went ye out for to see? A prophet? Yea, I say unto you, and much more than a prophet.

"For this is he, of whom it is written. Behold, I send my messenger before thy face, which shall prepare thy way before thee.

"For I say unto you, Among those that are born of women, there hath not risen a greater prophet than John the Baptist: Notwithstanding he that is least in the kingdom of God and heaven is greater than he.

"And from the days of John the Baptist until now, the kingdom of heaven suffereth violence, and the violent take it by force.

"For all the prophets and the law prophesied until John. "And if ye will receive it, this is Elias, which was for to come.

"He that hath ears to hear, let him hear."

For all the people that heard him and the publicans, justified God, being baptized with the baptism of John. But the Pharisees and lawyers rejected the counsel of God against themselves, being not baptized of him.

Part V – Events of Christ Jesus From His Second To His Third Passover
(His Main Galilean Ministry)

And the Lord said, *"Whereunto they shall I liken the men of this generation? And to what are they like?*

"They are like unto children sitting in the marketplace, and calling one to another, and saying, We have piped unto you and ye have not danced; we have mourned to you, and ye have not lamented or wept.

"For John the Baptist came neither eating bread nor drinking wine; and ye say, He hath a devil.

"The Son of man came eating and drinking; and ye say, Behold a gluttonous man, and a winebibber, a friend of publicans and sinners!

"But wisdom is justified of all her children."

Jesus Upbraids Chorazin, Bethsaida, and Capernaum and He Invites the Heavy Laden

Then he began to upbraid the cities wherein most of his mighty works were done, because they repented not:

"Woe unto thee, Chorazin! woe unto thee Bethsaida! for if the mighty works, which were done in you, had been done in Tyre and Sidon, they would have repented long ago in sackcloth and ashes.

"But I say unto you, it shall be more tolerable for Tyre and Sidon at the day of judgment, than for you.

"And thou, Capernaum, which art exalted unto heaven, shall be brought down to hell: for if the mighty works, which have been done in thee, had been done in Sodom, it would have remained until this day.

"But I say unto you, That it shall be more tolerable for the land of Sodom in the day of judgment, than for thee."

At that time Jesus answered and said, *"I thank thee, O Father, Lord of heaven and earth, because thou hast hid these things from the wise and prudent, and hast revealed them unto babes.*

"Even so, Father: for so it seemed good in thy sight. "All things are delivered unto me of my Father: and no man knoweth the Son, but the Father; neither knoweth any man the Father, save the son, and he to whomsoever the Son will reveal Him.

Part V – Events of Christ Jesus From His Second To His Third Passover
(His Main Galilean Ministry)

"Come unto me, all ye that labour and are heavy laden, and I will give you rest.

"Take my yoke upon you, and learn of me; for I am meek and lowly in heart: and ye shall find rest unto your souls.

"For my yoke is easy, and my burden is light.

Anointing of His Feet by the Sinful But Forgiven Woman in the House of Pharisee Simon

And one of the Pharisees desired him that he would eat with him. And he went into the Pharisee's house, and sat down to meat.

And, behold, a woman in the city, which was a sinner, when she knew that Jesus sat at meat in the Pharisee's house brought an alabaster box of ointment.

And stood at his feet behind him weeping and washed his feet with her tears and dried them with the hairs of her head, and kissed his feet, and anointed him with the ointment.

Now when the Pharisee, named Simon, saw it, he spake within himself saying, "If this man were a prophet, would have known who and what manner of woman this is that toucheth him: for she is a sinner."

And Jesus answering said unto him, *"Simon, I have somewhat to say unto thee."* And he saith, Master say on.

"There was a certain creditor which had two debtors: the one he owed five hundred pence, and other fifty.

"And when they had nothing to pay, he frankly forgave them both, tell me therefore, which of them will love him most?"

Simon answered and said, I suppose that he, to whom he forgave most. And he said unto him, *"Thou hast rightly judged."*

**Part V – Events of Christ Jesus From His Second To His Third Passover
(His Main Galilean Ministry)**

And he turned to the woman, and said unto Simon,

"Seeth thou this woman? I entered into thine house, thou gavest me no water for my feet: but she hath washed my feet with tears, and wiped them with the hairs of her head.

"Thou gavest me no kiss; but this woman since the time I came in hath not ceased to kiss my feet.

"My head with oil thou didst not anoint: but this woman hath anointed my feet with ointment.

"Wherefore I say unto thee, Her sins, which are many, are forgiven; for she loved much: but to whom little is forgiven, the same loveth little."

And he said unto her, *"Thy sins are forgiven."*

And they that sat at meat with him began to say within themselves, Who is this that forgiveth sins also?

And he said to the woman, *"Thy faith hath saved thee in peace."*

Returning to Capernaum, He Heals a Blind and Dumb Demoniac, the Pharisees Attribute the Miracle to Beelzebub

Then was one brought unto him one possessed with a devil, blind and dumb: and he healed him, insomuch that the blind and dumb both spake and saw.

And all the people were amazed and said, Is not this the son of David?

But the Pharisees said he cast out devils through Beelzebub the chief of the devils. And Jesus knew their thoughts and said unto them:

"Every kingdom divided against itself is brought to desolation; and every city or house divided against itself shall not stand: "And if Satan cast out Satan, he is divided against himself; how shall then his kingdom stand?

Part V – Events of Christ Jesus From His Second To His Third Passover
(His Main Galilean Ministry)

"And if I by Beelzebub cast out devils, by whom do your children cast them out? Therefore, they shall be your judges.

"But if I cast out devils, by whom do your children cast them out? therefore they shall be your judges.

"But if I cast out devils by the Spirit with the finger of God, then no doubt the kingdom of God is come unto you.

"Or else how can one enter unto a strong man's house and spoil his goods, except he first bind the strong man? and then he will spoil his house.

"When a strong man armed keepeth his palace, his goods are in peace:

"But when a stronger than he shall come upon him, he taketh from him all his armour wherein he trusted, and divideth his spoils.

"He that is not with me is against me: and he that gathereth not with me is against me: and he that gathereth not with me scattereth abroad.

<u>Blasphemy Against the Holy Ghost</u>

"Wherefore I say unto you, All manner of sin and blasphemy shall be forgiven unto men, Verily I say unto you, All sins shall be forgiven unto the sons of men, and blasphemies wherewith soever they shall blaspheme: but the blasphemy against the Holy Ghost shall not be forgiven unto men, and hath never forgiveness, but is in danger of eternal damnation.

"And whosoever speaketh a word against the Son of man, it shall be forgiven him: but whosoever speaketh against the Holy Ghost it shall not be forgiven him, neither in this world, neither in the world to come; but is in danger of eternal damnation. "Either make the tree good, and his fruit good; or else make the tree corrupt, and his fruit corrupt: for the tree is known by his fruit.

"O generation of vipers, how can ye, being evil, speak good things? for out of the abundance of the heart the mouth speaketh.

"A good man out of the good treasure of the heart bringeth forth good things: and evil man out of the evil treasure bringeth forth evil things.

Part V – Events of Christ Jesus From His Second To His Third Passover
(His Main Galilean Ministry)

"But I say unto you, That every idle word that men shall speak, they shall give account thereof in the day of judgment.

"For by thy words thou shall be justified, and by thy words thou shall be condemned."

Seeking a Sign and the Answer—Unclean Spirits

Certain scribes and Pharisees were seeking a sign from Jesus saying, Master, we would see a sign from thee.

But he answered and said unto them, *"An evil and adulterous generation seeketh after a sign; and there shall be no sign be given to it, but the sign of the prophet Jonas:*

"For as Jonas was three days and three nights in the whale's belly; so shall the Son of man be three days and three nights in the heart of the earth.

"The men of Nineveh shall rise in judgment with this generation, and shall condemn it: because they repented at the preaching of Jonas: and behold, a greater than Jonas is here.

"The queen of the south shall rise up in the judgment with this generation, and shall condemn it: for she came from the uttermost parts of the earth to hear the wisdom of Solomon; and, behold, a greater than Solomon is here.

"When the unclean spirit is gone out of a man, he walketh through dry places, seeking rest, and findeth none.

"Then he saith, I will return unto my house from whence I came out; and when he is come, he findeth it empty, swept and garnished.

"Then goeth he, and taketh with himself seven other spirits more wicked than himself, and they enter in and dwell there: and the last state of that man is worse than the first. Even so shall it be also unto this wicked generation."

Part V – Events of Christ Jesus From His Second To His Third Passover
(His Main Galilean Ministry)

<u>Behold My Mother and My Brethren</u>

While he yet talked to the people, behold, his mother and his brethren stood without desiring to speak with him. Then one said unto him, Behold thy mother and thy brethren stand without, desiring to speak with thee.

He answered, *"Who is my mother? and who are my bretheren?"*

And he stretched forth his hand toward his disciples and said, *"Behold my mother and my brethren!*

"For whosoever shall do the will of my Father which is in heaven, the same is my brother, and my sister, and mother.

"My mother and my brethren are those which hear the word of God, and do it."

NOTES: Scriptures of the Topics	Matt	Mark	Luke
- Healing of the Centurion's servant	8:7,10-13		7:9
- Healing of Peter's mother and all those that were sick and with infirmities	8:14-17		
- Raising of the widow's son at Nain			7:13,14
- John the Baptist's mission of inquiry from his dungeon Machareus	11:4-19		7:22-28, 31-35
- Jesus upbraids Chorazin, Bethsaida, Capernaum, and he invited the heavy laden	11:20-30		
- Anointing of His feet by the sinful but forgiven woman in the house of Pharisee Simon			7:40-50
- Returning to Capernaum, He heals a blind and dumb demoniac; the Pharisees attribute the miracle to Beelzebub	12:25-30	3:23-27	11:17-23
- Blasphemy against the Holy Ghost	12:31-37	3:28,29	
- Seeking a sign and the answer—unclean spirits	12:39-45		11:24-26
- Behold My Mother and My Brethren	12:48-50	3:33-35	8:21

Part V – Events of Christ Jesus From His Second To His Third Passover
(His Main Galilean Ministry)

Doctrines and Commandments

125. Christ Jesus has power to restore life into those who have died.

126. Many shall come from the east and west, and shall sit down with Abraham, Isaac, and Jacob in the Kingdom of Heaven.

127. As one truly believes, so be it done unto him.

128. The children of the kingdom shall be cast out into outer darkness.

129. Among those that are born of women, there is not a greater prophet than John the Baptist. But he that is least in the kingdom of God is greater than he.

130. From the days of John the Baptist until now, the kingdom of heaven suffered violence, and the violence take it by force.

131. All the prophets and the law prophesied until John. And if you will receive it, is Elias, which was to come.

132. Wisdom is justified of all her children.

133. For cities to remain until this day they should have mighty works and should be exalted unto heaven.

134. All things are delivered unto Christ Jesus of His Father.

135. No man knows Christ but God.

136. No man knows God except the Son, and he to whosoever
Christ will reveal to Him.

137. Go to Christ Jesus! All of you that labor and are heavy laden: He will give you rest.

138. You shall find rest unto your soul by taking Christ's yolk
upon yourself, and learn of Him for He is meek and lowly in heart.

139. His yolk is easy, and His burden is light.

140. Our sins are forgiven by Christ and oneself.

141. Your faith has saved you.

142. For those who have great love, many sins are forgiven; and those who have little love, little is forgiven.

143. Every kingdom divided against itself is brought to desolation: and every city or house divided against itself shall not stand.

144. The kingdom of God is come upon you if Christ cast out devils by the spirit of God.

145. Anyone that is not with Christ is against Him.

146. He that does not gather with Christ scatters abroad.

Part V – Events of Christ Jesus From His Second To His Third Passover
(His Main Galilean Ministry)

147. Unclean spirits walk and exist out of a person and look for a place to rest. They may enter into a person and in fact may take many other spirits more wicked than himself and enter in and dwell there: and the last state of that man is worse than the first.

148. Whosoever speaks against Christ Jesus, it shall be forgiven him. (See Luke 12:10)

149. Danger of eternal damnation to those who blasphemy against the Holy Ghost. (See Luke 12:10)

150. A person is known by his fruit. Either he is good and his fruit good; or else he is corrupt and his fruit corrupt. A good man out of the good treasures of the heart brings forth good things; and an evil man out of evil treasure bring forth evil things.

151. In the day of judgment every idle word that men shall speak they shall give account.

152. For by your words you shall be justified, and by your words you shall be condemned.

153. An evil and adulterous generation seeks after a sign and there shall be no sign given to it.

154. Whosoever shall hear and do the will of God in heaven shall be the mother, brethren, and sister of Christ.

Lessons We Should Learn

1.   By our faith we are healed and made whole, and by faith our sins are forgiven. As one truly believes, it shall be done unto him. Christ Jesus has the power to heal, to forgive sins, and to raise the dead. By one's true belief, faith and love in Christ, light and life are restored unto those who endure.

2.   John the Baptist, man and symbol of repenting and sinning no more was then baptized to serve God. He that is least in the kingdom of God is greater than he. One's preparation is continuous and ongoing to serve God and to do His will each day as children of God. Wisdom is justified in guiding all thought, words and actions and therefore His will be done in Earth as it is in Heaven.

3.   A great commandment of Christ Jesus, *"All of you that labour and are heavy laden, come unto me and I will give you rest."* Take his yolk and his burden is light. What a promise! By putting first things first, our love goes out to others, our sins are forgiven, and our burden is light as we become one with Christ. For those that are not with Christ are against Him. Our faith in those commandments will and has saved us. As we enter into His kingdom living according to His commandments, our house is His house— one's home shall stand, for it is not divided against itself and brought into desolation.

Part V – Events of Christ Jesus From His Second To His Third Passover
(His Main Galilean Ministry)

4.   Christ is the Light and the Word. All that is, is His word. It is important to realize the power in thought and word. For by our words we shall be justified, and by our words we shall be condemned—every idle word shall be accounted for. A person is known by his fruit. Either he is good and his fruit is good, or else he is corrupt and his fruit corrupt.

A good man out of the good treasures of the heart brings forth good things, and an evil man out of evil treasures brings forth evil things. Therefore one's words, actions, deeds, and works must be a true expression of our faith in Christ and His words, doctrines and commandments.

5.   We are taken with this world and all the temptations all the waking hours each day. We soon become as conditioned to accept temptation as a normal practice. As one becomes one with Christ, the temptation becomes intense. One's sins are forgiven and unclean spirits have gone out as one is cleansed. But Christ Jesus warns us saying, *"when the unclean spirit is gone out of a man, he walks through dry places, seeking rest, and findeth none."* Then he saith, *"I will return unto my house from whence I came out; and when he is come, he findeth it empty, swept, and garnished."*

Then goeth he and taketh with himself seven other spirits more wicked than himself and they enter in and dwell there.

And the last state of that man is worse than the first. Even so shall it be also unto this wicked generation. (Matt. 12:43-45)

One must be on guard and realize that to join the temptations of society under the justification of doing indulgences in moderation is only becoming partners with temptuous spirits. Each and every thought, word, and action should be of the spirit of God. The kingdom of God is come upon us if Christ cast out devils by the spirit of God.

6.   In this chapter there is a strong and great warning from Christ Jesus in His doctrines about "Eternal Damnation." Jesus says, *"All manner of sin and blasphemy shall be forgiven unto men: but the blasphemy against the Holy Ghost shall not be forgiven unto men. And whosoever speaketh a word against the Son of man it shall be forgiven him; but whosoever speaketh against the Holy Ghost, it shall not be forgiven him, neither in this world, neither in the world to come."*

Part V – Events of Christ Jesus From His Second To His Third Passover
(His Main Galilean Ministry)

My Thoughts About the Lessons

_____

_____

_____

_____

_____

_____

_____

_____

_____

_____

_____

_____

_____

_____

_____

_____

_____

_____

_____

_____

_____

_____

_____

_____

_____

NOTES

Part V – Events of Christ Jesus From His Second To His Third Passover
(His Main Galilean Ministry)

13

He Spoke Many Things To Them In Parables

The Sower

Jesus began again to teach by the sea side; and there was gathered unto him a great multitude, so that he entered into a ship, and sat in the sea; and the whole multitude was by the sea on the land.

And he taught them many things by parables, and said unto them in is doctrines, *"Behold, a sower went forth to sow;*

"And when he sowed, some seeds fell by the way side, and the fowls came and devoured them up:

"Some fell upon the stony places, where they had not much earth: and forthwith they sprung up, because they had no deepness of earth:

"And when the sun was up, they were scorched; and because they had no root, they withered away.

"And some fell among thorns; and the thorns sprung up, and choked them:

"But other fell into good ground, and brought forth fruit, some an hundred fold, some sixty fold, some thirtyfold.

"Who hath ears to hear, let him hear."

And the disciples came, and said unto him, Why speaketh thou unto them in parables?

He answered and said unto them,
"Because it is given unto you to know the mysteries of the kingdom of heaven: but unto them that are without, all these things are done in parables:

Part V – Events of Christ Jesus From His Second To His Third Passover
(His Main Galilean Ministry)

"For whosoever hath, to him shall be given, and he shall have more abundance: but whosoever hath not, from him shall be taken away even that he hath.
"Therefore speak I to them in parables: because they seeing see not; and hearing they hear not, neither do they understand.

"And in them is fulfilled the prophecy of Esaias, which saith, 'By hearing ye shall hear, and shall not understand; and seeing ye shall see, and shall not perceive:

"'For this people's heart is waxed gross, and their ears are dull of hearing, and their eyes they have closed; lest at any time they should see with their eyes, and hear with their ears and should understand with their heart, and should be converted, and I should heal them.'

"But blessed are your eyes, for they see: and your ears, for they hear.

"For verily I say unto you, that many prophets and righteous men have desired to see those things which ye see, and have not seen them; and to hear those things which ye hear, and have not heard them.

"Hear ye therefore the parables of the sower.

"The sower soweth the word.

"Now the parable is this: The seed is the word of God. "And these are they by the wayside, where the word is sown; but when they have heard, Satan cometh immediately, and taketh away the word that was sown in their hearts, lest they should believe and be saved.

"And these are they likewise which are sown on stony ground; who, when they have heard the word, immediately receive it with gladness;

"And have no root in themselves, and so endure but for a time: afterward, when affliction or persecution ariseth for the word's sake, immediately they are offended and in time of temptation fall away.

"And these are they which are sown among thorns; such as hear the word."

Part V – Events of Christ Jesus From His Second To His Third Passover (His Main Galilean Ministry)

"And the cares of this world, and the deceitfulness of riches, and the lusts of other things entering in, choke the word, and it becometh unfruitful, and bring no fruit to perfection.

"And these are they which are sown on good ground; such as hear the word, and receive it, and understandeth it, which in an honest and good heart, and bring forth fruit, some thirty fold, some sixty, and some an hundred.

"They on the rock are they, which, when they hear, receive the word with joy; and these have no root, which for a while believe, and in time of temptation fall away.

"And that which fell among thorns are they, which when they have heard go forth, and are choked with cares and riches and pleasures of this life, and bring no fruit to perfection.

"But that on good ground are they, which in an honest and good heart having heard the word, keep it, and bring forth fruit with patience."

Wheat and Tares

Another parable put he forth unto them saying, *"The kingdom of heaven is likened unto a man which sowed good seed in his field:*

"But while men slept, his enemy came and sowed tares among the wheat, and went his way.

"But when the blade was sprung up and brought forth fruit, then appeared the tares also.

"So the servants of the householder came and said unto him, Sir, didst not thou sow good seed in thy field? from whence then hath it tares?

"He said unto them, An enemy hath done this. The servants said unto him, wilt thou then that we go and gather them up?

"But he said, Nay; lest while ye gather up the tares, ye root up also the wheat with them.

"Let both grow together until the harvest: and in the time of harvest I will say to the reapers, Gather ye together first the tares and bind them in bundles to burn them: but gather the wheat into my barn."

Part V – Events of Christ Jesus From His Second To His Third Passover
(His Main Galilean Ministry)

Mustard Seed

Another parable put he forth unto them saying,

"Whereunto shall we liken the kingdom of God? or with what comparison shall we compare it?

"It is like a grain of mustard seed, which, when it is sown in the earth, is less than all the seeds that be in the earth:

"But when it is sown, it groweth up, and becometh greater than all herbs, and shooteth out great branches; so that the fowls of the air may lodge under the shadow of it."

Nothing is Secret, That Shall Not be Made Manifest

And he said unto them, *"No man when he hath lighted a candle, covereth it with a vessel, or putteth it under a bed; but setteth it on a candlestick, that they which enter in may see the light.*

"For nothing is secret, that shall not be made manifest; neither any thing hid, that shall not be known and come abroad. "If a man have ears to hear, let him hear.

"Take heed therefore how ye hear; with what measure ye mete, it shall be measured to you: and unto you that hear shall more be given: for whosoever hath, to him shall be given; and whosoever hath not, from him shall be taken even that which he seemeth to have."

The Kingdom of Heaven is Like Unto Leaven

Another parable spake he unto them;

"The kingdom of heaven is like unto leaven, which a woman took, and hid in three measures of meal, till the whole was leavened".

Part V – Events of Christ Jesus From His Second To His Third Passover
(His Main Galilean Ministry)

Sower of Seeds and the Tares

And he said, *"So is the kingdom of God, as if a man should cast seed into the ground.*

"And should sleep, and rise night and day, and the seed should spring and grow up, he knoweth not how.

"For the earth bringeth forth fruit of herself; first the blade, then the ear, after that the full corn in the ear.

"But when the fruit is brought forth, immediately he putteth in the sickle, because the harvest is come."

And with many such parables he spake the word unto them, as they were able to hear it. But without a parable he spake not unto them: and when they were alone, he expounded all things to his disciples: and his disciples came unto him, saying, declare unto us the parable of the tares of the field. He answered and said unto them,

"He that soweth the good seed is the Son of man;

"The field is the world; the good seed are the children of the kingdom; but the tares are the children of the wicked one;

"The enemy that sowed them is the devil; the harvest is the end of the world; and the reapers are the angels.

"As therefore the tares are gathered and burned in the fire; so shall it be in the end of this world.

"The Son of man shall send forth his angels, and they shall gather out of his kingdom all things that offend, and them which do iniquity;

"And shall cast them into a furnace of fire: there shall be wailing and gnashing of teeth.

"Then shall the righteous shine forth as the sun in the kingdom of their Father. Who hath ears to hear, let him hear."

Part V – Events of Christ Jesus From His Second To His Third Passover
(His Main Galilean Ministry)

The Kingdom of Heaven Is As...

"Again the kingdom of heaven is like unto treasure hid in a field; the which when a man hath found, he hideth, and for joy thereof goeth and selleth all that he hath, and buyeth that field.

"Again, the kingdom of heaven is like unto a merchant man, seeking goodly pearls: "Who, when he had found one pearl of great price, went and sold all that he had, and bought it.

"Again, the kingdom of heaven is like unto a net, that was cast into the sea, and gathered of every kind:

"Which, when it was full, they drew to shore, and set down, and gathered the good into vessels, but cast the bad away.

"So shall it be at the end of the world: the angels shall come forth, and sever the wicked from among the just,

"And shall cast them into the furnace of fire: there shall be wailing and gnashing of teeth."

Jesus said unto them, *"Have ye understood all these things?"*

They said unto him, Yea, Lord.

Then he said unto them, *"Therefore every scribe which is instructed unto the kingdom of heaven is like unto a man that is an householder, which bringeth forth out of his treasure things new and old."*

And it came to pass, that when Jesus had finished these parables, he departed thence.

NOTES: Scriptures of the Topics	Matt.	Mark	Luke
- The Sower	13:3-23	4:14-20	8:5-15
- Wheat and Tares	13:24-30		
- Mustard Seed	13:31-32	4:30-32	
- Nothing in Secret That Shall Not	4:21-25	8:16-18	
- The Kingdom of Heaven Is Like	13:33		
- Sower of Seeds and the Tares	13:37-43	4:26-29	
- The Kingdom of Heaven Is As...	13:44-52		

Part V – Events of Christ Jesus From His Second To His Third Passover
(His Main Galilean Ministry)

Doctrines and Commandments

155. They that hear the word, and the cares of this world, the deceitfulness of riches, and the lusts of other things choke the word and it becometh unfruitful. (They are like the seeds planted among the thorns.)

156. They that have the word sown in their hearts and when they have heard, Satan comes immediately and takes away the word. (They are like the seeds sown by the wayside.)

157. They that have an honest and good heart having heard the word, keep it and bring forth fruit with patience. (They are like the seeds planted on good ground.)

158. Many prophets and righteous men have desired to see those things which the disciples see, and have not seen them; and desired to hear those things which the disciples hear, and have not heard them.

159. Nothing is secret that shall not be made manifest; neither anything hid that shall not be known and come abroad.

160. Christ shall send forth His angels and they shall gather out of His kingdom all things that offend, and those that do iniquity.

161. Those that offend and do iniquities shall be cast into a furnace of fire.

162. The righteous shall shine forth as the sun in the kingdom of their Father.

163. The angels shall come forth, and sever the wicked from among the just at the end of the world.

164. Unto everyone that has shall be given, and he shall have abundance; but from he that has nothing shall be taken away even that which he has.

Lessons We Should Learn

1. One lesson in this chapter is made very clear in Christ's own words: His disciples came to Him and asked why He was speaking to the people in parables. Christ tells his disciples that it is given to them to know the mysteries of heaven and that many prophets and righteous men have desired to see and hear those things that they see and hear. However, the people do not see nor hear them. The people hearing do not understand and those seeing do not perceive. Therefore, Jesus speaks to us in parables. The reasons that people do not understand are that their hearts are not opened, their ears are dull of hearing, and their eyes are closed.

Christ can heal us that we should see with our eyes, hear with our ears, and understand with our heart and be converted. Christ Jesus loves us and wants each of us to understand His words and to have His words become manifest in our hearts. He keeps nothing from us and reveals all truth to us openly. Christ Jesus tells us of the world and the kingdom, and of those things that He hears and sees from His Father God.

Part V – Events of Christ Jesus From His Second To His Third Passover
(His Main Galilean Ministry)

2.   Christ openly warns us in the various parables about the temptations of the world, the lust after riches and worldly things, and the cares of the world. Most of us become so involved in those and other things, that we spend very little time with the Light of God and the word of Christ. Therefore, in time the word is choked out and it becomes unfruitful in our lives. Jesus says, *"But on good ground are they, which is and honest and good heart having heard the word, keep it, and bring forth fruit with patience."*

3.   To become fruitful in His word we must grow in His word, and by sowing His word we become as Christ.Jesus says, *"He that soweth the good seed is the Son of man"*.

4.   In our daily living we each have a choice to make in our behavior, thoughts, words, and actions. Our choice is to become either children of the Kingdom or children of the wicked one Satan. In one's choice to do righteousness and become fruitful in daily life by sowing the good seed becomes as Christ and by reaping, becomes as the angels. In the end, when all which do iniquity are finished, *"then shall the righteous shine forth as the sun in the kingdom of their Father. Who has ears to hear, let him hear,"* says Christ. Take time to search the scriptures to see where Jesus tells us, *"He that soweth the good seed is the Son of man"* (Matt. 13:37) *"and the reapers are the angels"* (Matt. 13:39).

5.   Every parent has a responsibility to their children to be as a scribe and instruct their children unto the kingdom of heaven. As parents we may become as the sower of Christ's words, and as either the Son of man or fathers of Satan. Our children observe the things parents do and often become as their parents.

That which one does in righteousness and unrighteousness is the fruit that he brings forth. And by our fruits we shall be known. Therefore, as a householder, the word of God should be brought forth and be made fruitful unto our greatest treasure on earth, our children. All things new and old should be brought forth unto the family members.

Part V – Events of Christ Jesus From His Second To His Third Passover
(His Main Galilean Ministry)

My Thoughts About the Lessons

_____
_____
_____
_____
_____
_____
_____
_____
_____
_____
_____
_____
_____
_____
_____
_____
_____
_____
_____
_____
_____
_____
_____

NOTES

Part V – Events of Christ Jesus From His Second To His Third Passover
(His Main Galilean Ministry)

14

Continuation of Our Lord's Ministry
Throughout Galilee

Jesus Calms the Storm

When Jesus finished explaining the meaning of parables to his disciples and evening had come, he saw a great multitude about him, he said unto them, *"Let us pass over unto the other side of the lake."*

And a certain scribe came, and said unto him, Master, I will follow thee withersoever thou goest.

And Jesus said unto him, *"The foxes have holes, and the birds of the air have nests; but the Son of man hath not where to lay his head."*

And another disciple said unto him, Lord, suffer me first to go and bury my Father.

But Jesus said unto him, *"Follow me; and let the dead bury their dead."*

And when Jesus and his disciple were in the ship, there arose a great tempest in the sea and Jesus was asleep. And his disciple awoke him, saying, Lord, save us: we perish.

And he said unto them, *"Why are ye fearful, O ye of little faith? Where is your faith?"*

And he arose, and rebuked the winds, and said unto the sea,

"Peace, be still." And the wind ceased, and there was a great calm.

And he said to them, *"Why are ye so fearful? How is it that ye have no faith?"*

Part V – Events of Christ Jesus From His Second To His Third Passover
(His Main Galilean Ministry)

He Cures a Demoniac of Gadara of Many Devils

And they came over unto the other side of the sea, into the country of the Gadarenes. And immediately he was met by a man, out of the tombs, with an unclean spirit. When he saw Jesus afar off, he ran and worshipped him.

And cried with a loud voice, what have I to do with thee, Jesus, thou Son of the most high God? I adjure thee by God, that thou torment me not.

Jesus said unto him, *"Come out of the man, thou unclean spirit."*

And he asked him, *"What is thy name?"* And he said, Legion: because many devils were entered unto him.

And they asked Jesus that he would not command them to go out into deep. And there was a herd of swine and they besought him that he would suffer them to enter into them. And he suffered them.

Then the devils went out of the man, and entered into the swine: and the herd ran violently down into the lake and were choked.

When the Gadarenes saw that the man that was possessed of the devils was healed they besought Jesus to depart from them, for they were taken with great fear, and he sent back into the ship, and returned back again.

The man out of whom the devils had departed from besought Jesus that he might be with him: but Jesus sent him away, saying, *"Return to thine own house, to thy friends, and shew how great things the Lord hath done for thee, and hath had compassion on thee."*
And he departed, and began to publish in Decapolis how great things Jesus had done for him.

He Raises Jairus's Daughter and Heals A Woman with A Blood Disease

When Jesus had returned to the seashore many people gathered and a ruler of the synagogue, named Jairus saw him and fell at his feet. And besought him greatly saying, "My little daughter lieth at the point of death: I pray thee come and lay thy hands on her, that she may be healed; and she shall live."

Part V – Events of Christ Jesus From His Second To His Third Passover
(His Main Galilean Ministry)

And Jesus went with him; and many people followed him, and thronged him.

And a certain woman who had an issue of blood for twelve years and had suffered many things of many physicians, and had spent all that she had, and was not bettered, but rather grew worse, When she had heard of Jesus, came in behind and touched his garment.

For she said, "If I may touch but his clothes, I shall be whole."

And right away her blood dried up and she felt in her body that she was healed of that plague.

And Jesus, immediately knowing in himself that virtue had gone out of him, turned himself about in the press, and said, *"Who touched my clothes? Somebody, hath touched me: for I perceive that virtue is gone out of me. Who touched me?"*

When the woman saw that she was not hid, she came trembling and fell at his feet and told Jesus how she was healed immediately when she had touched him.

And he said unto her, *"Daughter, be of good comfort: thy faith hath made thee whole; go in peace, and be whole of thy plague."*

There came one from the ruler of the synagogue's house and said to him, Thy daughter is dead, why trouble the Master any further?

As soon as Jesus heard the word he said to the ruler of the synagogue, *"Be not afraid, only believe. Fear not: believe only, and she shall be made whole."*

And when he came into the house he had no man go in save Peter, James, and John and the father and mother of the maiden.

And all wept, and be wailed her: but he said, *"Give place: Weep not; Why make ye this ado? she is not dead, but sleepeth."*

And they laughed him to scorn, knowing that she was dead.

Part V – Events of Christ Jesus From His Second To His Third Passover
(His Main Galilean Ministry)

And he put them all out, and took her by the hand, and called, saying, *"Maid, arise. Talitha cumi"* (Being interpreted, *"Damsel, I say unto thee, arise"*); and her spirit came again and she arose straight way: and he commanded give her meat. And her parents were astonished: and he charged them that they should tell no man what was done.

Jesus Heals Two Blind Men and Casts Out a Demon

And when Jesus departed thence, two blind men followed him, crying, and saying, Thou Son of David, have mercy on us.

And Jesus said unto them, *"Believe ye that I am able to do this?"* They said unto him, "Yea, Lord."

Then he touched their eyes, saying, *"According to your faith be it unto you."*

And their eyes were opened; and Jesus straightly charged them, saying, *"See that no man know it."* But when they departed, spread abroad his fame in all that country.

Jesus Visits Nazareth Again, When His Countrymen Disbelieve In Him

And Jesus departed and came into his own country; and his disciples followed him.

When the Sabbath day came he began to teach in the synagogue: and many hearing him were astonished, saying, From whence hath this man these things? and what wisdom is this which is given unto him, that even such mighty works are wrought by his hands?

Is not this the carpenter, the son of Mary, the brother of James, and Joses, and of Juda, and Simon? and are not his sisters here with us? And they were offended at him.

But Jesus said unto them, *"A prophet is not without honour, but in his own country, and among his own country, and kin, and in his own house."* And he could do no mighty work, save that he laid his hands upon a few sick folk, and healed them.

And he marveled because of their unbelief. And he went round about the villages, teaching.

Part V – Events of Christ Jesus From His Second To His Third Passover
(His Main Galilean Ministry)

Christ Finds the Harvest Plenteous But the Labourers Are Few

And Jesus went about all the cities and villages, teaching in their synagogues and preaching the gospel of the kingdom, and healing every sickness and every disease among the people.

But when he saw the multitudes, he was moved with compassion on them, because they fainted, and were scattered abroad, as sheep having no shepherd. Then he said unto his disciples, *The harvest truly is plenteous, but the labourers are few;*

" Pray ye therefore the Lord of the harvest, that he will send forth labourers into his harvest."

NOTES: Scriptures of the Topics	Matt.	Mark	Luke
-Jesus calms the storm	8:20,22,26		8:22,25 4:35,39,40
- He cures a demoniac of Gardara of many devils		5:8,9,19	8:30,39
- He raises Jairus' daughter and heals a woman with a blood disease	9:22,24	5:30,31, 34,36, 39,41	8:44-46,48,50,52,54
- Jesus heals two blind men and casts out a demon	9:28-30		
- Jesus visits Nazareth again, when his countrymen disbelieve in Him	13:57	6:4	
- Christ finds the harvest plenteous but the laborers are few	9:37,38		

Part V – Events of Christ Jesus From His Second To His Third Passover
(His Main Galilean Ministry)

Doctrines and Commandments

165. One is healed--made whole and of good comfort--by his faith, lack of fear, and belief only. (Matt. 9:22)

166. A prophet is not without honor in most places.

167. A prophet is without honor in his own country, and among his own kin, and in his own house. (Matt. 13:57)

168. The harvest truly is plenteous, but the laborers are few. Therefore, pray that the Lord will send forth laborers into His harvest.

Lessons We Should Learn

1.   Faith that Christ can heal affliction and all manner of illness is needed to be healed, made whole, and be in comfort and peace.

2.   Christ deals with demonic affliction and he casts out unclean spirits. In the Lord's prayer Jesus teaches us to pray, lead us not into temptation but deliver us from evil, and if one realizes that all that one asks in His name it shall be given. One would be very foolish to believe that Satan is not tempting our every thought and always waiting to tempt at the most opportune time.

3.   Those who choose to give themselves into the Lord and be as the sower and do the will of their Heavenly Father is as the Son of man and as the angels in the harvest. When serving the Lord one must see each day as a missionary unto the Father, in their daily routine job and life.

Part V – Events of Christ Jesus From His Second To His Third Passover
(His Main Galilean Ministry)

My Thoughts About the Lessons

_____

_____

_____

_____

_____

_____

_____

_____

_____

_____

_____

_____

_____

_____

_____

_____

_____

_____

_____

_____

_____

_____

NOTES

Part V – Events of Christ Jesus From His Second To His Third Passover
(His Main Galilean Ministry)

15

The Twelve Disciples Continue Their
Missions

The Twelve Are Sent Forth To Preach And Heal The Sick

Then Jesus called his twelve disciples together and gave them power and authority over all devils, and to cure diseases.

And he sent them to preach the kingdom of God, and to heal the sick.

And he said unto them, *"Take nothing for your journey, neither staves, nor scrip, neither bread, neither money; neither have two coats apiece.*

"And whatsoever house ye enter into, there abide, and thence depart, from that place. "And whosoever will not receive you, when ye go out of that city, shake off the very dust from your feet for a testimony against them.

"Verily I say unto you, it shall be more tolerable for Sodom and Gomorrah in the day of judgment, than for that city."

And they departed, and went through the towns, preaching the gospel, and healing everywhere.

The Disciples Return to Jesus: Telling All They Have Done And Taught

And the apostles gathered themselves together unto Jesus, and told him all things, both what they had done, and what they had taught.

And he said unto them, *"Come ye yourselves apart into a desert place, and rest awhile:"* for there were many coming and going, and they had no leisure so much as to eat.

And they departed into a desert place, belonging to the city called Bethsaida, by ship privately.

Part V – Events of Christ Jesus From His Second To His Third Passover (His Main Galilean Ministry)

Jesus Feeds Five Thousand People

After these things Jesus went over to the Sea of Galilee. And a great multitude followed him because they saw his miracles which he did on them that were diseased.

And Jesus went up into a mountain and there he sat with his disciples.

And the Passover, a feast of the Jews was nigh. When Jesus then lifted up his eyes, and saw a great company come unto him, he said unto them. *"They need not depart; give ye them to eat."*

And he said to Philip, *"Whence shall we buy bread, that these may eat?"* Philip answered him, "Two hundred penny worth of bread is not sufficient for them, that every one of them may take a little."

And he said to his disciples, *"Make them sit down by fifties in a company."*

Jesus asked them, *"How many loaves have ye? Go and see."* Andrew said unto him, there is a lad here, which hath five barley loaves, and two small fishes: but what are they among so many?"

Jesus said, *"Bring them hither to me."* And he took the five loaves and two fishes, and looking up to heaven, he blessed and brake and gave the loaves to his disciples, and the disciples to the multitude. And they did eat and were filled.

When they were filled, he said to his disciples,

"Gather up the fragments that remain, that nothing be lost." Therefore, they gathered them together, and filled twelve baskets with the fragments of the five barley loaves, which remained over and above unto them that had eaten. Then those men, when they had seen the miracle that Jesus did, said, This is of a truth that prophet that should come into the world.

Part V – Events of Christ Jesus From His Second To His Third Passover
(His Main Galilean Ministry)

Jesus Sends Disciples Westward To Bethsaida Across The Lake: He Walks To Them Across The Lake At Night

And straightway he constrained his disciples to get into the ship and to go to the other side unto Bethsaida, while he sent away the people.

And when he had sent them away, he departed into a mountain to pray.

And when evening was come, the ship was in the midst of the sea, and he alone was on land. The wind was contrary and the ship was now tossed with waves.

And in the fourth watch of the night Jesus went unto them, walking on the sea.

And when the disciples saw him walking on the sea, they were troubled, saying, It is a spirit; and they cried out for fear.

But straightway Jesus spake unto them, saying,

"Be of good cheer; it is I; be not afraid."

And Peter answered him and said, Lord if it be thou, bid me come unto thee on the water.

And he said, *"Come."* And Peter came out of the ship and walked on the water, to go to Jesus.

But when he saw the wind boisterous, he was afraid; and beginning to sink, he cried, saying, Lord save me.

And immediately Jesus stretched forth his hand, and caught him, and said unto him, *"O thou of little faith, wherefore didst thou doubt?"*

And when they were come into the ship, the wind ceased. Then they that were in the ship were sure amazed in themselves beyond measure, and wondered For they considered not the miracle of the loaves; for their heart was hardened. Then they came and worshipped him, saying, Of a truth thou art the Son of God.

Part V – Events of Christ Jesus From His Second To His Third Passover
(His Main Galilean Ministry)

Jesus The Bread of Life: His Words The Spirit of Life

The day following the miracle of feeding the five thousand, when the people which stood on the other side of the sea, where the miracle took place, saw that there was no other boat there, save that one where into his disciples were entered, and that Jesus went not with his disciples into the boat, but that his disciples were gone away alone;

(Howbeit there came other boats from Tiberias nigh unto the place where they did eat bread, after that the Lord had given thanks:)

When the people therefore saw that Jesus was not there, neither his disciples, they also took shipping, and came to Capernaum, seeking for Jesus.

And when they found him on the other side of the sea, they said unto him, Rabbi when camest thou hither?

Jesus answered them and said, *"Verily, verily, I say unto you, Ye seek me, not because ye saw the miracles, but because ye did eat of the loaves, and were filled.*

"Labour not for the meat which perisheth, but for that meat which endureth unto everlasting life, which the Son of man shall give unto you: for him hath God the Father sealed."

Then they said unto him, "What shall we do, that we might work the works of God?"

Jesus answered and said unto them, *"This is the work of God, that ye believe on him whom he hath sent."*

They said therefore unto him, What sign shewest thou then, that we may see, and believe thee? what dost thou work?

Our fathers did eat manna in the desert; as it is written. "He gave them bread from heaven to eat."

Then Jesus said unto them, *"Verily, verily, I say unto you, Moses gave you not that bread from heaven; but my Father giveth you the true bread from heaven.*

Part V – Events of Christ Jesus From His Second To His Third Passover
(His Main Galilean Ministry)

"For the bread of God is he which cometh down from heaven, and giveth life unto the world."

Then said they unto him, Lord, evermore give us this bread.

And Jesus said unto them, *"I am the bread of life: he that cometh to me shall never hunger: and he that believeth on me shall never thirst.*

"But I said unto you, That ye also have seen me, and believe not.

"All that the Father giveth me shall come to me; and him that cometh to me I will in no wise cast out.

"For I came down from heaven, not to do mine own will, but the will of him that sent me.

"And this is the Father's will which hath sent me, that of all which he hath given me I should lose nothing, but should raise it up again at the last day.

And this is the will of him that sent me, that every one which seeth the Son, and believeth on him, may have everlasting life: and I will raise him up at the last day."

The Jews then murmured at him because he said, *I am the bread which came down from heaven.*

And they said, Is this not Jesus, the son of Joseph, whose father and mother we know? how is it then that he saith, *I came down from heaven?*

Jesus therefore answered and said unto them, *"Murmur not among yourselves.*

"No man can come to me, except the Father which hath sent me draw him: and I will raise him up at the last day.

"It is written in the prophets, 'And they shall be all taught of God.' Every man therefore that hath heard, and hath learned of the Father, cometh unto me.

"Not that any man hath seen the Father, save he which is of God, he hath seen the Father.

Part V – Events of Christ Jesus From His Second To His Third Passover
(His Main Galilean Ministry)

"Verily, verily, I say unto you, He that believeth on me hath everlasting life.

"I am that bread of life.

"Your fathers did eat manna in the wilderness, and are dead.

"This is the bread which cometh down from heaven, that a man may eat thereof, and not die.

"I am the living bread which came down from heaven: if any man eat of this bread, he shall live for ever: and the bread

that I will give is my flesh, which I will give for the life of the world."

The Jews therefore strove among themselves, saying, how can this man give us his flesh to eat?

Then Jesus said unto them, *"Verily, verily, I say unto you, Except ye eat of the flesh of the Son of man, and drink his blood, ye have no life in you.*

"Whoso eateth my flesh, and drinketh my blood, hath eternal life; and I will raise him up at the last day.

"For my flesh is meat indeed, and my blood is drink indeed.

"He that eateth my flesh, and drinketh my blood, dwelleth in me, and I in him.

"As the living Father hath sent me, and I live by the Father: so he that eateth me, even he shall live by me.

"This is that bread which came down from heaven: not as your fathers did eat manna, and are dead; he that eateth of this bread shall live for ever."

These things said he in the synagogue as he taught in Capernaum.

Many therefore of his disciples, when they had heard this, said, "This is an hard saying; who can hear it?"

When Jesus knew in himself that his disciples murmured at it, he said unto them,

"Doth this offend you?

Part V – Events of Christ Jesus From His Second To His Third Passover
(His Main Galilean Ministry)

"What and if ye shall see the Son of man ascend up where he was before?

"It is the spirit that quickeneth; the flesh, profiteth nothing: the words that I speak unto you, they are spirit and they are life.

"But there are some of you that believe not." For Jesus knew from the beginning who they were that believed not, and who should betray him.

And he said, *"Therefore said I unto you, that no man can come unto me, except it were given unto him of my Father."*

From that time many of his disciples went back, and walked no more with him.

Then Jesus said to the twelve, *"Will ye also go away?"*

Then Simon Peter answered him, Lord, to whom shall we go? Thou hast the words of eternal life.

And we believe and are sure that thou art that Christ, the Son of the living God.

Jesus answered them, *"Have not I chosen you twelve, and one of you is a devil?"*

He spake of Judas Iscariot the son of Simon: for he it was that should betray him, being one of the twelve.

Part V – Events of Christ Jesus From His Second To His Third Passover
(His Main Galilean Ministry)

NOTES: Scriptures of the Topics	Matt	Mark	Luke	John
- The twelve are sent forth to preach and heal the sick		6:10,11	9:3-5	
- The disciples return to Jesus telling all they have done and taught	6:31	6:31		
- Jesus feeds five thousand people	14:16,17	6:37,38	9:13,14	6:5,10,12
- Jesus sends disciple westward to Bethsaida across the lake; He walks across the lake at night	14:27, 29,31	6:50		6:20
- Jesus is the Bread of Life; His words are the Spirit of life				6:26,27,29, 32,33,35-58, 61-65,67,70

Doctrines and Commandments

169. Go apart into a desert place and rest awhile.

170. One may walk upon the water as Peter if the Lord commands you to do so and if you have no doubt and have great faith.

171. Labor not for meat which will perish, but for that meat which will endure unto everlasting life.

172. God the Father has sealed for Christ that meat which will endure unto everlasting life.

173. Christ Jesus is the living bread which came down from heaven. God the Father gives you the true bread from heaven. The bread of God is Christ which came down from heaven and gives life unto the world. Christ Jesus is the bread of life and he that goes to Christ shall never hunger; he that believes on Christ shall never thirst. If any man eats of this bread he shall live forever. The bread that Christ will give is His flesh, which He will give for the life of the world.

174. All that God the Father gives to Christ Jesus shall go to Christ and those that go to Christ will not be cast out.

175. Christ came down from heaven not to do His own will but the will of our Father in Heaven.

Part V – Events of Christ Jesus From His Second To His Third Passover
(His Main Galilean Ministry)

176. The Father's will for Christ is that all that He had given to

Christ will not be lost and will be raised up again at the last day. And that everyone which sees Christ and believes on Him, may have everlasting life and Christ will raise him up at the last day.

177. No man can go to Christ Jesus except those that God has sent Christ to draw him, and Christ will raise him up at the last day.

178. Every man that has heard and has learned of the Father comes unto Christ.

179. He which is of God has seen the Father.

180. He that believes on Christ has everlasting life.

181. Except you eat the flesh of the Son of man, and drink His blood, you have no life in you.

182. As the living God has sent Christ and Christ Jesus lives by the Father, he that eats Christ, he shall live by Christ.

183. It is the spirit that quickens; the flesh profits nothing.

184. The words that Christ speaks unto you are spirit and they are life.

Also covered in Chapter 10

75.   Jesus gives commandments to disciples going on their mission and should be used in their daily missions.

1) Take no money with you for your trip. No staves, scrip, bread, or two coats.

2) Take the bare necessities for your traveling and salute no man by the way.

3) Inquire about the worthy in each place you may go.

4) Salute the house you enter and if worthy bless it.

5) Whosoever does not receive you as you depart, shake off the dust of your feet for a testimony against them when you leave that city.

Part V – Events of Christ Jesus From His Second To His Third Passover
(His Main Galilean Ministry)

Lessons We Should Learn

1.	Christ Jesus set standards to follow for missionaries and disciples to follow. Specifics of these rules, standards, and commandments can be identified in the doctrines and specifically in doctrine #75 (also found in Chapter 10)

2.	Jesus walks on water and commands Peter to do His will, have faith, and not to doubt. Christ has to express these miracles for His disciples to believe. Many of His disciples doubted when Christ fed the five thousand. As followers and disciples of Christ, many miracles may happen and come about if we believe and will not doubt.

3.	Jesus is the bread of life and His words are the spirit of life. One must partake of this bread and His words daily so that we may dwell in Christ Jesus, and that Christ dwells in us so that we may attain life everlasting.

4.	As we strive to do His will, God the Father may give us unto Christ Jesus.

Part V – Events of Christ Jesus From His Second To His Third Passover
(His Main Galilean Ministry)

My Thoughts About the Lessons

_____

_____

_____

_____

_____

_____

_____

_____

_____

_____

_____

_____

_____

_____

_____

_____

_____

_____

_____

_____

_____

_____

_____

_____

_____

NOTES

Part VI – From Third Passover to the Beginning of the Last Passover Week

16

Jesus Teaches The Commandments of God

Transgressions and Hypocrites Bound by Tradition

Then came to Jesus scribes and Pharisees, which were of Jerusalem, saying, Why do thy disciples transgress the tradition of the elders? for they wash not their hands when they eat bread. But he answered and said unto them, *"Why do ye also transgress the commandments of God by your tradition?*

"For God commanded, saying and Moses said, 'Honour thy father and mother:' and,' He that curseth father and mother, let him die the death.'

"But ye say, Whosoever shall say to his father or his mother, It is a gift, by whatsoever thou mightest be profited by me; he shall be free.

"And honour not his father or his mother, he shall be free. Thus have ye made the commandment of God of none effect by your tradition, which ye have delivered: and many such like things do ye.

"Ye hypocrites, well did Esaias prophesy of you, saying, "'This people draweth nigh unto me with their mouth, and honoureth me with their lips; but their hearts is far from me.

"But in vain they do worship me teaching for doctrines the commandments of men."'

"For laying aside the commandments of God, ye hold the tradition of men, as the washing of pots and cups: and many other such like things ye do."

And he called to the multitude, and said unto them,
"Hearken unto me every one of you and understand: "Not that which goeth into the mouth defileth a man: but that which cometh out of the mouth, this defileth a man.

Part VI – From Third Passover to the Beginning of the Last Passover Week

"If any man have ears to hear, let him hear."

Then came his disciples, and said unto him, Knowest thou that the Pharisees were offended, after they heard this saying?

But he answered and said, *"Every plant, which my heavenly Father hath not planted, shall be rooted up.*

"Let them alone: they be blind leaders of the blind. And if the blind lead the blind, both shall fall into the ditch."

Then answered Peter and said unto him, "Declare unto us this parable."

And Jesus said, *"Are ye also yet without understanding? Do ye not perceive, that whatsoever thing from without entereth into the man, it cannot defile him;*

"Do ye not understand that whatsoever entereth in at the mouth goeth into the belly, and is cast out into the draught?

"But those things which proceed out of the mouth come forth from the heart; and they defile the man.

"For out of the heart proceed evil thoughts, murders, adulteries, fornication, thefts, false witness, blasphemies, covetousness, wickedness, deceit, lasciviousness, an evil eye, pride, foolishness:

"All these evil things come from within, and defile the man.
"These are the things that defile a man: but to eat with unwashen hands defileth not a man."

Jesus Goes Into the Coast of Tyre and Sidon: the Syrophenician Woman's Faith Gains a Cure for Her Daughter

Then Jesus went thence, and departed into the coasts of Tyre and Sidon. And beheld a woman of Canaan, she was a Greek, a Syrophenician by nation; and she besought him that he would cast forth the devil out of her daughter.

Part VI – From Third Passover to the Beginning of the Last Passover Week

But he answered her not a word. And his disciples came and besought him, saying, send her away; for she crieth after us.

But he answered and said, *"I am not sent but unto the lost sheep of the house of Israel."*

Then she came and worshipped him, saying, Lord, help me.

But he answered and said, *"Let the children first be filled: It is not meet to take the children's bread, and cast it to the dogs."*

And she said, "Truth, Lord: yet the dogs eat the crumbs which fall from the masters' table."

Then Jesus answered and said unto her, *"O woman, great is thy faith: be it unto thee even as thou wilt.*

"For this saying go thy way; the devil is gone out of thy daughter."

And her daughter was made whole from that very hour..

He Returns to the Sea of Galilee Through Decapolis: Healing Many and Feeds Four Thousand

And departing from the coast of Tyre and Sidon, he came unto the sea of Galilee, through the midst of the coasts of Decapolis.

And great multitudes came unto him, having with them those that were lame, blind, dumb, maimed, and many others and cast them down at Jesus' feet; and he healed them: and they brought him one that was deaf, and had a speech impediment.

And Jesus took him aside from the multitude, and put his finger into his ears, and he spit, and touched his tongue; and looking up to heaven, he sighed, and saith unto him, *"Ephphatha"* that is, *"be opened."*

And straightway his ears were opened, and the string of his tongue was loosed, and he spake plain. The multitudes wondered, when they saw the dumb to speak, the maimed to be whole, the lame to walk and the blind to see: and they glorified the God of Israel.

Part VI – From Third Passover to the Beginning of the Last Passover Week

The multitude being very great, and having nothing to eat, Jesus called his disciples unto him and said,

"I have compassion on the multitude, because they have now been with me three days, and have nothing to eat:

"And if I send them away fasting to their own houses, they will faint by the way; for divers of them came from far."

And his disciples say unto him, "Whence should we have so much bread in the wilderness, as to fill so great a multitude?"

And Jesus said, *"How many loaves have ye?"* And they said, Seven and a few little fishes.

And he commanded the multitude to sit down on the ground.

And he took the seven loaves and the fishes, and gave thanks, and broke them, and gave to his disciples, and the disciples to the multitude.

And they did all eat, and were filled: and they took up of the broken meat that was left seven baskets full.

There were four thousand men beside women and children that did eat.

And he sent away the multitude, and took ship, and came into the coast of Magdala.

The Pharisees and Sadducees Require a Sign

The Pharisees also with the Sadducees came, and tempting desired him that he would shew them a sign from heaven.

He answered and said unto them, *"Why doth this generation seek after a sign? Verily I say unto you, There shall no sign be given unto this generation?"*

Part VI – From Third Passover to the Beginning of the Last Passover Week

"When it is evening, ye say, It will be fair weather: for the sky is red.

"And in the morning, It will be foul weather to day: for the sky is red and lowring. O ye hypocrites, ye can discern the face of the sky; but can ye not discern the signs of the times?

"A wicked and adulterous generation seeketh after a sign; and there shall no sign be given unto it, but the sign of the prophet Jonas."

And he left them, and departed.

He Warns Against Leaven Doctrine of Bethsaida

And when his disciples were come to the other side of the sea of Galilee, they had forgotten to take bread.

Then Jesus said unto them, *"Take heed and beware of the leaven of the Pharisees and of the Sadducees and of Herod."*

And they reasoned among themselves, saying, It is because we have taken no bread.

Which then Jesus perceived, he said unto them,

"O ye of little faith, why reason among yourselves, because ye have brought no bread?

Perceive ye not yet, neither understand? Have ye your heart yet hardened?
"Having eyes, see not? and having ears, hear ye not? and do ye not remember. Do ye not understand, neither remember the five loaves of the five thousand, and how many baskets full of fragments ye took up?"

They say unto him, Twelve.

"Neither the seven loaves of the four thousand, and how many baskets ye took up?" And they said seven.
"How is it that ye do not understand that I spake it not to you concerning bread, that ye should beware of the leaven of the Pharisees and of the Sadducees?"

Part VI – From Third Passover to the Beginning of the Last Passover Week

Healing of a Blind Man

And Jesus went to Bethsaida and they brought a blind man unto him. And he took the blind man by the hand and led him out of town; and when he had spit on his eyes, and put his hands upon him, he asked him if he could see.

And he looked up and said, "I see men as trees, walking." Jesus put his hands again upon his eyes, and he was restored, and saw every man clearly.

And he sent him away to his house, saying,

"Neither go into the town, nor tell it to any in the town."

NOTES: Scriptures of the Topics	Matt	Mark
- Transgressions and Hypocrites bound by tradition	15:3-9-11,13-20	7:6-16,18-23
- Jesus goes into the Coast of Tyre and Sidon: the Syrophenician woman's faith gains a cure for her daughter	15:24,26,28	7:27
- He returns to the Sea of Galilee through Decopolos: healing many and feeds four thousand	15:32,34	7:34, 8:2,3,5
- The Pharisees and Sadducees require a sign	16:2-4	8:12
- He warns against leaven of doctrine in Bethsaida	16:6,8-12	8:15,17,21
- Healing of a blind man		8:26

Part VI – From Third Passover to the Beginning of the Last Passover Week

Doctrines and Commandments

185. By our traditions we transgress the commandments of God and by these traditions we make the commandments of God of none effect.

186. People draw near to Christ Jesus with their mouth and honor Christ with their lips; but their heart is far from Christ Jesus. They are hypocrites, in vain they worship Christ, not His teachings or His doctrines, but the commandments of men.

187. That which goes into the mouth does not defile man, but that which comes out of the mouth, for it comes forth from the heart, defiles the man.

188. Out of the heart proceed evil thoughts, murders, adulterers, fornication, thefts, false witness, blasphemies, covetousness, wickedness, deceit, lasciviousness, an evil eye, pride, and foolishness. All these evil things come from within, and defile the man.

189. Every plant which our Heavenly Father hath not planted, shall be rooted up.

190. Let them alone: they be blind leaders of the blind, and if the blind lead the blind, both shall fall into the ditch.

Lessons We Should Learn

1.   By family and social conditioning we allow tradition to be paramount over our behavior--right or wrong. Seldom does one take time to compare the word of God with one's traditions and the expression of one's speech and heart.

2.   All forms of evil enter the mind and heart. As masters of our own being we can express any form of that evil or none at all. The words of Christ Jesus may be allowed to enter into the mind and heart for His words are the light of the world and are also everywhere present. All is within one's being: the light and the dark. Which shall be the expression of one's faith? The choice is to be made before uttering one word and continued judgment must be made of one's self, or else evil traditions of man shall defile one's being in all manner of evil thoughts, words, and acts.

Part VI – From Third Passover to the Beginning of the Last Passover Week

My Thoughts About the Lessons

_____

_____

_____

_____

_____

_____

_____

_____

_____

_____

_____

_____

_____

_____

_____

_____

_____

_____

_____

_____

_____

_____

_____

_____

Part VI – From Third Passover to the Beginning of the Last Passover Week

17

Jesus is the Christ: The Christ of God

Peter's Confession

W hen Jesus came into the coasts of Caesarea Philippi, He asked his disciples, saying,

"Whom do men say that I the Son of man am?"

And they said, Some say that thou art John the Baptist: some Elias; and others Jeremias, and others say that one of the old prophets is risen again.

He said unto them, *"But whom say ye that I am?"*

And Simon Peter answered and said, Thou art the Christ, the Son of the living God; The Christ of God.

And Jesus answered and said unto him, *"Blessed art thou Simon Barjona: for flesh and blood hath not revealed it unto thee, but my Father which is in heaven.*

"And I say also unto thee, that thou art Peter, and upon this rock I will build my church; and the gates of hell shall not prevail against it.

"And I will give unto thee the keys of the kingdom of heaven: and whatsoever thou shalt bind on earth shall be bound in heaven: and whatsoever thou shalt loose on earth shall be loosed in heaven."

Then charged his disciples that they should tell no man that he was Jesus the Christ.

Part VI – From Third Passover to the Beginning of the Last Passover Week

He Foretells His Death and Resurrection: Reproof of Peter

From that time forth Jesus began to show his disciples, how that he must go unto Jerusalem, saying,

"The Son of man must suffer many things, and be rejected of the elders and chief priests and scribes, and be slain, and be raised the third day."

Then Peter took him, and began to rebuke him, saying, Be it far from thee Lord: this shall not be unto thee.

But he turned and said unto Peter, *"Get thee behind me, Satan: thou art an offence unto me: for thou savourest not the things that be of God, but those that be of men."*

Then said Jesus unto his disciples and the people, *"If any man will come after me, let him deny himself, and take up his cross daily and follow me.*

"For whosoever will save his life shall lose it: and whosoever will lose his life for my sake and the gospels, the same shall save it.

"For what is a man profited, if he shall gain the whole world, and lose his own soul? or be cast away? or what shall a man give in exchange for his soul?

"For whosoever shall be ashamed of me and my words in this adulterous and sinful generation; of him shall the Son of man be ashamed, when he shall come in his own glory, and in the glory of his father with the holy angels.

"For the Son of man shall come in the glory of his Father with his angels; and then he shall reward every man according to his works.

"Verily I say unto you, There be some of them standing here, which shall not taste of death, till they see the Son of man coming in his kingdom and see the kingdom of God come with power."

Part VI – From Third Passover to the Beginning of the Last Passover Week

NOTES: Scriptures of the Topics	Matt.	Mark	Luke
- Peter's confession	16:13,15-19	8:27, 29	9:18,20
- He foretells his death and resurrection: reproof of Peter	16:23	8:33	9:22
- Man must take up his cross and follow Jesus	16:24-28	8:34-38 9:1	9:23-27

Doctrines and Commandments

191. Blessed are the followers of Christ who recognize Jesus as the Christ of God.

192. Blessed are they that receive revelation from God the Father and not from men.

193. Thou art Peter, and upon this rock I will build my church; and the gates of hell shall not prevail against it.

194. Christ will give unto you the keys of the kingdom of heaven: and whatsoever you shalt bind on earth shall be bound in heaven: and whatsoever you shall loose on earth shall be loosed in heaven.

195. When one does those things that are not morally pleasing and of God, but of man, they are of Satan.

196. If any man will come after Christ, let him deny himself, and take up his cross daily and follow Christ.

197. Whosoever will save his life shall lose it; and whosoever will lose his life for Christ's sake and the gospel (his teachings) shall find it.

198. For what is a man profited, if he shall gain the whole world, and lose his own soul? Or what shall a man give in exchange for his soul.

199. Christ Jesus shall come in the glory of his Father with his angels; and then he shall reward every man according to his works.

200. There are some which shall not taste of death, until they see Christ Jesus coming in his kingdom, in God's power and with the holy angels.

Part VI – From Third Passover to the Beginning of the Last Passover Week

The Lessons We Should Learn

1.   One should continually realize and honor Christ Jesus as the Christ of God.

2.   One should never seek the revelation from man, but always be open to the revelation from God the Father.

3.   God will give to us the knowledge and enlightenment to know how and what to bind on earth knowing that it shall also be bound in heaven and what we loose, and fail to bind on earth, shall be lost in heaven.

4.   As we seek those things that are of men and not of God we become an offence to Christ and God and we may be giving glory to Satan.

5.   When one becomes eager and sincere to seek Christ with all the heart and all of his soul, he must deny himself, and take up his cross daily and follow Christ.

6.   If one selfishly does those things to save his own life, he shall lose it! One should not worry about his life, but should follow after Christ being precautious, and do the will of God the Father. If his life is given for Christ's sake, he shall find it.

7.   One should not work for his own self, but must work to do the will of God knowing that the work is a labor of love for God and his fellow man, and that work is the manifestation of one's belief and faith in God.

Part VI – From Third Passover to the Beginning of the Last Passover Week

My Thoughts About the Lessons

_____
_____
_____
_____
_____
_____
_____
_____
_____
_____
_____
_____
_____
_____
_____
_____
_____
_____
_____
_____
_____
_____
_____

NOTES

Part VI – From Third Passover to the Beginning of the Last Passover Week

18

The Transfiguration

Jesus Comforts His Disciples After They Experience a Vision and Hear Words From God

And it came to pass about six to eight days after these sayings, Jesus took Peter, John, and James, and went up into a mountain to pray.

And as he prayed, the fashion of his countenance was altered, and his raiment was white and glistening, shining and exceeding white as the light and his face did shine as the sun.

And behold there appeared unto them Moses and Elias talking with him. Who appeared in glory, and spake of his decease which he should accomplish at Jerusalem.

Then answered Peter, and said unto Jesus, Lord, is it good for us to be here: and let us make three tabernacles; one for thee, and one for Moses, and one for Elias. For he wist not what to say; for they were sure afraid. While he yet spake, a bright cloud overshadowed them: and behold a voice out of the cloud, which said, "This is my beloved Son, in whom I am well pleased; hear ye him."

And when the disciples heard it they fell on their face, and were sore afraid.

And when Jesus came and touched them and said,

"Arise and be not afraid."

And when they lifted their eyes, they saw no man, save Jesus only.

And as they came down from the mountain, Jesus charged them, saying, *"Tell the vision to no man, until the Son of man be risen again from the dead."*

Part VI – From Third Passover to the Beginning of the Last Passover Week

The Son of Man Shall Suffer of Them as Elias - Elias Shall first Come, and Restore all Things

And his disciples asked him, saying, Why then say the scribes that Elias must first come?

And Jesus answered and said unto them, *"Elias truly shall first come, and restore all things; and how it is written of the Son of man, that he must suffer many things, and be set at nought.*

"But I say unto you, That Elias is come already and they knew him not, but they have done unto him whatsoever they listed, as it is written of him. Likewise shall also the Son of man suffer of them."

Then the disciples understood that he spake unto them of John the Baptist.

Jesus Casts Out a Demon, Which the Disciples Could Not Cast Out; Have Faith as a Mustard Seed to Move Mountains

And the next day when he came to his disciples, he saw a great multitude about them, and the scribes questioning with them.

And straightway all the people, when they beheld him, were greatly amazed, and running to him saluted him.

And he asked the scribes, *"What question ye with them?"*

And one of the multitude answered and said, "Master, I have brought unto thee my son, which hath a dumb spirit:

And wheresoever he taketh him, he teareth him: and he foameth, and gnasheth with his teeth, and pineth away: and I spake to thy disciples that they should cast him out; and they could not cure him.

Jesus answered him and said, *"O faithless and perverse generation, how long shall I be with you? how long shall I suffer you? bring him hither unto me."*

Part VI – From Third Passover to the Beginning of the Last Passover Week

And they brought him unto him: and when he saw him, straightway the spirit tare him; and he fell on the ground, and wallowed foaming.

And he asked his father,

"How long is it ago since this came unto him?"

And he said, of a child. And of times it hath cast him into the fire, and into the waters, to destroy him: but if thou canst do any thing, have compassion on us, and help us.

Jesus said unto him, *"If thou canst believe, all things are possible to him that believeth."*

And straightway the father of the child cried out, and said with tears, Lord, I believe; help thou mine unbelief.

When Jesus saw that the people came running together, he rebuked the foul spirit, the devil, saying unto him, *"Thou dumb and deaf spirit, I charge thee, come out of him, and enter no more into him."*

And the spirit cried, and rent him sore, and came out of him: and he was as one dead; insomuch that many said, He is dead.

But Jesus took him by the hand, and lifted him up; and he arose.

Then came the disciples to Jesus apart, and asked him privately, Why could not we cast him out?

And Jesus said unto them,
"Because of your unbelief: for verily I say unto you. If ye have faith as a grain of mustard seed, ye shall say unto this mountain, Remove hence to yonder place; and it shall remove: and nothing shall be impossible unto you.

"Howbeit this kind goeth not out and this kind can come forth by nothing, but by prayer and fasting."

Part VI – From Third Passover to the Beginning of the Last Passover Week

<u>Jesus Again Foretells His Death and Resurrection</u>

And they departed thence while they abode in Galilee; and he would not that any man should know it. For he taught his disciples, and said unto them,

"The Son of man shall be betrayed and delivered into the hands of men:

"And they shall kill him; and after that he is killed, and the third day he shall be raised again.

"Let these sayings sink down into your ears: for the Son of man shall be delivered into the hands of men."

But they understood not this saying, and it was hid from them, that they perceived it not: and they feared to ask him of that saying, and they were exceedingly sorry.

<u>Temple Tribute Money Provided From a Fish at Capernaum</u>

And when they went into Capernaum, they that received tribute money came to Peter, and said, doth not your master pay tribute?

He saith, Yes. And when he was come into the house, Jesus prevented him, saying, *"What thinkest thou, Simon? Of whom do the kings of the earth take custom or tribute? of their own children, or of strangers?"*

Peter saith unto him, Of strangers. Jesus said unto him, *"Then are the children free.*

"Not withstanding, lest we should offend them, go thou to the sea, and cast an hook, and take up the fish that first cometh up; and when thou hast opened his mouth; thou shalt find a piece of money: that take, and give it unto them for me and thee."

Part VI – From Third Passover to the Beginning of the Last Passover Week

NOTES: Scriptures of the Topics	Matt	Mark	Luke
- Jesus comforts His disciples after they experience a vision and hear words from God	17:7,9		
- The Son of man shall suffer of them as Elias: Elias shall first come, and restore all things	17:11,12	9:12,13	
- Jesus casts out a demon, which the disciples could not cast out: Have faith as a mustard seed to move mountains.	17:17,20, 21	9:16,19 21,23,25,29	9:41
- Jesus again foretells his death and resurrection.	17:22,23	9:31	9:44
- Temple tribute money miraculously provided from a fish of Capernaum.	17:24-27		

Doctrines and Commandments

201. Elias and John the Baptist shall first come and restore all things and that Elias is indeed come.

202. All things are possible to him that believes. Nothing shall be impossible unto you.

203. Christ Jesus casts out deaf and dumb spirits with His command.

204. If you have faith as a grain of a mustard seed, you could say to a mountain move to another place and it shall move.

205. By prayer and fasting nothing shall be impossible unto you.

206. Christ foretells His death and His resurrection the third day.

207. Christ Jesus was delivered into the hands of man and they killed Him.

208. Jesus foretells of temple tribute money miraculously provided from the mouth of a fish.

Part VI – From Third Passover to the Beginning of the Last Passover Week

Lessons We Should Learn

1.   Our relationship with Christ Jesus is changed with the realization of the restoration of John the Baptist of all things that is indeed here as one comes to this realization. First repent as John did teach and a greater awareness and fullness of Christ's teaching shall be known.

2.   Nothing shall be impossible unto each of us by prayer, fasting, belief, and faith. Things that may seem impossible could be mountains. Mountains could be your anxieties, illness, evil doings, etc.

3.   Christ did foretell the things that would happen to Him, even years in advance. He knew that He would be delivered into the hands of men and would be put to death by them. Yet His faith and desire to do the will of God never faltered.

Part VI – From Third Passover to the Beginning of the Last Passover Week

My Thoughts About the Lessons

_____

_____

_____

_____

_____

_____

_____

_____

_____

_____

_____

_____

_____

_____

_____

_____

_____

_____

_____

_____

_____

_____

_____

NOTES

Part VI – From Third Passover to the Beginning of the Last Passover Week

19

The Kingdom of Heaven

Be Converted and Become as Little Children

And He came to Capernaum: and being in the house he asked them, *"What was it that ye disputed among yourselves by the way?"*

For a while they held their peace, then the disciples came to Jesus saying, Who should be the greatest in the kingdom of heaven?

And he sat down and called the twelve, and said unto them, *"If and man desire to be first, the same shall be last of all,*

and servant of all."

"For he that is least among you all, the same shall be great."

And Jesus called a little child unto him, and set him in the midst of them.

And said, *"Verily I say unto you, except ye be converted, and become as little children, ye shall not enter into the kingdom of heaven.*

"Whosoever therefore, shall humble himself as this little child, the same is greatest in the kingdom of heaven.

"And whoso shall receive one such little child in my name receiveth me: and whosoever shall receive me receiveth him that sent me: for he that is least among you all, the same shall be great."

And John answered and said, Master, we saw one casting out devils in thy name: and he followeth not us: and we forbad him because he followeth not us.

But Jesus said, *"Forbid him not: for there is no man which shall do a miracle in my name, that can lightly speak evil of me*

Part VI – From Third Passover to the Beginning of the Last Passover Week

"For he that is not against us is on our part, is for us

"For whosoever shall give you a cup of water to drink in my name, because ye belong to Christ, verily I say unto you, he shall not lose his reward.

"But whoso shall offend one of these little ones which believe in me, it were better for him that a millstone were hanged about his neck, and he were cast into the sea, and that he were drowned in the depth of the sea."

Woe unto the World Because of Offenses

"Woe unto the world because of offences! for it must needs be that offences come; but woe to that man by whom the offence cometh!

"Wherefore if thy hand or thy foot offend thee, cut them off, and cast them from thee: it is better for thee to enter into life halt or maimed, rather than having two hands or two feet to be cast into hell, into everlasting fire.

"Where their worm dieth not, and the fire is not quenched.

"And if thine eye offend thee, pluck it out, and cast it from thee: it is better for thee to enter into life with one eye, rather than having two eyes to be cast into hell fire.

"For every one shall be salted with fire, and every sacrifice hall be salted with salt.

"Salt is good: but if the salt have lost his saltness, wherewith will ye season it? Have salt in yourselves, and have peace one with another.

"Take heed that ye despise not one of these little ones; for I say unto you, that in heaven their angels do always behold the face of my Father which is in heaven."

Part VI – From Third Passover to the Beginning of the Last Passover Week

Jesus Came to Save That Which Was Lost

"For the Son of man is come to save that which was lost. "How think ye? if a man have an hundred sheep, and one of them be gone astray, doth he not leave the ninety and nine, and goeth into the mountains, and seeketh that which is gone astray?

"And if so be that he find it, verily I say unto you, he rejoiceth more of that sheep, than of the ninety and nine which went not astray.

"Even so it is not the will of your Father which is in heaven, that one of these little ones should perish."

How to Handle Your Brother When He Trespasses Against You

"Moreover if thy brother shall trespass against thee, go and tell him his fault between thee and him alone: if he shall hear thee, thou hast gained thy brother.

"But if he will not hear thee, then take with thee one or two more, that in the mouth of two or three witnesses every word may be established.

"And if he shall neglect to hear them, tell it unto the church: but if he neglect to hear the church, let him be unto thee as an heathen man and a publican."

Then came Peter to him, and said, Lord, how oft shall my brother sin against me, and I forgive him? till seven times?

Jesus saith unto him, *"I say not unto thee, until seven times: but until seventy time seven."*

What You Bind On Earth Shall be Bound in Heaven

"Verily I say unto you, whatsoever ye shall bind on earth shall be bound in heaven: and whatsoever ye shall loose on earth shall be loosed in heaven."

Part VI – From Third Passover to the Beginning of the Last Passover Week

There I am Where Two or Three Are Gathered in My Name

"Again I say unto you, that if two of you shall agree on earth as touching anything that they shall ask, it shall be done for them of my father which is in heaven.

"For where two or three are gathered together in my name, there am I in the midst of them."

Parable of the Unmerciful Debtor: Forgive From Your Heart

"Therefore is the kingdom of heaven likened unto a certain king, which would take account of his servants.

"And when he had begun to reckon one was brought unto him, which owed him ten thousand talents.

"But forasmuch as he had not to pay, his lord commanded him to be sold, and his wife, and children, and all that he had, and payment to be made.

"The servant therefore fell down and worshipped him, saying, Lord, have patience with me, and I will pay thee all.'

"Then the lord of that servant was moved with compassion, and loosed him, and forgave him the debt.

"But the same servant went out, and found one of his fellow servants, which owed him an hundred pence: and he laid hands on him, and took him by the throat, saying, 'Pay me that thou owest.'

"And his fellowservant fell down at his feet, and besought him saying, 'Have patience with me, and I will pay thee all.'

"And he would not: but went and cast him into prison, till he should pay the debt.

Part VI – From Third Passover to the Beginning of the Last Passover Week

"So when his fellow servants saw what was done, they were very sorry, and came and told unto their lord all that was done.

"Then his lord, after that he had called him, said unto him,

'O thou wicked servant, I forgave thee all that debt, because thou desiredst me:

"'Shouldest not thou also have had compassion on thy fellowservant, even as I had pity on thee?'

"And his lord was wroth, and delivered him to the tormentors, till he should pay all that was due unto him.

"So likewise shall my heavenly Father do also unto you, if ye from your heart forgive not every one his brother their trespasses."

NOTES: Scriptures of the Topics	Matt.	Mark	Luke
- Be converted and become as little children	18:3-6	9:33,35 37-42	9:48,50
- Woe unto the world because of offences	18:7-10		
- Jesus came to save that which was lost	18:11-14		
- How to handle your brother when he trespasses	18:15-17,22		
- What you bind in earth shall be bound in heaven	18:18		
- There I am where two or three are gathered in My name	18:19,20		
- Parable of the unmerciful debtor: forgive from your heart.	18:23-35		

Part VI – From Third Passover to the Beginning of the Last Passover Week

Doctrines and Commandments

209. Man who desires to be first and greatest in the kingdom shall be least among men, and shall be last of all and servant of all.

210. To enter into the kingdom of heaven, be converted and become as little children.

211. The greatest in the kingdom of heaven is whosoever shall humble himself as this little child.

212. Whoso shall receive one little child in Christ's name receives Christ.

213. Whoever offends one of the little children that believe in the Lord, it would be better that he was drowned in the depth of the sea.

214. Christ will give unto you the keys of the kingdom of heaven and whatsoever you shalt bind on earth shall be bound in heaven and whatsoever you shall loose on earth shall be loosed in heaven.

215. It is better to enter into life halt or maimed, rather than to have two hands, or two feet, or two eyes and to be cast into everlasting fire for offending you.

216. Children have angels in heaven that always behold the face of God the Father which is in heaven.

217. Christ Jesus came to save that which was lost.

218. It is not the will of your Father which is in heaven that one little one should perish.

219. If your brother shall trespass against you, you shall go and tell him his faults between you and him alone. If he will not hear you, then take with you one, two, or three witnesses that every word may be established. If he shall refuse or neglect to hear them, tell it unto the church. If he neglect to hear the church, let him be as a heathen man and a publican.

220. Forgive one's sins against you seventy times seven times: 490 times.

221. Christ Jesus is in the midst of them, where two or three are gathered together in His name.

222. If you will not from your heart forgive every one of their trespasses, God the Father shall likewise do unto you. If you forgive men their trespasses, your Heavenly Father will also forgive you.

Part VI – From Third Passover to the Beginning of the Last Passover Week

Lessons We Should Learn

1.   Our desire should be to serve God and to do His will, not our own. We should not look for a certain position: to be first, or to be next to Christ. Only God the Father and His will shall be done, and he will choose those to high places, or to whatever position. For many are called but few are chosen. To truly live by Christ's doctrine and truth one should be willing to serve and do that which God has for him.

2.   To be that willing servant one must repent—give up worldly sins of all manner and become as a little child, desiring not the human traits, but pure and innocent in heart. As one does these things unto the end, he will enter into the kingdom of God.

3.   Each adult person should be willing to receive little children in the true spirit. Children are innocent and naïve and look to the adult as a model: a person to respect, to follow, and to copy. Children develop their virtues and habits—good or bad—from adults first and then from their peers. One must realize that children have angels in heaven that behold the face of God the Father and one's closeness and guidance and love of children is being close and one with the love of God.

4.   Each person is an individual expression of God. Within us is the godchild which is given to all children. Also, the body is the temple to the soul.

In the Lord's prayer we ask our Heavenly Father to lead us not into temptation but to deliver us from evil. However, if temptation comes it would be better to realize it. If your eye is offending you remove it and live with one eye that is good and sees good. If your hand offends you, remove it so it will not offend you again and then you may enter the rest of your life on earth. But your being will be in His light and the rest of you a child of God. There is no compromising with temptation—one is either a child of God or a child of Satan and to be lukewarm is to be a lost child.

5.   Christ Jesus came to save that which was lost. One's life can be transformed and as one becomes as little children by repenting all sins so that once again one is pure in heart as little children. As this transformation takes place one becomes a performing Christ, being in likeness of Christ, and one with Christ.

Part VI – From Third Passover to the Beginning of the Last Passover Week

6. If your brother shall trespass against you, beware of the temptation of retribution. Very often one uses this hurt to hurt back. At that very time temptation of talking against that brother enters one's thought and the adversary takes over the heart with hate—which in fact could be the very hate to prevent reconciliation from taking place. Christ's doctrines and teachings say to forgive one's sins against you seventy times seven, which is 490 times. And if you will not from your heart forgive every one of their trespasses, God the Father shall likewise do unto you.

7. It seems that we bind certain things on earth, such as; contracts with men about our home and other worldly things about our families, which are of prime importance in the kingdom. But how about the words of Christ? One's most devout covenant with God should be to bind the teachings of Christ in his heart and then all temptation is not bound to you and cannot enter the heart. What a blessing to know that the Lord's prayer is being fulfilled each day, in one's heart, that is: His will be done on earth as it is in heaven. And the keys of the kingdom shall be manifest in one's heart. By doing this we shall know that Christ Jesus is in us, as He is in God the Father. Also, we are loving both Jesus and God by keeping Jesus' words. And this is a much greater love than words without covenants to keep Jesus' commandments.

8. The will of God is that not "one little one should perish."

A mother carrying a child, a child of God our Father which is in heaven, and the father of that little one should know the blessings of the coming of the birth of this child and should never contemplate an abortion which does take the child's will and God's blessing from the child whom is the procreation, of His, a child of God.

Part VI – From Third Passover to the Beginning of the Last Passover Week

My Thoughts About the Lessons

_____

_____

_____

_____

_____

_____

_____

_____

_____

_____

_____

_____

_____

_____

_____

_____

_____

_____

_____

_____

_____

_____

_____

_____

_____

_____

_____

NOTES

Part VI – From Third Passover to the Beginning of the Last Passover Week

20

Journey to the Feast of Tabernacles:
He Teaches in the Temples

Jesus Declares His Time Is Not Yet Come

Before going to the Jews' feast of tabernacles, which was at hand, Jesus walked in Galilee: for he would not walk in Jewry, because the Jews sought to kill him.

His brethren asked to see his works for neither did his brethren believe in him.

Then Jesus said unto them, *"My time is not yet come: but your time is always ready.*

"The world cannot hate you; but me it hateth, because I testify of it, that the works thereof are evil.

"Go ye up unto this feast: I go not up yet unto this feast; for my time is not yet full come."

When his brethren were gone, then he also went to the feast not openly, but as it were in secret.

Then the Jews sought him at the feast and no man spake openly for him for fear of the Jews.

My Doctrine Is Not Mine: But His That Sent Me

Now about the midst of the feast Jesus went up into the temple, and taught.
And the Jews marvelled, saying, How knoweth this man letters, having never learned?
Jesus answered them, and said, *"My doctrine is not mine, but his that sent me.*

"If any man will do his will, he shall know of the doctrine, whether it be of God, or whether I speak of myself.

Part VI – From Third Passover to the Beginning of the Last Passover Week

He that speaketh of himself seeketh his own glory: but he that seeketh his glory that sent him, the same is true, and no unrighteousness is in him.

"Did not Moses give you the law, and yet none of you keepeth the law? Why go ye about to kill me?

Healing on the Sabbath Day

The people answered and said, Thou hast a devil: who goeth about to kill thee?

Jesus answered and said unto them, *"I have done one work, and ye all marvel.*

"Moses therefore gave unto you circumcision: (not because it is of Moses, but of the fathers;) and ye on the sabbath day circumcise a man.

"If a man on the sabbath day receive circumcision, that the law of Moses should not be broken: are ye angry at me, because I have made a man every whit whole on the Sabbath day?

"Judge not according to the appearance, but judge righteous judgment."

Christ Testifies That He Is Sent of God

Then said some of them of Jerusalem, Is not this he, whom they seek to kill? But he speaks boldly, and they say nothing unto him. Do the rulers know indeed that this is the very Christ?

Howbeit we know this man whence he is: but when Christ cometh, no man knoweth whence he is.

Then cried Jesus in the temple as he taught, saying,

"Ye both know me, and ye know whence I am: and I am not come of myself, but he that sent me is true, whom ye know not.

"But I know him: for I am from him, and he hath sent me."

Then they sought to take him: but no man laid hands on him, because his hour was not yet come.

Part VI – From Third Passover to the Beginning of the Last Passover Week

Jesus Foretells His Return to the Father

The Pharisees heard that the people murmured such things concerning him; and the Pharisees and the chief priests sent officers to take him.

Then said Jesus unto them, *"Yet a little while I am with you, and then I go unto him that sent me.*

"Ye shall seek me, and shall not find me: and where I am thither ye cannot come?"

The Jews talked among themselves and thought he would go among the Gentiles and teach them. They didn't understand his saying,

"Ye shall seek me, and shall not find me: and whence I am, thither ye cannot come."

He Preaches at the Feast

In the last day, that great day of the feast, Jesus stood and cried, saying, *"If any man thirst, let him come unto me, and drink.*

"He that believeth on me, as the scripture hath said, out of his belly shall flow rivers of living water."

(But this spake he of the Spirit which they that believe on him should receive: for the Holy Ghost was not yet given; because that Jesus was not yet glorified.)

Many of the people when they heard this saying, said, Of a truth this is the prophet.

Others said, This is the Christ.

Part VI – From Third Passover to the Beginning of the Last Passover Week

An Adulterous Taken to Jesus to Judge

After the feast was over and every man went their way, Jesus went unto the Mount of Olives.

And early in the morning he came again into the temple, and all the people came unto him; and he sat down and taught them.

And the scribes and Pharisees brought unto him a woman taken in adultery. They said unto him, Master this woman was taken in adultery, in the very act.

Now Moses in the law commanded us, that such should be stoned: but what sayest thou?

This they said, tempting him, that they might have to accuse him. But Jesus stooped down and with his finger wrote on the ground, as though he heard them not.

So when they continued asking him, he lift up himself, and said unto them, *"He that is without sin among you let him first cast a stone at her."*

And again he stooped down, and wrote on the ground. And they which heard it, being convicted by their own conscience, went out one by one; and Jesus was left alone, and the woman standing in the midst.

When Jesus stood up and saw none but the woman, he said unto her, *"Woman where are those thine accusers? hath no man condemned thee?"*

She said, No man, Lord.

And Jesus said unto her,

"Neither do I condemn thee: go, and sin no more."

Part VI – From Third Passover to the Beginning of the Last Passover Week

NOTES: Scriptures of the Topics	John
- Jesus declares his time is not yet come	7:6-8
- My doctrine is not Mine, but His that sent Me	7:16-19
- Healing on the Sabbath Day	7:21-24
- Christ testifies that He is sent by God	7:28-29
- Jesus foretells His return to the Father	7:33-34,36
- Jesus preaches at the feast	7:37,38
- An adulterous taken to Jesus to judge	8:7,10,11

Doctrines and Commandments

222. The world hated Christ and crucified Him because He testified of it that the works thereof are evil.

223. Christ declares and testifies that His doctrine is not His but His that sent Him—God the Father's.

224. If anyone will do His will, he shall know of the doctrine, whether it be of God, or whether Christ Jesus speaks of Himself.

225. He that speaks of himself seeks His own glory and there is unrighteous in him.

226. He that seeks the glory of God, there is no unrighteousness in him.

227. Judge not according to the appearance, but judge righteous judgment.

228. Christ did not come of Himself, but of God, who Christ testifies is true, and that He knows Him and that Christ is from Him and that God sent Jesus the Christ.

229. Christ declares and testifies that He goes to God the Father, He states, *"I go unto him that sent me."* (Him, a personal Father, God.)

230. One may seek Christ, but where he is with God, one cannot go.

231. Those who thirst, let them go to Christ and drink.

232. He that believes Christ with all his mind and all his soul

and believes all the scriptures about Christ, out of his being shall flow rivers of living water.

233. Christ does not condemn the sinner, but He says, "go and sin no more."

Part VI – From Third Passover to the Beginning of the Last Passover Week

Lessons We Should Learn

1.   One can observe in this chapter there are twelve major doctrines (beliefs, teachings of Christ) that He testifies. First is that the world, the worldly people and their works are evil.

The last, He declares that He does not condemn the worldly people and their sinful works. Instead, He says, "to go," to continue in the world, but, "to sin no more," meaning to stop all sin forever. Give it up, go cold turkey, don't try to compromise; "<u>SIN NO MORE.</u>" When one does that, he is truly testifying about Christ. Our first testimony to Christ should be: (a) to repent (judge our own worldly works. This means each thought, word, and the very act itself). Then: (b) sin no more. The act of faith and our true testimony to Christ is not to sin again.

For Christ did not come to judge us but He leaves that to each of us to do. We each have that free will and agency to choose right from wrong, and to do whatever one wants to do. However, one should remember that words are empty and become continuous lies if one's works are evil; for the works are the actual manifestation of one's heart. This is why He states, "Go and sin no more!"

When one makes that decision right then, there is no sin in us and we again have Christ in our hearts! Also, we show our love of God and Christ Jesus.

Remember, where sin is, Christ is not there. For His first testimony after being baptized by John the Baptist is to rebuke Satan. He teaches us, each of us, to do the same. He gives us examples how to do it. But what a blessing there is when one's sin is given up—Christ is there in one's heart in the place of that sin. He was actually there all the time and we pushed Him out with our sins. We each can get rid of our sins one at a time. He has shown us how, for He makes all things known to us. We should partake of His light, for He is the word, truth, and light.

Part VI – From Third Passover to the Beginning of the Last Passover Week

2.	One may read all of the doctrines of Christ and wonder if they are true, and wonder how to approach them to understand them. There seems to be so many beliefs and teachings that Christ has given to us. It seems almost an impossible task to truly understand.

Remember that Christ's doctrines are of God the Father, and that Christ has and does reveal everything to us. However, one may never know the entire truth in any of the doctrines, for only God the Father can do that in our heart.

Christ Jesus has shown us how to understand and have knowledge of His doctrines. He says, "If any man do His will, he shall know of the doctrine, whether it be of God, or whether I speak of myself."

So the key to know, to have knowledge, is to do His will. The will of God. The same will of God that Christ did. For Christ's testimony is, that He does the will of His Father not His own, and this is stated repeatedly in the scriptures.

3.	One must see himself as he really is. Not one's appearance, but rather judge righteous judgment. One must monitor each thought, before saying anything; each word, before doing anything. In this righteous judgment if one sees himself speaking of himself, he is seeking his own glory and within him he has unrighteousness. One is to seek the glory of God and then there is no unrighteousness in him.

Part VI – From Third Passover to the Beginning of the Last Passover Week

My Thoughts About the Lessons

_____

_____

_____

_____

_____

_____

_____

_____

_____

_____

_____

_____

_____

_____

_____

_____

_____

_____

_____

_____

_____

_____

_____

_____

Part VI – From Third Passover to the Beginning of the Last Passover Week

21

Jesus Announces He Is the Light of the World

Then spake Jesus again unto them saying,

"I am the light of the world: he that followeth me shall not walk in darkness, but shall have the light of life."

The Pharisees therefore said unto Him, thou bearest record of thyself; thy record is not true.

Jesus answered and said unto them, *"Though I bear record of myself, yet my record is true: for I know whence I came and wither I go: but ye cannot tell me whence I come, and whither I go."*

Witness of Christ Judgment by Christ

Jesus said, *"Ye judge after the flesh; I judge no man. "And yet if I judge, my judgment is true: for I am not alone, but I and the father tha t sent me".*

Witness of Christ and Testimony

"It is also written in your law, that the testimony of two men is true."

"I am one that bear witness of myself, and the Father that sent me beareth witness of me".

Then said they unto him, Where is thy Father?

Jesus answered, *"Ye neither know me, nor my Father: if ye had known me, ye should have known my Father also."*

Part VI – From Third Passover to the Beginning of the Last Passover Week

Worldly People Can't Go To Christ: Where He Is

These words spake Jesus in the treasury, as he taught in the temple: and no man laid hands on him; for his hour was not yet come.

Then said Jesus again unto them,

"I go my way, and ye shall seek me, and shall die in your sins: whither I go, ye cannot come."

Then said the Jews Will he kill himself? because he saith, Whither I go, ye cannot come."

And he said unto them, *"Ye are from beneath; I am from above: ye are of this world; I am not of this world.."*

"I said therefore unto you, that ye shall die in your sins: for if ye believe not that I am he, ye shall die in your sins."

Christ Told Us These Truths From The Beginning

Then said they unto him, Who art thou? And Jesus saith unto them, *"Even the same that I said unto you from the beginning."*

"I have many things to say and to judge of you: but he that sent me is true; and I speak to the world those things which I have heard of him."

They understood not that he spake to them of the Father.

Part VI – From Third Passover to the Beginning of the Last Passover Week

We Must Lift Up the Son of Man and Know That Jesus Is the Christ Sent by God

Then said Jesus unto them,

"When ye have lifted up the Son of man, then shall ye know that I am he, and that I do nothing of myself; but as my Father hath taught me, I speak these things."

And he that sent me is with me: the Father hath not left me alone; for I do always those things that please him."

As he spake these words, many believed on him.

How To Be Disciples of Christ

Then Jesus said to those Jews which believe on him,

"If ye continue in my word, then ye are my disciple indeed;
"And ye shall know the truth, and the truth shall make you free."

Those Who Sin Are the Servants of Sin

The Jews told Jesus, We be Abraham's seed, and were never in bondage to any man: how sayest thou, *"Ye shall be made free?"*

Jesus answered them, *"Verily, verily, I say unto you, Whosoever committeth sin is the servant of sin."*

"And the servant abideth not in the house for ever: but the Son abideth ever."

"If the Son therefore shall make you free, ye shall be free indeed."

Part VI – From Third Passover to the Beginning of the Last Passover Week

Abraham's Seed Are Not of God

"I know that ye are Abraham's seed; but ye seek to kill me, because my word hath no place in you.

"I speak that which I have seen with my Father: and ye do that which ye have seen with your father."

They answered and said unto him, Abraham is our father.

Jesus saith unto them, *"If ye were Abraham's children, ye would do the works of Abraham.*

"But now ye seek to kill me, a man that hath told you the truth, which I have heard of God: this did not Abraham. "Ye do the deeds of your father.

"If God were your Father, ye would love me: for I proceeded forth and came from God; neither came I of myself, but he sent me."

Man Is of His Worldly Father, the Devil, and Not of God

"Why do ye not understand my speech? even because ye cannot hear my word.

"Ye are of your father the devil, and the lust of your father ye will do. He was a murderer from the beginning, and abode not in the truth, because there is no truth in him. When he speaketh a lie, he speaketh of his own: for he is a liar, and the father of it.

"And because I tell you the truth, ye believe me not.

"Which of you concieveth me of sin? And if I say the truth, why do ye not believe me?

"He that is of God heareth God's words: ye therefore hear them not, because ye are not of God."

Part VI – From Third Passover to the Beginning of the Last Passover Week

Christ Does Not Seek His Own Glory

Then the Jews said, Thou art a Samaritan, and hast a devil.

Jesus answered, *"I have not a devil: but I honour my Father and ye do dishonour me*
"And I seek not mine own glory: there is one that seeketh and judgeth."

We Shall Never See Death If We Keep His Sayings

"Verily, verily, I say unto you, if a man keep my saying, he shall never see death."
Then said the Jews, now we know that thou hast a devil.

Abraham is dead, and the prophets; and thou sayest, If a man keep my saying, he shall never taste of death.

Art thou greater than our father Abraham, which is dead? and the prophets are dead: whom makest thou thyself?

God Honors Christ: Before Abraham Was, I Am

Jesus answered, *"If I honour myself, my honour is nothing: it is my Father that honoureth me; of whom ye say, that he is your God:*

"Yet ye have not known him; but I know him; and if I should say, I know him not, I shall be a liar like unto you: but I know him, and keep his saying.
"Your father Abraham rejoiced to see my day; and he saw it, and was glad."

Then said the Jews unto them, Thou art not yet fifty years old, and hast thou seen Abraham?

Jesus said unto them,
"Verily, verily, I say unto you, Before Abraham was, I am."
Then they took stones to cast at him, but Jesus hid himself and left the temple, going through the midst of them.

Part VI – From Third Passover to the Beginning of the Last Passover Week

Healing the Blind Man of Siloam

And Jesus passed by, he saw a man which was blind form his birth. And his disciples ask him, saying, Master, who did sin, this man, or his parents, that he was born blind.

Jesus answered, *"Neither hath this man sinned, or his parents: but that the works of God should be made manifest in him.*

"I must work the works of him that sent me, while it is day: the night cometh, when no man can work.

"As long as I am in the world, I am the light of the world."

When he had thus spoken, he spat on the ground, and made clay of the spittle, and anointed the eyes of the blind man with the clay,

And said unto him, *"Go wash in the pool of Siloam."* He went his way therefore, and washed, and came seeing.

The Jews questioned the blind man who now has regained his sight and they felt that Jesus was a sinner. But the man that was born blind but could now see, said, "if this man were not of God, he could do nothing." They answered, saying, "Thou wast born in sins, and dost thou teach us? And they cast him out.

Jesus heard that they had cast him out; and when he had found him, he said unto him,

"Does thou believe on the Son of God?"

He answered and said, who is he, Lord, that I might believe on him?

And Jesus said unto him, *"Thou hast both seen him, and it is he that talketh with thee."*

And he said, Lord, I believe. And he worshipped him.

* * *

Part VI – From Third Passover to the Beginning of the Last Passover Week

And Jesus said, *"For judgment I am come into this world, that they which see not might see; and that they which see might be made blind."*

And some of the Pharisees which were with him heard these words and said unto him, are we blind also?

Jesus said unto them, *"If ye were blind, ye should have no sin: but now ye say, we see; therefore your sin remaineth."*

NOTES: Scriptures of the Topics	John
- Record of Christ	8:12,14
- Judgment of Christ	8:15,16
- Witness of Christ and testimony	8:17-19
- Worldly people can't go to Christ; where He is	8:21-24
- Christ told us these truths from the beginning	8:25,26
- We must lift up the Son of Man and know that Jesus is the Christ, sent by God	8:28,29
- How to be disciples of Christ	8:31,32
- Those who sin are the servants of sin	8:33-36
- Abraham's seed are not of God	8:37-42
- Man is of his worldly father, the devil, and not of God	8:43-47
- Christ does not seek His own glory	8:49-51,54
- We shall never see death, if we keep his sayings	8:51,52
- God honors Christ; before Abraham was, I am	8:55,56,58
- Healing the blind man of Siloam	9:3-7,11,35-41

Doctrines and Commandments

234. Christ is the light of the world and he that follows shall not walk in darkness, but shall have the light of life. (Jn. 9:5)

235. Christ bears record of Himself and His record is true: and He knows from what place He came and what place He goes; but you can't tell from what place He comes and to what place He goes.

Part VI – From Third Passover to the Beginning of the Last Passover Week

236. Christ judges no man; you judge after the flesh. If Christ judges, His judgment is true; for He is not alone but He and the Father.

237. If you know Christ, you know God also.

238. Christ is not of this world He is from above.

239. You are from beneath.

240. *"If you do not believe that I am He,"* Christ said, *"You shall die in your sins."*

241. We were with Christ in the beginning. *"Even the same that I said unto you from the beginning."* (Jn. 8:25)

242. God is true. *"He that sent me is true: and I speak to the world those things which I have heard of Him."*

41. Whatever God the Father does, the Son does likewise (see Jn. 8:28)

42. Heavenly Father loves the Son and shows Him all things that He does. *"I do nothing of myself; but as my Father hath taught me, I speak these things."* (Jn. 8:28)

243. When you have lifted up the Son of Man, then shall ye know that I am He and that I do nothing of Myself.

244. God is with Christ; God has not left Christ Jesus alone.

245. Christ Jesus always does those things that please God.

246. You are Christ's disciple if you continue in His word. And you shall know the truth, and the truth shall make you free.

247. Those who sin are the servants of sin.

248. Christ abides forever and if He shall make you free, you shall be free indeed.

249. Man is of his worldly father, the devil, and not of God. (John 8:42-49)

250. He that is of God hears God's words.

251. You that are not of God don't hear God's words.

252. Christ and I am. (Jn. 8:58 and Jn. 9:5)

253. Christ came into this world, that they which see not might see; and they which see might be made blind. *"If ye were blind, ye should have no sin; but now ye say, we see, therefore your sin remaineth."* (Jn. 9:39,41)

63. Seek honor from God only (Jn. 8:49-51)

Part VI – From Third Passover to the Beginning of the Last Passover Week

Lessons We Should Learn

1.   Within Christ's teachings we see that by being a follower of Christ, we shall have the light of life. For Christ tells us those things that He hears and sees from God and He makes all things known to us. He sends the promise of His Father upon us and we are endued with power from on high. Christ Jesus speaks openly about His doctrines to the world, and in secret He says nothing. And as Christ Jesus makes his doctrines and commandments known to us, He tells that: we shall do the same works as His, we may be children of light, and that we may be one with our Heavenly Father and Christ Jesus. We are Christ's disciples if we continue in his word and we shall know the truth and the truth shall make us free.

2.   Christ bears record of Himself and His record is true and He knows from what place He came and to what place He goes. However, we can't tell from what place He come sand to what place He goes unless he tells us. For He is from above and we are from beneath. We judge after the flesh and Christ judges no man. But our choice is to follow Christ and be open to only those things that He shows us. We must realize that we are of worldly fathers that are of the devil and works of the devil and not of God. We need to break from these worldly traditions of the devil and return to the truth, the light, and the words of Christ. By so doing, we judge the flesh and our choice is to be a child of light or of darkness.

3.   Our choice is to follow or not follow Christ. If we don't believe in our hearts that Jesus is the "I am He," the Christ of God, we shall die in our sins. By not believing in the Christ we can see only those worldly things and we are in darkness. When we believe in Him, we have lifted up the Christ and we shall know that Jesus is the Christ and He does nothing of Himself. As we know Christ, we know God.

4.   Those who sin are the servants of sin and we all are sinners. But I realize that I don't want to serve two masters and my choice has to be one or the other. One must realize that you shall not abide in sin forever, so the choice should be to follow Christ, now! The time is now so that He may abide in us and we may abide in His house. For Christ abides forever and if He shall make us free, we shall be free indeed. There is no greater freedom, joy, and happiness than to be free from sin and be a true follower of Christ. The glory is to our Heavenly Father. We are then of God and hear God's words. We learn God's words that are the words from Jesus Christ. Jesus says, *"If ye continue in my word, then ye are my disciple indeed." "And ye shall know the truth, and the truth shall make you free." " Verily, verily I say unto you, if a man keep my sayings, he shall never see death."*

Part VI – From Third Passover to the Beginning of the Last Passover Week

My Thoughts About the Lessons

_____

_____

_____

_____

_____

_____

_____

_____

_____

_____

_____

_____

_____

_____

_____

_____

_____

_____

_____

_____

_____

Part VI – From Third Passover to the Beginning of the Last Passover Week

22

Christic the Good Shepherd

I am the Door and the Good Shepherd

" *Verily, verily, I say unto you, He that entereth not by the door into the sheepfold, but climbeth up some other way, the same is a thief and a robber.*

"But he that entereth in by the door is the shepherd of the sheep.

"To him the porter openeth; and the sheep hear his voice and he calleth his own sheep by name, and leadeth them out. "And when he putteth forth his own sheep, he goeth before them, and the sheep follow him: for they know his voice. "And a stranger will they not follow, but will flee from him: for they know not the voice of strangers."

This parable spake Jesus unto them: but they understood not what things they were which he spake unto them.

Then Jesus said unto them,

"Verily, verily, I say unto you, I am the door of the sheep.

"All that ever came before me are thieves and robbers: but the sheep did not hear them.

"I am the door; by me if any man enter in, he shall be saved, and shall go in and out, and find pasture.

"The thief cometh not, but for to steal, and to kill, and to destroy: I am come that they might have life, and that they might have it more abundantly."

I Lay Down My Life For the Sheep

"I am the good shepherd: the good shepherd giveth his life for the sheep, But he that is an hireling, and not the shepherd, whose own the sheep are not, seeth the wolf coming, and leaveth the sheep, and fleeth: and the wolf catcheth them, and scattereth the sheep."

Part VI – From Third Passover to the Beginning of the Last Passover Week

"The hireling fleeth, because he is an hireling, and careth not for the sheep.

"I am the good shepherd, and know my sheep, and am known of mine.

"As the Father knoweth me, even so know I the Father: and I lay down my life for the sheep."

Other Sheep Have I Which Are Not of This Fold

"And other sheep I have, which are not of this fold: them also I must bring, and they shall hear my voice; and there shall be one fold, and one shepherd."

Commandments Received From God

"Therefore doth my Father love me, because I lay down my life, that I might take it again.

"No man taketh it from me, but I lay it down of myself. I have power to lay it down, and I have power to take it again. This commandment have I received of my Father."

There was a division again among the Jews for these sayings. And many of them said, He hath a devil, and is mad; why hear ye him?

Others said, These are not the words of him that hath a devil. Can a devil open the eyes of the blind?

NOTES: Scriptures of the Topics   <u>John</u>

- I am the Door and the Good Shepherd   10:1-5,7-10
- I lay down My life for the sheep   10:11-15
- Other sheep have I which are not of this fold   10:16
- Commandments received from God   10:17,18

Part VI – From Third Passover to the Beginning of the Last Passover Week

Doctrines and Commandments

254. He that does not enter into the sheepfold by the door is the same as a thief and a robber.

255. He that enters into the sheepfold by the door is the shepherd of the sheep.

256. Christ is the door of the sheep. By Christ Jesus if any man enters in, he shall be saved, and shall go in and out, and find pasture.

All that ever came before Christ are the thieves and robbers: but the sheep did not hear them. The thief came not, but to steal, and to kill, and to destroy.

257. Christ Jesus came that his sheep (followers) might have life and that they might have it more abundantly.

258. Christ is the good shepherd; he knows his sheep, and they know him. As God knows Christ, Christ knows the Father; and Christ lays down his life for the sheep.

259. Christ has other sheep which are not of this fold. Christ must bring them and they shall hear his voice; and there shall be one fold, and one shepherd.

260. Christ has power to lay down his life, and he has power to take it again. This commandment he received of God. God loves Christ because he layed down his life for his fold and has given Christ the power.

Lessons We Should Learn

1.   Christ is the way and the door to life, and if any one enters in he shall be saved, and shall go in and out and find pasture. One may ask, "Saved from what?" The thief and the robber that is mentioned in the scriptures is Satan who comes to steal, to kill, and to destroy. Therefore, if we try to enter other than by Christ and his doctrines and commandments, we are then as the thief and the robber, and we have joined Satan.

2.   What a new life it is by joining the right flock that we might be reborn into this new life by being a follower of Christ and that we might have life more abundantly. To know that we hear Christ's voice and know his voice, and we flee and don't know the voice of Satan.

3.   We are the followers of Christ and to lay our life down for him as he layed his life down for us. And the commandment is received from God. Only God can give the power to take up life again and the glory is His.

Part VI – From Third Passover to the Beginning of the Last Passover Week

My Thoughts About the Lessons

_____

_____

_____

_____

_____

_____

_____

_____

_____

_____

_____

_____

_____

_____

_____

_____

_____

_____

_____

_____

_____

_____

• • •

Part VI – From Third Passover to the Beginning of the Last Passover Week

23

Christ's Final Departure From Galilee to Jerusalem Through Samaria

Jesus Came Not to Destroy Men's Lives, But to Save Them

And it came to pass, when the time was come that he should be received up, he steadfastly set his face to go to Jerusalem, and sent messengers before his face: and they went, and entered into a village of the Samaritans, to make ready for him.

And they did not receive him, because his face was as though he would go to Jerusalem.

And when his disciples James and John saw this, they said, "Lord, wilt thou that we command fire to come down from heaven, and consume them, even as Elias did?"

But he turned, and rebuked them, and said, *"Ye know not what manner of spirit ye are of.*

"For the Son of man is not come to destroy men's lives, but to save them." And they went to another village.

Jesus Gives a Warning to Certain Would-Be Followers

And it came to pass, that, as they went in the way, a certain man said unto him, "Lord, I will follow thee whithersoever thou goest."

And Jesus said unto him, *"Foxes have holes, and birds of the air have nests; but the Son of man hath not where to lay his head."*

And he said to another, *"Follow me."* But he said, "Lord, suffer me first to go and bury my father."

Jesus said unto him, *"Let the dead bury their dead: but go thou and preach the kingdom of God."*

Part VI – From Third Passover to the Beginning of the Last Passover Week

And another man saith, "Lord, I will follow thee: but let me go bid them farewell, which are not at home at my house."

And Jesus said unto him, *"No man, having put his hand to the plough, and looking back, is fit for the kingdom of God."*

NOTES: Scriptures of the Topics   <u>Luke</u>

- Jesus came not to Destroy men's lives, but to   9:55,56
save them
- Jesus gives a warning to certain would-be   9:58-60,62
followers

Doctrines and Commandments

261. Christ Jesus is come to save men's lives; not to destroy them.

262. A true follower of Christ hears only the shepherd's voice and will follow him. As the gifts of God are bestowed upon one, he shall not look back to the ways of the world and worldly desires and temptations, but shall keep with the work and will of God; and keep fit for the Kingdom of God.

Lessons We Should Learn

1.   Christ Jesus brings all things to him through gifts from his Heavenly Father by doing God's will, not His own, with faith, love, patience, and steadfast knowledge and devotion, knowing that one shall be saved from the temptations and destruction of Satan and shall become fit for the Kingdom of God. For He is come giving men life and saving them from the ways and bondage of Satan and does not destroy man, but uplifts him to be free of bondage and truly saved.

2.   Christ says, *"Follow me."* He doesn't say this sometimes, and say other times to instead go and do the things of the world, be tempted and bound by Satan and give me what is left over. He says in his commandment from God, *"Go and sin no more;"* and when he does this with all his heart and soul and the power of God giving up sin each day. We need to do this each day and follow Christ. By doing those things that Christ is teaching us to do we shall be steadfast to hear only his voice and be a true devout followers of Christ. A devout follower of Christ wrote, *"I will die with my hands on the plough."* What a vow to make! And as one keeps these types of vows he shall be fit for the Kingdom of God.

Part VI – From Third Passover to the Beginning of the Last Passover Week

My Thoughts About the Lessons

_____

_____

_____

_____

_____

_____

_____

_____

_____

_____

_____

_____

_____

_____

_____

_____

_____

_____

_____

_____

_____

_____

_____

_____

NOTES

Part VI – From Third Passover to the Beginning of the Last Passover Week

24

Jesus Sends Other Seventy Disciples Forth

<u>Jesus Gives Commandments to His Disciples</u>

The Lord appointed other seventy also, and sent them two by two before his face into every city and place, whither he himself would come.

Therefore said he unto them, *"The harvest truly is great, but the labourers are few: pray ye therefore the Lord of the harvest, that he would send forth labourers into his harvest.*

"Go your ways: behold, I send you forth as lambs among wolves.

"Carry neither purse, nor scrip, nor shoes: and salute no man by the way.

"And into whatsoever house ye enter, first say, Peace be to this house.

"And if the son of peace be there, your peace shall rest upon it: if not, it shall turn to you again.

"And in the same house remain, eating and drinking such things as they give: for the labourer is worthy of his hire. Go not from house to house.

"And into whatsoever city ye enter, and they receive you, eat such things as are set before you:

"And heal the sick that are therein, and say unto them, The kingdom of God is come nigh unto you.

"But into whatsoever city ye enter, and they receive you not, go your ways out into the streets of the same, and say,

"Even the very dust of your city, which cleaveth on us, we do wipe off against you: notwithstanding be ye sure of this, that the kingdom of God is come nigh unto you.

Part VI – From Third Passover to the Beginning of the Last Passover Week

"But I say unto you, that it shall be more tolerable in that day for Sodom than for that city.

"Woe unto thee, Chorazin! woe unto thee, Bethsaida! for if the mighty works had been done in Tyre and Sidon, which have been done in you, they had a great while ago repented, sitting in sackcloth and ashes.

"But it shall be more tolerable for Tyre and Sidon at the judgment, than for you.

"And thou Capernaum, which art exalted to heaven, shalt be thrust down to hell.

"He that heareth you heareth me; and he that despiseth you despiseth me; and he that despiseth me despiseth him that sent me."

And the seventy returned again with joy, saying, Lord even the devils are subject unto us through thy name.

And he said unto them, *"I beheld Satan as lightning fall from heaven.*

"Behold I give unto you power to tread on serpents and scorpions, and over all the power of the enemy: and nothing shall by any means hurt you. "Not withstanding in this rejoice not, that the spirits are subject unto you; but rather rejoice, because your names are written in heaven.

Christ Thanks His Heavenly Father: God is Lord of Heaven and Earth

In that hour Jesus rejoiced in spirit, and said,

"I thank thee, O Father, Lord of heaven and earth, that thou hast hid these things from the wise and prudent, and hast revealed them unto babes: even so, Father; for so it seemed good in thy sight.

All Things are Delivered to Jesus of God

"All things are delivered to me of my Father; and no man knoweth who the Son is, but the Father; and who the Father is, but the Son, and he to whom the Son will reveal him."

Part VI – From Third Passover to the Beginning of the Last Passover Week

His Disciples are Blessed to See the Things That God Has for Them to See

And he turned to his disciples, and said privately, *"Blessed are the eyes which see the things that ye see: "For I tell you, that many prophets and kings have desired to see those things which ye see, and have not seen them; and to hear those things which ye hear, and have not heard them."*

Story of Good Samaritan: a Lawyer Asks Jesus What He Must Do to Inherit Eternal Life

And behold, a certain lawyer stood up, and tempted him, saying, Master what shall I do to inherit eternal life?

Jesus said unto him, *"What is written in the law? How readest thou?"*

And the lawyer answered, 'Thou shalt love the Lord thy God with all thy heart, and with all thy soul, and with all thy strength, and with all thy mind; and thy neighbor as thyself.'

And Jesus said unto him, *"Thou hast answered right: this do, and thou shalt live."*

But the lawyer, willing to justify himself, said unto Jesus, And who is my neighbor?

And Jesus answering said, *"A certain man went down from Jerusalem to Jericho, and fell among thieves which stripped him of his raiment, and wounded him, and departed, leaving him half dead.*

"And by chance there came down a certain priest that way: and when he saw him, he passed by on the other side.

"And likewise a Levite, when he was at the place, came and looked on him, and passed by on the other side.

"But a certain Samaritan as he journeyed, came where he was: and when he saw him, he had compassion on him.

Part VI – From Third Passover to the Beginning of the Last Passover Week

"And went to him, and bound up his wounds, pouring in oil and wine, and set him on his own beast, and brought him to an inn, and took care of him.

"And on the morrow when he departed, he took out two pence, and gave them to the host, and said unto him, Take care of him; and whatsoever thou spendest more, when I come again, I will repay thee.

"Which now of these three, thinkest thou, was neighbor unto him that fell among the thieves?"

And he said, He that shewed mercy on him. Then Jesus said unto him, *"Go and do thou likewise."*

<u>Martha and Her Sister Mary Speak to Jesus</u>

Now it came to pass, as they went that he entered into a certain village: and a certain woman named Martha received him into her house.

And she had a sister called Mary, which also sat at Jesus' feet, and heard his word. But Martha was cumbered about much serving, and came to him, and said, Lord dost thou not care that my sister hath left me to serve alone? bid her therefore that she help me.

And Jesus answered and said unto her, *"Martha, Martha thou art careful and troubled about many things:*

"But one thing is needful; and Mary hath chosen that good part, which shall not be taken away from her."

Part VI – From Third Passover to the Beginning of the Last Passover Week

NOTES: Scriptures of the Topics	Luke
- Jesus gives commandments to his disciples	10:2-20
- Christ thanks His Heavenly Father: God is Lord of Heaven and Earth	10:21
- All things are delivered to Jesus of God	10:22
- His disciples are blessed to see the things that God has for them to see	10:23,24
- Story of Good Samaritan	10:30-37
- A lawyer asks Jesus what he must do to inherit eternal life	10:26,28
- Martha and her sister Mary speak to Jesus	10:41,42

Doctrines and Commandments

263. There is great need in the world today to go forth with the words of Christ Jesus, but there are few disciples and missionaries to send forth.

264. Christ Jesus beheld Satan as lightning from heaven

265. The power of God is given to you over all power of the enemy, and nothing shall hurt you as you become a disciple of Christ.

266. As disciples of Christ, rejoice because your names are written in heaven.

267. For those who are wise and prudent, the light and truth is lost and unknown and revealed to those who become a disciple of Christ and are as babes (little children).

268. Christ will reveal all things of God.

269. He that hears the disciples of Christ hears Christ.

270. He that despises the disciples of Christ despises Christ.

271. Christ's disciples are blessed to see the things that God has for them to see.

272. We are neighbors and to do neighborly things to those who have fallen among sinners, or in the hands of sinners.

273. One must choose the good part, Christ's doctrines and commandments, and put them forth first in his life, above all other needs, and the good part shall not be taken from him.

42. Christ knows all truth and untruth, He knows all things of God

Part VI – From Third Passover to the Beginning of the Last Passover Week

75.   Jesus gives commandments to disciples going on their missions and should be used in our daily mission in life. (See Chapter 10, Doctrines 75-1 to 75-27)

Lessons We Should Learn

1.   As you become a true serving and giving disciple of Christ the blessings and power are given to you and nothing shall hurt you. The need for Christ's words to be known and lived in the world today is greatly needed and there are few that are humble and serving to Him.

2.   As true Christians our daily life becomes given to serve the Lord. If we are as little children His truth and light shall not be lost. Christ reveals all things of God to us. How tempting it is to be busy in our daily lives with daily worldly things and give only the left over time to Christ's words. To live Christ's commandments and teachings with all our heart and all our soul we have chosen the first things first and in order of rightful priority over worldly things. Then we are true disciples of Christ and our daily lives are testimonies of Christ. As true disciples of Christ their names are written in heaven.

Part VI – From Third Passover to the Beginning of the Last Passover Week

My Thoughts About the Lessons

_____

_____

_____

_____

_____

_____

_____

_____

_____

_____

_____

_____

_____

_____

_____

_____

_____

_____

_____

_____

_____

_____

_____

_____

_____

NOTES

Part VI – From Third Passover to the Beginning of the Last Passover Week

25

Christ Teaches Us to Pray

Jesus Again Teaches His Disciples How to Pray

And it came to pass, that, as he was praying in a certain place, when he ceased, one of his disciples said unto him, Lord, teach us to pray, as John also taught his disciples.

And he said unto them, *"When ye pray, say, Our Father which art in heaven, Hallowed be thy name. Thy kingdom come. Thy will be done, as in heaven, so in earth.*

"Give us day by day our daily bread.

"And forgive us our sins; for we also forgive everyone that is indebted to us. And lead us not into temptation; but deliver us from evil."

And he said unto them, *"Which of you shall have a friend, and shall go unto him at midnight, and say unto him, Friend, lend me three loaves;*

"For a friend of mine in his journey is come to me, and I have nothing to set before him?

"And he from within shall answer and say, Trouble me not: the door is now shut, and; my children are with me in bed; I cannot rise and give thee.

"I say unto you, though he will not rise and give him, because he is his friend, yet because of his importunity he will rise and give him as many as he needeth."

Part VI – From Third Passover to the Beginning of the Last Passover Week

Ask and It Shall Be Given: Knock and It Shall Be Opened

"And I say unto you, Ask and it shall be given you; seek and ye shall find; knock, and it shall be opened unto you.

"For every one that asketh receiveth; and he that seeketh findeth; and to him that knocketh it shall be opened.

"If a son shall ask bread of any of you that is a father, will he give him a stone? or if he ask a fish, will he for a fish give him a serpent?
"Or if he shall ask an egg, will he offer him a scorpion?"

Your Heavenly Father Will Give the Holy Spirit to Them That Ask Him

"If ye then, being evil, know how to give good gifts unto your children: how much more shall your Heavenly Father give the Holy Spirit to them that ask him?"

NOTES: Scriptures of the Topics — Luke

- He again teaches the disciples how to pray — 11:2-8
- Ask and it shall be given: knock and it shall be opened — 11:9-12
- Our Heavenly Father will give the Holy Spirit to them that ask him — 11:13

Doctrines and Commandments

102. Use the Lord's Prayer
274. Ask, and it shall be given you; for everyone that asks receives.
275. Seek and you shall find; and he that seeks finds.
276. Knock and it shall be opened unto you
277. God will give the Holy Spirit to those that ask Him.

Part VI – From Third Passover to the Beginning of the Last Passover Week

Lessons We Should Learn

1.   Christ taught us to pray, to commune with God the Father, to talk with Him. If we would follow these commandments:

-   Ask and it shall be given

-   Seek and you shall find

-    Knock and it shall be opened, and the truth, the light and the kingdom shall be given.

What light and beauty Christ Jesus gave us in his prayer to his and our Heavenly Father.

"Our Father"

His Father and our Father; what assurances we have to know that God our creator is alive and does love us and create us in His image.

"Hallowed be thy name"

His name is the Holy of Holy in the most exalted being; and all glory is unto Him, His name and His right for all love to return to honor Him and His name.

"Thy kingdom come"

His kingdom, the most precious, His children! As we become one with Christ we also are one with God.

"Thy will be done in earth as it is in heaven"

His children shall do His will each day, day by day, right here on earth. We are in high places within our hearts with Christ, with God, each day, and now this moment with God! Just as if we were in heaven. It is the same and it must manifest the same right here on earth.

"Give us this day our daily bread"

Give us Christ each day—he is the bread of life—he is the word, the light, the truth. Let him be in us, in our heart each day, each moment to be one with us, each one. As we ask it, it shall be given.

"And forgive us our sins as we forgive those who sin against us"

As we do, we are! As we do, the same manifests unto us. As we repent, we have a new righteousness within us. God's will is done—the door is closed to Satan. We have overcome! But we each must bear our cross each day to be in the power of God! Then, we can each be one with Christ; and one with God! God forgives us of all trespasses against him. As we go and sin no more—then we are truly forgiven.

Part VI – From Third Passover to the Beginning of the Last Passover Week

"Lead us not into temptation, but deliver us from evil"

We ask for the protection of God—for the world tempts each of us severely. We need all His power to protect us from the forces and will of Satan. The closer we become to God and Christ—the more the adversary works to see us backslide. So ask it and it shall be given.

Ask for God's power! His power is greater than all power in the world and in the universe. Direct this power to protect oneself, daily and continuously—each hour and each moment.

"And the Power"

There is only one power in all Creation—in all the heavens—the Cosmos—the Earth and any other place. God is the Power that put all the life into motion, reality and existence!

"And the Glory"

All is in His Glory! We exemplify Him, in all that we do, when we do His will! And we see the Light—the Christ! We do His will—we are healed—

we are in his Joy and our own—we love one another—we succeed—all is in Glory to God—we give Him the praise—it is Him in us. For of ourselves we do nothing. It is only God expressing in each of us and the Glory belongs to God!

"Forever"

In all eternity—God is in the beginning and is forever—life eternal—life everlasting—that God is—that we are, as we become one with God—right now in earth as it is in heaven.

Amen. (One with God, God is True)

Part VI – From Third Passover to the Beginning of the Last Passover Week

My Thoughts About the Lessons

NOTES

Part VI – From Third Passover to the Beginning of the Last Passover Week

26

Christ's Warnings: Commandments and Discourses

Christ Warns Against an Evil Generation

And when the people were gathered thick together, he began to say, *"This is an evil generation: they seek a sign; and there shall no sign be given it, but the sign of Jonas the prophet. "For as Jonas was a sign unto the Ninevites, so shall also the Son of man be to this generation.*

"The queen of the south shall rise up in the judgment with the men of this generation, and condemn them: for she came from the utmost parts of the earth to hear the wisdom of Solomon; and behold, a greater than Solomon is here.

"The men of Nineve shall rise up in the judgment with the men of this generation, and shall condemn it, for they repented at the preaching of Jonas; and, behold, a greater than Jonas is here.

"No man, when he hath lighted a candle, putteth it in a secret place, neither under a bushel, but on a candlestick, that they which come in may see the light.

"The light of the body is the eye: therefore when thine eye is single, thy whole body also is full of light; but when thine eye is evil, thy body also is full of darkness.

"Take heed therefore, that the light which is in thee be not darkness.

"If thy whole body therefore be full of light, having no part dark, the whole shall be full of light, as when the bright shining of a candle doth give thee light."

Part VI – From Third Passover to the Beginning of the Last Passover Week

Christ Warns Against Hypocrisy

And as he spake, a certain Pharisee besought him to dine with him: and he went in, and sat down to meat.

And when the Pharisee saw it, he marveled that he had not first washed before dinner.

And the Lord said unto him, *"Now do ye Pharisees make clean the outside of the cup and the platter; but your inward part is full of ravening and wickedness. "Ye fools did not he that made that which is without make that which is within also?*

"But rather give alms of such things as ye have; and, behold, all things are clean unto you.

"But woe unto you, Pharisees! for ye tithe mint and rue all manner of herbs, and pass over judgment and the love of God: these ought ye to have done. And not to leave the other undone.

"Woe unto you, Pharisees! for ye love the uppermost seats in the synagogues, and greetings in the markets.

"Woe unto you, scribes and Pharisees, hypocrites! for ye are as graves which appear not, and the men that walk over them are not aware of them."

Then answered one of the lawyers, and said unto him, Master, thus saying thou reproachest us also.

And he said, *"Woe unto you also, ye lawyers! for ye lade men with burdens grievous to be borne, and ye yourselves touch not the burdens with one of your fingers.*

"Woe unto you! for ye build the sepulchers of the prophets, and your fathers killed them.

"Truly ye bear witness that ye allow the deeds of your fathers: for they indeed killed them, and ye build their sepulchers.

Part VI – From Third Passover to the Beginning of the Last Passover Week

"Therefore also said the wisdom of God, I will send them prophets and apostles, and some of them they shall slay and persecute:

"That the blood of all the prophets, which was shed from the foundation of the world, may be required of this generation;

"From the blood of Abel unto the blood of Zacharias, which perished between the altar and the temple: verily I say unto you, It shall be required of this generation.

"Woe unto you, lawyers! for ye have taken away the key of knowledge: ye entered not in yourselves, and them that were entering in ye hindered."

And as he said these things unto them, the scribes and Pharisees began to urge him vehemently, and to provoke him to speak of many things:

Laying wait for him, and seeking to catch something out of his mouth, that they might accuse him.

Christ Warns Against Covetousness

And one of the company said unto him, Master, speak to my brother, that he divide the inheritance with me.

And he said unto them, *"Man, who made me a judge or a divider over you?"*
And he said unto them, *"Take heed, and beware of covetousness: for a man's life consisteth not in the abundance of the things which he possesseth."*

And he spake a parable unto them, saying, *"The ground of a certain rich man brought forth plentifully:*

"And he thought within himself, saying, What shall I do, because I have no room where to bestow my fruits?

"And he said, This will I do: I will pull down my barns, and build greater; and there will I bestow all my fruits and my goods.

Part VI – From Third Passover to the Beginning of the Last Passover Week

"And I will say to my soul, Soul, thou hast much goods laid up for many years; take thine ease, eat, drink, and be merry.

"But God said unto him, Thou fool, this night thy soul shall be required of thee: then whose soul shall those things be, which thou hast provided?

"So is he that layeth up treasure for himself, and is not rich toward God."

Exhortation to His Disciples

When there were gathered together an innumerable multitude of people, he began to say unto his disciples first of all,

"Beware ye of the leaven of the Pharisees, which is hypocrisy.

"For there is nothing covered, that shall not be revealed; neither hid, that shall not be known.

"Therefore whatsoever ye have spoken in darkness shall be heard in the light; and that which ye have spoken in the ear in closets shall be proclaimed upon the housetops.

"And I say unto you my friends, Be not afraid of them that kill the body, and after that have no more that they can do.

"But I will forewarn you whom ye shall fear: Fear him, which after he hath killed hath power to cast into hell; yea, I say unto you, Fear him.

"Are not five sparrows sold for two farthings, and not one of them is forgotten before God?

"But even the very hairs of your head are all numbered. Fear not therefore; ye are of more value than many sparrows.

"Also I say unto you, Whosoever shall confess me before men, him shall the Son of man also confess before the angels of God:

Part VI – From Third Passover to the Beginning of the Last Passover Week

"But he that denieth me before men shall be denied before the angels of God.

"And whosoever shall speak a word against the Son of man, it shall be forgiven him: but unto him that blasphemeth against the Holy Ghost it shall not be forgiven.

"And when they bring you unto the synagogues, and unto magistrates, and powers, take ye no thought how or what thing ye shall answer, or what ye shall say:

"For the Holy Ghost shall teach you in the same hour what ye ought to say."

Your Father Knows What Your Needs Are

And he said unto his disciples, *"Therefore I say unto you, Take no thought for your life, what ye shall eat; neither for the body, what ye shall put on.*

"The life is more than meat, and the body is more than raiment.

"Consider the ravens; for they neither sow nor reap, which neither have storehouse nor barn; and God feedeth them: how much more are ye better than the fowls?

"And which of you with taking thought can add to his stature one cubit?

"If ye then be not able to do that thing which is least, why take ye thought for the rest?

"Consider the lilies how they grow: they toil not, they spin not; and yet I say unto you, that Solomon in all his glory was not arrayed like one of these.

"If then God so clothe the grass, which is to day in the field, and to morrow is cast into the oven; how much more will he clothe you, O ye of little faith?

"And seek not ye what ye shall eat, or what ye shall drink, neither be ye of doubtful mind.

"For all these things do the nations of the world seek after: and your Father knoweth that ye have need of these things.

Part VI – From Third Passover to the Beginning of the Last Passover Week

Seek the Kingdom of God and All Things Shall Be Added unto You

"But rather seek ye the kingdom of God; and all these things shall be added unto you.

"Fear not, little flock; for it is your Father's good pleasure to give you the kingdom.

"Sell that ye have and give alms; provide yourselves bags which wax not old, a treasure in the heavens that faileth not, where no thief approacheth, neither moth corrupteth.

"For where your treasure is, there will your heart be also."

Be Ready For the Son of Man Comes At an Unknown Hour

"Let your loins be girded about, and your lights burning; "And ye yourselves like unto men that wait for their Lord, when he will return from the wedding; that when he cometh and knocketh, they may open unto him immediately.

"Blessed are those servants, whom the lord when he cometh shall find watching: verily I say unto you, that he shall gird himself, and make them to sit down to meat, and will come forth and serve them.

"And if he shall come in the second watch, or come in the third watch, and find them so, blessed are those servants.

"And this know, that if the goodman of the house had known what hour the thief would come, he would have watched, and not have suffered his house to be broken through.

"Be ye therefore ready also: for the Son of man cometh at an hour when ye think not."

Part VI – From Third Passover to the Beginning of the Last Passover Week

Then Peter said unto him, Lord, speakest thou this parable unto us, or even to all?

And the Lord said, *"Who then is that faithful and wise steward, whom his Lord shall make ruler over his household, to give them their portion of meat in due season?*

"Blessed is the servant, whom his lord when he cometh shall find so doing.

"Of a truth I say unto you, that he will make him ruler over all that he hath.

"But and if that servant say in his heart, My lord delayeth his coming; and shall begin to beat the men servants and maidens, and to eat and drink, and to be drunken;

"The lord of that servant will come in a day when he looketh not for him, and at an hour when he is not aware, and will cut him in sunder, and will appoint him his portion with the unbelievers.

"And that servant, which knew his Lord's will, and prepared not himself, neither did according to his will, shall be beaten with many stripes.

"But that he knew not, and did commit things worthy of stripes shall be beaten with few stripes. For unto whomsoever much is given, of him shall be much required: and to whom men have committed much, of him they will ask the more."

Jesus Has a Baptism to Be Baptized With

"I am come to send fire on the earth; and what will I, if it be already kindled?

"But I have a baptism to be baptized with; and how am I straitened till it be accomplished!

"Suppose ye that I am come to give peace on earth? I tell you, Nay; but rather division:

"For from henceforth there shall be five in one house divided, three against two, and two against three

Part VI – From Third Passover to the Beginning of the Last Passover Week

"The father shall be divided against the son, and the son against the father; the mother against the daughter, and the daughter against the mother; the mother in law against her daughter in law, and the daughter in law against her mother in law."

And he said also to the people, *"When ye see a cloud rise out of the west, straightway ye say, There cometh a shower; and so it is.*

"And when ye see the south wind blow, ye say, There will be heat; and it cometh to pass.

"Ye hypocrites, ye can discern the face of the sky and of the earth; but how is it that ye do not discern this time?

"Yea, and why even of yourselves judge not what is right?"

When You Go With Your Adversary to The Magistrate

"When thou goest with thine adversary to the magistrate, as thou art in the way, give diligence that thou mayest be delivered from him; lest he hale thee to the judge, and the judge deliver thee to the officer, and the officer cast thee into prison.
"I tell thee, thou shalt not depart thence, till thou hast paid the very last mite."

God's Judgments: Motive to Repentance

There were present at that season some that told him of the Galileans, whose blood Pilate had mingled with their sacrifices.

And Jesus answering said unto them,

"Suppose ye that these Galileans were sinners above all the Galileans, because they suffered such things?
"I tell you, Nay: but, except ye repent, ye shall all likewise perish.
"Or those eighteen, upon whom the tower in Siloam fell, and slew them, think ye that they were sinners above all men that dwelt in Jerusalem?
"I tell you, Nay: but, except ye repent, ye shall all likewise perish."

Part VI – From Third Passover to the Beginning of the Last Passover Week

Parable of the Barren Fig Tree

He spake also this parable, *"A certain man had a fig tree planted in his vineyard; and he came and sought fruit thereon, and found none.*

"Then said he unto the dresser of his vineyard, Behold, these three years I come seeking fruit of this fig tree, and find none: cut it down; why cumbereth it the ground?

"And he answering said unto him, Lord, let it alone this year also, till I shall dig about it, and dung it:

"And if it bear fruit, well: and if not, then after that thou shall cut it down."

Cure of a Woman With a Spirit of Infirmity on the Sabbath Day

And he was teaching in one of the synagogues on the Sabbath.

And there was a woman which had a spirit of infirmity eighteen years, and was bowed together, and could in no wise lift up herself.

And when Jesus saw her, he called her to him, and said unto her, *"Woman, thou art loosed from thine infirmity."*

And he laid his hands on her: and immediately she was made straight, and glorified God.

And the ruler of the synagogue answered with indignation, because Jesus had healed on the Sabbath day, and said unto the people, There are six days in which men ought to work: in them therefore come and be healed, and not on the Sabbath day.

The Lord then answered him, and said, *"Thou hypocrite, doth not each one of you on the Sabbath loose his ox or his ass from the stall, and lead him away to watering?*

Part VI – From Third Passover to the Beginning of the Last Passover Week

"And ought not this woman, being a daughter of Abraham, whom Satan hath bound, lo, these eighteen years, be loosed from this bond on the Sabbath day?"

And when he had said these things, all his adversaries were ashamed: and all the people rejoiced for all the glorious things that were done by him.

Jesus Asks, *"What is the kingdom of God like?"*

Then he said, *"Unto what is the kingdom of God like? and whereunto shall I resemble it?*

"It is like a grain of mustard seed, which a man took, and cast into his garden; and it grew, and waxed a great tree; and the fowls of the air lodged in the branches of it."

And again he said, *"Whereunto shall I liken the kingdom of God?*

"It is like leaven, which a woman took and hid in three measures of meal, till the whole was leavened."

And he went through the cities and villages, teaching, and journeying toward Jerusalem.

Part VI – From Third Passover to the Beginning of the Last Passover Week

NOTES: Scriptures of the Topics	Luke
- Christ warns against an evil generation	11:29-36
- Christ warns against hypocrisy	11:39-52
- Christ warns against covetousness	12:14-21
- Exhortation to his disciples; blasphemy against the Holy Ghost	12:1-12
- Your Father knows what your needs are	12:22-30
- Seek the kingdom of God and all things shall be added unto you	12:31-34
- Be ready for the Son of man comes at an unknown hour	12:35-48
- Jesus has a baptism to be baptized with: and of yourself judge what is right	12:49-53 54-57
- When you go with your adversary to the magistrate	12:58,59
- God's judgments: motive to repentance	13:2-5
- Parable of the barren fig tree	13:6-9
- Cure of a woman with a spirit of infirmity on the Sabbath day	13:12,15,16
- Jesus asks, *"What is the kingdom of God like?"*	13:18-21

Doctrines and Commandments

108. The light of the body is the eye; if your eye is righteous, your whole body shall be full of light. But if your eye be evil your whole body is full of darkness (See Luke. 11:34-36)

278. No sign is given an evil generation.

279. Christ Jesus warns against hypocrites: who make clean the outside of the cup and the platter; but their inward part is full of ravening and wickedness; who love the uppermost seats in the churches and greetings in the markets; who tithe with all manner of riches but Passover judgment and the love of God (Those you ought to have done and leave the other undone).

Part VI – From Third Passover to the Beginning of the Last Passover Week

280. Christ warns against covetousness: beware of covetousness; for your life does not consist in the abundance of the things that you possess. One is a fool to lay up treasurers for himself and not rich toward God.

281. Christ warns against lawyers; for they burden men with burdens grievous to be born and they are free of the burdens themselves; they bear witness of their fathers' deeds, that their fathers killed the prophets and the lawyers build their sepulchers; they take away the key of knowledge; they do not enter in themselves and hinder those who were entering in.

75.

14) Fear not those who kill the body, for after that there is nothing more they can do.

15) Christ forewarns us to fear him which is able to destroy both soul and body in hell

16) Whosoever shall confess Christ Jesus before men, him will I confess also before my Father which is in heaven (See Luke. 12:8)

17) Whosoever shall deny me before men him will I also deny before my Father.

148. Whosoever shall speak a word against Christ Jesus it shall be forgiven him.

149. He that blaspheme against the Holy Ghost it shall not be forgiven.

282. The Holy Ghost shall teach you what you ought to say before magistrates and powers.

283. Seek the kingdom of God and all things shall be added unto you.

284. Be ready, for the Christ comes at an hour when you think not. You hypocrites, you can discern the weather and the sky, but you are not discerned about this time. Why don't you even judge yourself what is right?

285. *"From henceforth there shall be five in one house divided, three against two and two against three. The father shall be divided against the son, and the son against the father; the mother against the daughter, and the daughter against the mother; the mother in law against her daughter in law, and the daughter in law against her mother in law."*

286. Unless you repent, you shall all likewise perish.

287. Go to the magistrate with your adversary and you shall not leave there until you have paid the very last mite.

288. Hypocrites don't do the Lord's work on the Sabbath day.

110. God knows of each hair upon your head so we should fear not for God will take care of us.

107. Where your treasure is, there will your heart be also. Sell what you have and give alms.

Part VI – From Third Passover to the Beginning of the Last Passover Week

Lessons We Should Learn

1.   Christ's warning to hypocrites really makes one realize what hypocrites we really are at times and in different situations. It seems we spend so much time with worldly business that at the time seems to take most of our time. Also, one needs to examine the motives for taking positions in life and at church. And to examine each thought, word and action with all those we meet each day and with our neighbors.

2.   Covetousness of worldly possessions and our neighbor's goods and family; we must know that God knows our every need and we need not spend any more days, months, and years striving for things of our own desires that may not be what God has for us. As Christ Jesus teaches us, seek first the kingdom of God and all things shall be added unto you.

3.   We need to repent daily. Judge our behavior each day to be sure that we are putting Christ's doctrines and commandments to work in our lives. That we are always a living testimony to God by living the gospels of Christ Jesus. We should always do the will of God and know that it must be done with all our strength and all our heart whether it be the Sabbath day or any other day. Then we shall be seeking the kingdom of God and if the hour arrives when the Lord is come we shall be ready.

Part VI – From Third Passover to the Beginning of the Last Passover Week

My Thoughts About the Lessons

_____

_____

_____

_____

_____

_____

_____

_____

_____

_____

_____

_____

_____

_____

_____

_____

_____

_____

_____

_____

_____

_____

_____

_____

_____

Part VI – From Third Passover to the Beginning of the Last Passover Week

27

Jesus Proclaims His Divine Oneness With God at the Feast of Dedication

The Christus

<u>The Christ</u>

A nd it was at Jerusalem at the feast of the dedication, and it was winter. And Jesus walked in the temple in Solomon's porch. Then came the Jews round about him, and said unto him, How long dost thou make us doubt? If thou be the Christ tell us plainly.

Jesus answered them, *"I told you, and ye believed not: the works that I do in my Father's name, they bear witness of me.* "But ye believe not, because ye are not of my sheep, as I said unto you.

"My sheep hear my voice, and I know them, and they follow me:

"And I give unto them eternal life; and they shall never perish, neither shall any man pluck them out of my hand."

<u>I and My Father are One</u>

"My Father, which gave them me, is greater than all; and no man is able to pluck them out of my Father's hand.

"I and my Father are one."

Then the Jews took up stones again to stone him.

Jesus answered them, *"Many good works have I shewed you from my Father; for which of those works do ye stone me?"*

Part VI – From Third Passover to the Beginning of the Last Passover Week

Christ Says He is the Son of God

The Jews answered him saying, For a good work we stone thee not; but for blasphemy; and because that thou, being a man, makest thyself God.

Jesus answered them, *"Is it not written in your law, I said, Ye are gods?*

"If he called them gods, unto whom the word of God came, and the scripture cannot be broken;

"Say ye of him, whom the Father hath sanctified, and sent into the world, Thou blasphemest; because I said, I am the Son of God?"

The Father is in Christ, and Christ in Him

"If I do not the works of my Father, believe me not.

"But if I do, though ye believe not me, believe the works: that ye may know, and believe, that the Father is in me, and I in him."

Therefore they sought again to take him; but he escaped out of their hand, And went away again beyond Jordan into the place where John at first baptized; and there he abode.

And many resorted unto him, and said, John did no miracle: but all things that John spake of this man were true.

And many believed on him there.

NOTES: Scriptures of the Topics   John

- The Christ   10:25-28
- I and My Father are one   10:29,30,32
- Christ says He is the Son of God   10:34-36
- The Father is in Christ, and Christ in Him   10:37,38

Part VI – From Third Passover to the Beginning of the Last Passover Week

Doctrines and Commandments

258. Christ is the good shepherd; he knows his sheep and they know him. As God knows Christ, Christ knows the Father: and Christ lays down his life for the sheep. They follow Christ.

289. Christ gives his sheep eternal life; and they shall never perish, neither shall any man pluck them out of his hand.

290. Christ and God are one.

291. Christ is the Son of God.

292. The Father is in Christ and Christ is in the Father.

Lessons We Should Learn

1.   Christ is one with God. God created us in his image and we may be one with Christ and therefore, one with God. As we become one with Christ and follow him, we are one of his flock and no man shall pluck you from the hands of Christ. As he is our shepherd we will only follow his sayings and shall be deaf to the voice of Satan, and to those who follow Satan.

2.   What a blessing it is to know that Christ Jesus is the Savior, our Savior, he is the Word, he is the Light, he is in the image of God, and that he is the True Image of God and that he is One with God; and that he may choose us to be one of his flock and may have eternal life with him and God our Father.

Part VI – From Third Passover to the Beginning of the Last Passover Week

My Thoughts About the Lessons

_____

_____

_____

_____

_____

_____

_____

_____

_____

_____

_____

_____

_____

_____

_____

_____

_____

_____

_____

_____

_____

_____

_____

_____

_____

Part VI – From Third Passover to the Beginning of the Last Passover Week

28

Discipleship For Christ

Jesus Returns Toward Bethany on Hearing of the Sickness of Lazarus

And he went through the cities and villages, teaching, and journeying toward Jerusalem.

Then said one unto him, Lord, are there few that be saved? And he said unto them,

"Strive to enter in at the strait gate: for many, I say unto you, will seek to enter in, and shall not be able.

"When once the master of the house is risen up, and hath shut the door, and ye begin to stand without, and to knock at the door, saying, Lord, Lord, open unto us; and he shall answer and say unto you, I know you not whence ye are:

"Then shall ye begin to say, we have eaten and drunk in thy presence, and thou hast taught in our streets.

"But he shall say, I tell you, I know you not whence ye are; depart from me, all ye workers of iniquity.

"There shall be weeping and gnashing of teeth, when ye shall see Abraham and Isaac, and Jacob, and all the prophets, in the kingdom of God, and you yourselves thrust out.

"And they shall come from the east, and from the west, and from the north, and from the south, and shall sit down in the kingdom of God.

"And behold, there are last which shall be first, and there are first which shall be last."

Now a certain man was sick, named Lazarus, of Bethany, the town of Mary and her sister Martha.(It was Mary which anointed the Lord with ointment, and wiped his feet with her hair, whose brother Lazarus was sick.)

Part VI – From Third Passover to the Beginning of the Last Passover Week

Therefore, his sisters sent unto him, saying Lord, behold he whom thou lovest is sick.

When Jesus heard that, he said, *"This sickness is not unto death, but for the glory of God, that the Son of God might be glorified thereby."*

Now Jesus loved Martha, and her sister, and Lazarus.

When he had heard therefore that he was sick, he abode two days still in the same place where he was.

Then after that saith he to his disciples, *"Let us go into Judea again."*

His disciples say unto him, Master, the Jews of late sought to stone thee; and goest thou thither again?

Jesus answered, *"Are there not twelve hours in the day? If any man walk in the day, he stumbleth not, because he seeth the light of this world,*

"But if a man walk in the night, he stumbleth, because there is no light in him."

After that he said unto them, *"Our friend Lazarus sleepeth; but I go, that I may awake him out of sleep."*

Then his disciples question him about Lazarus taking a rest in sleep.

Then said Jesus unto them plainly, *"Lazarus is dead."*

"And I am glad for your sakes that I was not there, to the intent ye may believe; nevertheless let us go unto him."

Part VI – From Third Passover to the Beginning of the Last Passover Week

Jesus Answers Herod

The same day there came certain of the Pharisees, saying unto him, Get thee out, and depart hence: for Herod will kill thee.

And Jesus said unto them *"Go ye, and tell that fox, Behold, I cast out devils, and I do cures to day and to morrow, and the third day I shall be perfected.*

"Nevertheless I must walk to day, and to morrow, and the day following: for it cannot be that a prophet perish out of Jerusalem.

"O Jerusalem, Jerusalem, which killest the prophets, and stonest them that are sent unto thee; how often would I have gathered thy children together, as a hen doth gather her brood under her wings, and ye would not!

"Behold, your house is left unto you desolate: and verily I say unto you, Ye shall not see me, until the time come when ye shall say, Blessed is he that cometh in the name of the Lord."

Cure of a Man with Dropsy

And it came to pass, as he went unto the house of one of the chief Pharisees to eat bread on the Sabbath day, that they watched him.

And there was a certain man before him which had the dropsy.

And Jesus answering spake unto the lawyers and Pharisees, saying, *"Is it lawful to heal on the Sabbath day?"*

And they held their peace. And he took him, and healed him, and let him go.

Jesus answered them, saying, *"Which of you shall have an ass or an ox fallen into a pit and will not straightway pull him out on the Sabbath day?"*

And they could not answer him again to these things.

Part VI – From Third Passover to the Beginning of the Last Passover Week

Parable of the Great Supper

And Jesus put forth a parable to those which were bidden, when he marked how they chose out the chief rooms; saying unto them,

"When thou art bidden of any man to a wedding, sit not down in the highest room; lest a more honorable man than thou be bidden of him;

"And he that bade thee and him come and say to thee, Give this man place; and thou begin with shame to take the lowest room.

"But when thou art bidden, go and sit down in the lowest room; that when he that bade thee cometh, he may say unto thee, Friend, go up higher: then shalt thou have worship in the presence of them that sit at meat with thee.

"For whosoever exalteth himself shall be abased; and he that humbleth himself shall be exalted."

Then said he also to him that bade him, *"When thou makest a dinner or a supper, call not thy friends, nor thy brethren, neither thy kinsmen, nor thy rich neighbours; lest they also bid thee again, and a recompence be made thee.*

"But when thou makest a feast, call the poor, the maimed, the lame, the blind:
"And thou shalt be blessed; for they cannot recompense thee: for thou shalt be recompensed at the resurrection of the just."

And when one of them that sat at meat with him heard these things, he said unto him, blessed is he that shall eat bread in the kingdom of God.

Then said he unto him, *"A certain man made a great supper, and bade many:*
"And sent his servant at supper time to say to them that were bidden, Come; for all things are now ready.

"And they all with one consent began to make excuse. The first said unto him, I have bought a piece of ground, and I must needs go and see it: I pray thee have me excused.

Part VI – From Third Passover to the Beginning of the Last Passover Week

"And another said, I have bought five yoke of oxen, and I go to prove them: I pray thee have me excused.

"And another said, I have married a wife and therefore I cannot come.

"So that servant came, and showed his lord these things. Then the master of the house being angry said to his servant, Go out quickly into the streets and lanes of the city, and bring in hither the poor, and the maimed, and the halt, and the blind.

"And the servant said, Lord, it is done as thou hast commanded and yet there is room.

"And the lord said unto the servant, go out into the highways and hedges, and compel them to come in, that my house may be filled.

"For I say unto you, That none of those men which were bidden shall taste of my supper."

Who Can Be Christ's Disciples?

And there went great multitudes with him: and he turned and said unto them,

"If any man come to me, and hate not his father, and mother, and wife, and children, and brethren, and sisters, yea, and his own life also, he cannot be my disciple.

"And whosoever doth not bear his cross, and come after me, cannot be my disciple.

"For which of you, intending to build a tower, sitteth not down first, and counteth the cost, whether he have sufficient to finish it?

"Lest haply, after he hath laid the foundation, and is not able to finish it, all that behold it begin to mock him.

"Saying, this man began to build, and was not able to finish.

Part VI – From Third Passover to the Beginning of the Last Passover Week

"Or what king, going to make war against another king, sitteth not down first, and consulteth whether he be able with ten thousand to meet him that cometh against him with twenty thousand?

"Or else, while the other is yet a great way off, he sendeth an embassage, and desireth conditions of peace.

"So likewise, whosoever he be of you that forsaketh not all that he hath, he cannot be my disciple.

"Salt is good: but if the salt have lost its savour, wherewith shall it be seasoned?

"It is neither fit for the land, nor yet for the dunghill; but men cast it out. He that hath ears to hear, let him hear."

NOTES: Scriptures of the Topics	Luke	John
- Jesus returns toward Bethany on hearing the sickness of Lazarus	13:24-30	11:4-7 9:11,14,15
- Jesus answers Herod	13:32-35	
- Cure of a man with dropsy	14:3,5	
- Parable of the Great Supper	14:8-14,16-24	
- Who can be Christ's disciples?	14:26-35	

Doctrines and Commandments

293. All you that are workers of iniquity shall depart from Christ and Christ does not know where you are.

294. You shall not see Christ Jesus until the time comes when you shall say, "Blessed is he that comes in the name of the Lord."

295. Healing and the work of our Heavenly Father is permitted within the doctrines of Christ, even on the Sabbath day.

296. Whosoever shall exalt himself shall be lowered in rank, and he that shall humble himself shall be exalted.

297. "When you make a dinner or a feast, call the poor, the maimed, the lame, the blind." "Not your friends, your brethren, your kinsman, and your rich neighbors, and you shall be blessed and recompensed at the resurrection of the just."

Part VI – From Third Passover to the Beginning of the Last Passover Week

298. Whosoever does not bear his cross, and come after Christ, cannot be Christ's disciple.

299. Any man who goes to Christ and does not hate his father, and mother, and wife, and children and brethren and sisters and his own life also, he cannot be Christ's disciple.

300. There is a resurrection of the just.

301. There is a blessing for the just, and that blessing and compensation is at the resurrection of the just.

Lessons We Should Learn

1.   We are unjust in our works and actions and sinners and workers of iniquities; we are then depart of Christ and He knows not where we are. His light does shine upon the just and the unjust, rather only those who choose not to do iniquities and live each day His teachings and doctrines shall know Christ and He shall know His followers. The choice of that decision is ours each day to make and we should repent all iniquities of the past.

2.   The work of our Heavenly Father in all types of healings, manifestation of Christ's words in man and within the Holy Spirit does take place each day, including the Sabbath day. There is no special day for the will of God to be done.

3.   As we strive to get ahead of our neighbor and others we lower ourselves in the exaltation of oneself in the kingdom of God. For all we have done is to seek the honor of man by exalting ourselves before man; we are saying look at me I am successful, and great, and prosperous. We should be humble as we are blessed with whatever God gives us to have. For all comes from Him and in His graciousness and love; the glory should to be to Him for our use of these things. As we use them we should never put them before Him, His work, and His will in our lives. As we put God first in all things and at all times we are humble and are in His light and doing His will. And all things that we do each day should be in the Spirit of truth or temptation may come unto us and then the exaltation is unto the adversary who will darken our mind to think it is o.k. to exalt oneself. After all, we are here on earth to know, to try, and to sample these things! But, be sure it is in the Spirit of truth and the light of Christ Jesus, according to His beliefs and teachings, not our own.

Part VI – From Third Passover to the Beginning of the Last Passover Week

4.	What a blessing of plenty to be living in a land of plenty to have dinner feasts, such as Thanksgiving Day meals with our family and what a blessing it would be to prepare the same meal for those in need and invite them to come into our home to break the bread of the words of Christ!

5.	To be a true disciple of Christ, he tells us that one should bear his own cross and come after Him. Each of us must seek Him out. We may come unto Christ as a family but to be a true disciple the will of God must come before the will of man, our earthly father, mother, spouse, children and brethren and in fact one's life—all should be given willingly—just as one does for his nation in the time of war. For Christ says, *"Whosoever he be of you that forsaketh not all that he hath, he cannot be my disciple."*

Part VI – From Third Passover to the Beginning of the Last Passover Week

My Thoughts About the Lessons

_____

_____

_____

_____

_____

_____

_____

_____

_____

_____

_____

_____

_____

_____

_____

_____

_____

_____

_____

_____

_____

_____

_____

NOTES

Part VI – From Third Passover to the Beginning of the Last Passover Week

29

Christ the Shepherd and the Lost Sheep; The Prodigal Son and Other Parables

The Lost Sheep

Then drew near unto him, all the publicans and sinners, for to hear him.

And the Pharisees and scribes murmured, saying, This man receiveth sinners, and eateth with them.

And he spake this parable unto them, saying,

"What man of you, having an hundred sheep, if he lose one of them doth not leave the ninety and nine in the wilderness, and go after that which is lost, until he find it?

"And when he hath found it, he layeth it on his shoulders, rejoicing.

"And when he cometh home, he calleth together his friends and neighbours, saying unto them, Rejoice with me; for I have found my sheep which was lost.

"I say unto you, that likewise joy shall be in heaven over one sinner that repenteth, more than over ninety and nine just persons, which need no repentance."

Part VI – From Third Passover to the Beginning of the Last Passover Week

The Lost Coin

"Either what woman having ten pieces of silver, if she lose one piece, doth not light a candle, and sweep the house, and seek diligently till she find it?

"And when she hath found it, she calleth her friends and her neighbours together, saying, Rejoice with me; for I have found the piece which I had lost.

"Likewise, I say unto you, there is joy in the presence of the angels of God over one sinner that repenteth.

The Prodigal Son

And he said, *"A certain man had two sons:*

"And the younger of them said to his father, Father, give me the portion of goods that falleth to me. And he divided unto them his living.

"And not many days after the younger son gathered all together, and took his journey into a far country, and there wasted his substance with riotous living.

"And when he had spent all, there arose a mighty famine in that land; and he began to be in want.

"And he went and joined himself to a citizen of that country; and he sent him into his fields to feed swine.

"And he would fain have filled his belly with the husks that the swine did eat; and no man gave unto him.

"And when he came to himself, he said, How many hired servants of my father's have bread enough and to spare, and I perish with hunger!

"I will arise and go to my father, and will say unto him, Father, I have sinned against heaven, and before thee.

Part VI – From Third Passover to the Beginning of the Last Passover Week

"And am no more worthy to be called thy son: make me one as of thy hired servants.

"And he arose, and came to his father. But when he was yet a great way off, his father saw him, and had compassion, and ran, and fell on his neck, and kissed him.

"And the son said unto him, Father, I have sinned against heaven, and in thy sight, and am no more worthy to be called thy son.

"But the father said to his servants, Bring forth the best robe, and put it on him; and put a ring on his hand, and shoes on his feet:

"And bring hither the fatted calf, and kill it, and let us eat, and be merry"

"For this my son was dead, and is alive again; he was lost, and is found, and they began to be merry.

"Now his elder son was in the field: and as he came and drew nigh to the house, he heard music and dancing.

"And he called one of the servants, and asked what these things meant:

"And he said unto him, Thy brother is come; and thy father hath killed the fatted calf, because he hath received him safe and sound.

"And he was angry, and would not go in: therefore came his father out, and intreated him.

"And he answering said to his father, Lo, these many years do I serve thee, neither transgressed I at any time thy commandment: and yet thou never gavest me a kid, that I might make merry with my friends:

"But as soon as this thy son was come, which hath devoured thy living with harlots, thou hast killed for him the fatted calf.

Part VI – From Third Passover to the Beginning of the Last Passover Week

"And he said unto him, Son, thou art ever with me, and all that I have is thine.

"It was meet that we should make merry, and be glad: for this thy brother was dead, and is alive again; and was lost, and is found."

The Unjust Steward: You Cannot Serve God and Mammon

And he said also unto his disciples, *"There was a certain rich man, which had a steward; and the same was accused unto him that he had wasted his goods.*

"And he called him, and said unto him, How is it that I hear this of thee? give an account of thy stewardship; for thou mayest be no longer steward.

"Then the steward said within himself, What shall I do? for my lord taketh away from me the stewardship: I cannot dig; to beg I am ashamed.

"I am resolved what to do, that, when I am put out of the stewardship, they may receive me into their houses.

"So he called every one of his lord's debtors unto him, and said unto the first, How much owest thou unto my lord?

"And he said, An hundred measures of oil. And he said unto him, Take thy bill, and sit down quickly, and write fifty.

"Then said he to another, and how much owest thou? And he said, an hundred measures of wheat. And he said unto him, take thy bill, and write fourscore.

"And the lord commended the unjust steward, because he had done wisely; for the children of this world are in their generation wiser than the children of light.

"And I say unto you, Make to yourselves friends of the mammon of unrighteousness; that, when ye fail, they may receive you into everlasting habitations.

"He that is faithful in that which is least is faithful also in much: and he that is unjust in the least is unjust also in much.

Part VI – From Third Passover to the Beginning of the Last Passover Week

"If therefore ye have not been faithful in the unrighteous mammon, who will commit to your trust the true riches?

"And if ye have not been faithful in that which is another man's, who shall give you that which is your own?

"No servant can serve two masters: for either he will hate the one, and love the other; or else he will hold to the one and despise the other. Ye cannot serve God and mammon."

The Pharisees also, who were covetous, heard all these things: and they derided him.

And he said unto them, *"Ye are they which justify yourselves before men; but God knoweth your hearts: for that which is highly esteemed among men is abomination in the sight of God.*

"The law and the prophets were until John; since that time the kingdom of God is preached, and every man presseth into it.

"And it is easier for heaven and earth to pass, than one tittle of the law to fail.
"Whosoever putteth away his wife, and marrieth another, committeth adultery: and whosoever marrieth her that is put away from her husband committeth adultery."

The Rich Man and Lazarus

"There was a certain rich man, which was clothed in purple and fine linen, and fared sumptuously everyday:

"And there was a certain beggar named Lazarus, which was laid at his gate full of sores.

"And desiring to be fed with the crumbs which fell from the rich man's table: moreover the dogs came and licked his sores.

"And it came to pass, that the beggar died, and was carried by the angles into Abraham's bosom: the rich man also died, and was buried;

Part VI – From Third Passover to the Beginning of the Last Passover Week

"And in hell he lift up his eyes, being in torments and seeth Abraham afar off, and Lazarus in his bosom.

"And he cried and said, Father Abraham, have mercy on me, and send Lazarus, that he may dip the tip of his finger in water, and cool my tongue; for I am tormented in this flame.

"But Abraham said, Son, remember that thou in thy lifetime recievedst thy good things, and likewise Lazarus evil things: but now he is comforted, and thou art tormented.

"And beside all this, between us and you there is a great gulf fixed: so that they which would pass from hence to you cannot; neither can they pass to us, that would come from thence.

"Then he said, I pray thee therefore, father, that thou wouldest send him to my father's house:

"For I have five brethren; that he may testify unto them, lest they also come into this place of torment.

"Abraham saith unto him, They have Moses and the prophets; let them hear them.

"And he said, Nay, Father Abraham: but if one went unto them from the dead, they will repent.

"And he said unto him, If they hear not Moses and the prophets, neither will they be persuaded, though one rose from the dead."

Sayings As to Offenses

Then said he unto the disciples, *"It is impossible but that offences will come: but woe unto him, through whom they come!*

"It were better for him that a millstone were hanged about his neck, and he cast into the sea, than that he should offend one of these little ones.

"Take heed to yourselves: If thy brother trespass against thee, rebuke him; and if he repent, forgive him,

Part VI – From Third Passover to the Beginning of the Last Passover Week

"And if he trespass against thee seven times in a day, and seven times in a day turn again to thee saying, I repent; thou shalt forgive him."

And the apostles said unto the Lord, Increase our faith. And the Lord said, *"If ye had faith as a grain of a mustard seed, ye might say unto this sycamine tree, Be thou plucked up by the root, and be thou planted in the sea; and it should obey you.*

"But which of you, having a servant plowing or feeding cattle, will say unto him by and by, when he is come from the field, Go and sit down to meat?

"And will not rather say unto him, Make ready wherewith I may sup, and gird myself, and serve me, till I have eaten and drunken; and afterward thou shalt eat and drink?

"Doth he thank that servant because he did the things that were commanded him? I trow not.

"So likewise ye, when ye shall have done all those things which are commanded you, say, We are unprofitable servants: we have done that which was our duty to do."

Jesus Raises Lazarus From the Dead

Now a certain man was sick, named Lazarus, of Bethany, the town of Mary and her sister Martha. His sisters sent word unto him, saying, Lord, behold he whom thou lovest is sick.

When heard that, he said, *"This sickness is not unto death, but for the glory of God, that the Son of God might be glorified thereby."*

When he heard therefore that he was sick, he abode two days in the same place where he was.

Then after that he saith to his disciples, *"Let us go into Judaea again."*

His disciples say unto him, Master, the Jews of late sought to stone thee; and goest thou thither again?

Part VI – From Third Passover to the Beginning of the Last Passover Week

Jesus answered, *"Are there not twelve hours in the day?*

If any man walk in the day, he stumbleth not, because he seeth the light of this world.
"But if a man walk in the night, he stumbleth, because there is no light in him."
After that he saith unto them, *"Our friend Lazarus sleepeth; but I go that I may awake him out of sleep."*

Then said his disciples, Lord, if he sleep, he shall do well. Howbeit Jesus spake of his death: but they thought that he had spoken of taking of rest in sleep.

Then Jesus said unto them plainly, *"Lazarus is dead. "And I am glad for your sakes that I was not there, to the intent ye may believe; nevertheless let us go unto him."*

Then when Jesus came, he found that he had lain in the grave four days already.

Now Bethany was nigh unto Jerusalem, about fifteen furlongs off:

And many Jews came to Martha and Mary to comfort them concerning their brother.

Then Martha, as soon as she heard that Jesus was coming, went and met him: but Mary sat still in the house.

Then said Martha unto Jesus, Lord, if thou hadst been here, my brother had not died.

But I know, that even now, whatsoever thou wilt ask of God, God will give it thee.

Jesus saith unto her, *"Thy brother shall rise again."*

Martha said unto him, I know that he shall rise again in the resurrection at the last day.

Part VI – From Third Passover to the Beginning of the Last Passover Week

Jesus said unto her, *"I am the resurrection, and the life: he that believeth in me though he were dead, yet shall he live: "And whosoever liveth and believeth in me shall never die. Believest thou this?"*

She saith unto him, Yea, Lord: I believe that thou art the Christ, the Son of God, which should come into the world.

And when she had so said, she went her way, and called Mary her sister secretly, saying, The Master is come, and calleth for thee.

As soon as she heard that, she arose quickly, and came unto him.

Then when Mary was come where Jesus was, and saw him, she fell down at his feet, saying unto him, Lord, if thou hadst been here, my brother had not died.

When Jesus therefore saw her weeping, and the Jews also weeping which came with her, he groaned in the spirit and was troubled.

And said, *"Where have ye laid him?"* They said unto him, Lord, come and see. Jesus wept.

Then said the Jews, behold how he loved him!

And some of them said, Could not this man, which opened the eyes of the blind and have caused that even this man should not have died?

Jesus therefore again groaning in himself cometh to the grave. It was a cave, and a stone lay upon it.

Jesus said, *"Take ye away the stone."* Martha, the sister of him that was dead, saith unto him, Lord, by this time he stinketh: for he hath been dead four days.

Jesus saith unto her, *"Said not unto thee, that, if thou wouldest believe, thou shouldest see the glory of God?"*

Part VI – From Third Passover to the Beginning of the Last Passover Week

Then they took away the stone from the place where the dead was laid. And Jesus lifted up his eyes, and said, *"Father, I thank thee that thou hast heard me.*

"And I knew that thou hearest me always: but because of the people which stand by I said it, that they may believe that thou hast sent me."

And when he had thus spoken, he cried with a loud voice,

"Lazarus, come forth."

And he that was dead came forth, bound hand and foot with grave clothes: and his face was bound about with a napkin. Jesus saith unto them, *"Loose him, and let him go."*

Then many of the Jews which came to Mary, and had seen the things which Jesus did, believed on him.

But some of them went their ways to the Pharisees, and told them what things Jesus had done.

NOTES: Scriptures of the Topics	Luke	John
- The lost sheep	15:4-7	
- The lost coin	15:8-10	
- The prodigal son	15:11-32	
- The unjust steward: you cannot serve God and Mammon	16:1-13	
- The rich man and Lazarus	16:19-31	
- Sayings as to offenses	17:1-4,6-10	
- Jesus raises Lazarus from the dead		11:4,7,9-11,14,15,23,25 26,34,39-45

Doctrines and Commandments

302. Joy shall be in heaven over one sinner that repents, more than over ninety-nine just persons, which need no repentance.

303. Our Heavenly Father rejoices in glory when a sinner repents and returns to him. (Luke. 15:11-32)

Part VI – From Third Passover to the Beginning of the Last Passover Week

304. You cannot serve God and Mammon. No servant can serve two masters: for either he will hate the one, and love the other; or else he will hold to the one, and despise the other.

305. God knows your heart.

306. That which is highly esteemed among men is abomination in the sight of God; you are they which justify yourselves before men.

307. The law and the prophets were until John the Baptist.

308. Since the time of John, the Kingdom of God is preached and every person is pressed into it.

309. It is easier for heaven and earth to pass than one tittle of the law to fail.

91. Whosoever puts away his wife and marries another, commits adultery.

91. Whosoever marries the woman that is put away from her husband commits adultery.

310. After death on earth one may be in a place of being tormented or a place being comforted.

311. In those places after death where one is tormented and the other is comforted there is a great gulf fixed so that they cannot pass from one to another.

312. Those who have died and are being comforted are not sent to the living in earth to testify so those on earth shall repent; for the sinner will not be persuaded.

313. The sinners on earth are to listen to Moses and the prophets.

213. Those who offend little children: it would be better for him that a millstone were hanged about his neck, and be cast into the sea.

314. If thy brother trespass against you, rebuke him, and if he repents, forgive him.

315. If a person trespasses against you seven times a day, and seven times each day he says, "I repent," you shall forgive him.

204. If you had faith as a mustard seed you might say to a tree to be uprooted and planted in the sea, and it should obey you.

316. When you have done all those things that are commanded you, say, "We are unprofitable servants; we have done that which was our duty to do."

317. We shall rise again.

318. Christ is the resurrection, and the life; he that believes

Christ though he were dead, yet shall he live.

319. Whosoever lives and believes in Christ Jesus shall never die.

Part VI – From Third Passover to the Beginning of the Last Passover Week

320. If we will believe in the words, commandments and doctrines of Christ, and believe in Him, we shall see the glory of God.

321. God hears us, our prayers, and our thanks to Him always.

322. We should pray to God as a testimony to God, for others to hear who may be near.

323. Our prayers of thanks to our Father should be given in gratitude and thanksgiving even before our prayers are answered, and have faith knowing they shall be answered according to His will, not ours.

Lessons We Should Learn

1.   When one truly repents, the joy shall be known in heaven.

Our Heavenly Father rejoices in glory when one sinner repents and returns to him.

2.   As we give ourselves to God we should give our all and love Him, worship Him, and serve Him with all of our minds, hearts, souls and power--for He knows our hearts. We cannot serve two masters; we can't serve and seek the honor of man and material worldly things and desires before God. God should be first and come before all things and others in one's life. And then all things that He wants for one to have shall be made manifest.

3.   Before John the Baptist there were the laws and the prophets and since the time of John, the Christ, the Messias, is with us, and the kingdom of God is preached. Every person is under His light not that we are not to obey the laws and the prophets but as Christ Jesus is the fulfillment of the laws we too should fulfill all the laws. Christ Himself tells us that, *"It is easier for heaven and earth to pass than one tittle of the law to fail."*

4.   Anyone who leaves his wife her husband and marries another commits adultery. One should realize that vows to one another are as vows to God. If we can't keep vows to oneself and to our spouses, how can we keep the vows to God? When adulterous acts are committed there is a chain reaction of offenses for the person who marries the wife that has been left by her spouse also commits adultery.

Part VI – From Third Passover to the Beginning of the Last Passover Week

5.   Our loved ones who have died can see the torment caused by sin and would like to warn us but cannot. There is a great gulf fixed so that one who has died cannot warn or comfort those still living but the word of Christ can let us each know that they are trying to persuade us to repent. Christ tells us to listen to Moses: to Him, His words, and commandments; and the prophets: for His Word is the light of the world and His word is available to each of us. When we really and truly believe in Him we will live our own lives without sinning and following His will and knowingly will sin no more and be in the light by living according to His word and endure forever in that light.

6.   There are many offenses that we are doing—knowingly and unknowingly. Several offenses that one must be keenly aware of are: the offenses against the Holy Ghost and the offenses against little ones. For Christ says, *"It would be better for him that a millstone were hanged about his neck, and be cast into the sea."* Also, all of the daily and regular offenses the Lord guides us to forgive those who trespass against us continuously shall be forgiven if they repent. After all, God forgives our sins even before they are committed, if they are repented.

7.   Christ Jesus has so very explicitly shown us the faith displayed in all of the miraculous healing and works and He says, *"If you had faith as a mustard seed you might say to a tree to be uprooted and planted in the sea and it should obey you."* In other words, many great things may happen as we have the unbending faith that Christ is teaching us to have.

8.   We must do all things that are commanded for each of us to do in a great spirit; a spirit of serving the Lord and doing the will of our Heavenly Father; a spirit of giving without thought or reward for we are to be unprofitable servants; we do all things as it is our duty to do.

We should never do things thinking, "If I do these things I will surely be blessed."

9.   Believers in Christ know and believe in His resurrection and if we would believe in Christ though we may die and be dead, then shall we live and rise again. As we rise, we live and believe in Christ Jesus and shall never die.

Part VI – From Third Passover to the Beginning of the Last Passover Week

10.   In believing and living all the words and commandments of Christ Jesus, one is demonstrating his own faith and belief in Christ. Christ gives us the promise that God the Father has promised to Christ—for all that Christ has He gives to us. That promise is that if each of us will live and do these things we shall see the Glory of God.

11.   One should never doubt that God hears our prayers. He knows our heart and our prayers before we pray. Each prayer should be a testimony to Him and any light, power and healing that is given, is given by Him. We are only the instrument and all glory is to be given to God; for whatever works and gifts are received and given in prayer are of God and from God and of His will, not your will or my will and all praise and glory is to God!

Part VI – From Third Passover to the Beginning of the Last Passover Week

My Thoughts About the Lessons

_____

_____

_____

_____

_____

_____

_____

_____

_____

_____

_____

_____

_____

_____

_____

_____

_____

_____

_____

_____

_____

_____

_____

_____

_____

NOTES

Part VI – From Third Passover to the Beginning of the Last Passover Week

30

The Last Journey to Jerusalem Through Samaria and Galilee

Jesus therefore walked no more openly among the Jews; but went thence unto a country near to the wilderness, into a city called Ephraim, and there continued with His disciples.

And it came to pass, as He went to Jerusalem, that He passed through the midst of Samaria and Galilee.

He Heals the Lepers on the Samaritan Frontier

And as he entered into a certain village, there met him ten men that were lepers, which stood afar off:

And they lifted up their voices, and said, Jesus, Master, have mercy on us.

And when he saw them, he said unto them, *"Go shew yourselves unto the priests."* And it came to pass, that, as they went, they were cleansed.

And one of them, when he saw that he was healed, turned back, and with a loud voice glorified God,

And fell down on his face at his feet, giving him thanks: and he was a Samaritan.

And Jesus answering said, *"Were there not ten cleansed ?but where are the nine?"*

"There are not found that returned to give glory to God, save this stranger."

And he said unto him, *"Arise, go thy way: thy faith hath made thee whole."*

Part VI – From Third Passover to the Beginning of the Last Passover Week

When Should the Kingdom of God Come? Jesus Says that The Kingdom of God is Within Us

And when he was demanded of the Pharisees, when the kingdom of God should come, he answered them and said, *"The kingdom of God cometh not with observation:*

"Neither shall they say, lo here! or, lo there! For, behold, the kingdom of God is within you."

And he said unto the disciples, *"The days will come, when ye shall desire to see one of the days of the Son of man, and ye shall not see it.*

"And they shall say to you, See here; or, see there: go not after them, nor follow them.

"For as the lightning, that lighteneth out of the one part under heaven, shineth unto the other part under heaven; so shall also the Son of man be in his day.

"But first must he suffer many things, and be rejected of this generation.

"And as it was in the days of Noe, so shall it be also in the days of the Son of man.

"They did eat, they drank, they married wives, and they were given in marriage, until the day that Noe entered into the ark, and the flood came, and destroyed them all.

"Likewise also as it was in the days of Lot; they did eat, they drank, they bought, they sold, they planted, they builded;

"But the same day that Lot went out of Sodom it rained fire and brimstone from heaven, and destroyed them all.

"Even thus shall it be in the day when the Son of man is revealed.

"In that day, he which shall be upon the housetop, and his stuff in the house, let him not come down to take it away: and he that is in the field, let him likewise not turn back.

Part VI – From Third Passover to the Beginning of the Last Passover Week

"Remember Lot's wife.

"Whosoever shall seek to save his life shall lose it; and whosoever shall lose his life shall preserve it.

"I tell you, in that night there shall be two men in one bed; the one shall be taken, and the other shall be left.

"Two woman shall be grinding together; the one shall be taken, and the other left.

"Two men shall be in the field; the one shall be taken, and the other left."
And they answered and said unto him, Where, Lord? And he said unto them, "Wheresoever the body is, thither will the eagles be gathered together.

Parable of Importunate Widow and the Pharisee and Publican

And he spake a parable unto them to this end, that men ought always to pray and not to faint;

Saying, *"There was in a city a judge, which feared not God, neither regarded man:*
"And there was a widow in that city; and she came unto him, saying, avenge me of mine adversary.

"And he would not for a while: but afterward he said within himself, Though I fear not God, nor regard man;

"Yet because this widow troubleth me, I will avenge her, lest by her continual coming she weary me".

And the Lord said, *"Hear what the unjust judge saith. "And shall not God avenge his own elect, which cry day and night unto him, though he bear long with them?*

"I tell you that he will avenge them speedily.

Part VI – From Third Passover to the Beginning of the Last Passover Week

Nevertheless when the Son of man cometh, shall he find faith on the earth?"

And he spake this parable unto certain which trusted in themselves that they were righteous, and despised others:

"Two men went up into the temple to pray; the one a Pharisee, and the other a publican. "The Pharisee stood and prayed thus with himself, God, I thank thee, that I am not as other men are, extortioneres, unjust, adulterers, or even as this publican.

"I fast twice a week, I give tithes of all that I possess. "And the publican, standing afar off, would not lift up so much as his eyes unto heaven, but smote upon his breast, saying, God be merciful to me a sinner.

"I tell you, this man went down to his house justified rather than the other: for everyone that exalteth himself shall be abased; and he that humbleth himself shall be exalted."

Jesus is Questioned About Divorce

The Pharisees also came unto him, tempting him, and saying unto him, Is it lawful for a man to put away his wife for every cause?

And he answered and said unto them,

"What did Moses command you? Have ye not read, that he which made them at the beginning made them male and female.

"And said, for this cause shall a man leave father and mother, and shall cleave to his wife: and they twain shall be one flesh?

"Wherefore they are no more twain, but one flesh. What therefore God hath joined together, let not man put asunder."

They say unto him, Why did Moses then command to give a writing of divorcement, and to put her away?

Part VI – From Third Passover to the Beginning of the Last Passover Week

He saith unto them, *"Moses because of the hardness of your hearts suffered you to put away your wives: but from the beginning it was not so.*

"But from the beginning of the creation God made them male and female.

"And I say unto you, Whosoever shall put away his wife, except it be for fornication, shall marry another, committeth adultery: and whoso marrieth her which is put away doth commit adultery.

"And if a woman shall put away her husband, and be married to another, she committeth adultery."

His disciples say unto him, If the case of the man be so with his wife, it is not good to marry.

But he said unto them, *"All men cannot receive this saying, save they to whom it is given.*

"For there are some eunuchs, which were so born from their mother's womb: and there are some eunuchs, which were made eunuchs of men: and there be eunuchs, which have made themselves eunuchs for the kingdom of heaven's sake. He that is able to receive it let him receive it."

NOTES: Scriptures of the Topics

	Matt	Mark	Luke
- He heals ten lepers on the Samaritan frontier			17:14,17-19
- When should the Kingdom of God come? Jesus says that it is within us.			17:20-37
- Parable of importunate widow and the Pharisee and Publican			18:2-14
-Jesus is question about divorce	19:4-6,8,9,11,12	10:3,5-9,11,12	

Doctrines and Commandments

324. Give glory to God only.

325. Healing faith, "one's faith will make him well and whole."

Part VI – From Third Passover to the Beginning of the Last Passover Week

326. The Kingdom of God is within you; it is not here, or there.

327. The Kingdom of God does not come with observation; they will tell you to see here or there; but do not go there or follow them.

328. Wheresoever the body is, there will the eagles be gathered together.

329. This generation, like the generation when Christ Jesus is on earth, are rejecting Him and causing Him to suffer many things as He did then.

330. Many shall hear His word but few will be chosen. (Even in the day when the Son of man is revealed)

331. Whosoever shall seek to save his life shall lose it for Jesus' sake;

and whosoever shall lose his life shall preserve it.

332. Even in the day when the Son of man is revealed, they may all be destroyed as in the day of Noe, and in the day of Lot.

333. God bears long with each of His children.

334. God shall avenge His own elect.

335. God will avenge them speedily.

336. When Christ Jesus comes, shall God find faith on the earth?

337. One should not pray to God giving thanks to God for not being like men who are extortioners, unjust, adulterers, and as the publican or any other sinners.

338. One should pray, saying, "God be merciful to me a sinner."

339. Everyone that exalts himself (elevates himself in rank, honor and power) shall be abased (reduced in rank).

340. Everyone that humbles himself (lowers himself in station, importance and power) shall be exalted.

341. God in the beginning made His children male and female.

342. Because of God's plan to join man and woman together, a man shall leave his father and mother and shall cleave to his wife and the two of them shall be one flesh.

343. What God has joined together, let no man (no person) separate them.

344. Whosoever shall put away his wife, except, it be for fornication and shall marry another, commits adultery.

345. If a woman shall put away her husband, and be married to another, she commits adultery.

346. Whosoever marries a woman who has been put away by her husband, does commit adultery.

347. All men cannot receive the doctrine of being single and unmarried, for the kingdom of heaven's sake except for they to whom it is given.

Part VI – From Third Passover to the Beginning of the Last Passover Week

Lessons We Should Learn

1.   We should show ourselves to the priests and give honor to God only when we are healed and testify of all of our healings not only once but often. As we are made whole by our faith we should know we are well and go as all is well in our ways of life and glorify God this way and with our testimony.

2.   As we become one with Christ as Christ is one with God we shall behold the kingdom, for "Behold the Kingdom of God is within you." Therefore as we hear that the kingdom is here, or there, we should not follow.

3.   Each of us should live each day for God our Father and His will as Christ has shown us; for no one knows the hour or day when Christ shall be revealed. Each should be willing to give his or her life for God and if it is lost then God has taken them.

4.   We should be together as families and bretheren in the light and love of Christ so that when the time comes we shall be there to be gathered by the angels.

5.   Our generation is as evil in their ways as generations before. As one goes their own way and rationalizes that I am okay, I am not doing anything others are not doing I am doing these things in moderation; this kind of rationalization is rejecting Christ for He has taught each of us to do God's will only and not our own; when we do that, we become one with Christ.

By not holding close to the doctrines and light of Christ we cause Him to suffer many things for us as He did then. At Gethsemane Christ prayed for and received from our Heavenly Father atonement for each of us that we might be one with Christ Jesus as he is one with God. We each are sealed to Christ. For this to take place we must be reconciled to God in light, not sin, and we must be delivered from temptation and realize that we can overcome the consequences of sin, past and present, through this atonement. But one principal needs to be followed that Christ Jesus has taught each of us. That is, to go and sin no more, and with that commitment we are showing our faith in God and the atonement He made for us, and if we continue in our own way, may we cause Christ Jesus to suffer still for us? Many hear His words but few will be chosen. For our lesson is to ask, "What will I do with His words after I hear them, what shall manifest in my life? What lessons are for me?" Each of us should be sensitive each day to the spirit and the directions we get therein and then follow that quiet voice from within.

Part VI – From Third Passover to the Beginning of the Last Passover Week

My Thoughts About the Lessons

_____

_____

_____

_____

_____

_____

_____

_____

_____

_____

_____

_____

_____

_____

_____

_____

_____

_____

_____

_____

_____

_____

_____

Part VI – From Third Passover to the Beginning of the Last Passover Week

31

Jesus Blesses Little Children

A nd they brought young children and infants to him, that he should teach them: and his disciples rebuked those that brought them.

But when Jesus saw it, he was much displeased, and said unto them,

"Suffer the little children to come unto me, and forbid them not: to come unto me: for of such is the kingdom of heaven and of God.

"Verily I say unto you, whosoever shall not receive the kingdom of God as a little child, he shall in no wise enter therein."

And he took them up in his arms, put his hands upon them, and blessed them.

Christ Tells How to Inherit Eternal Life

And when he was gone forth into the way, there came a certain ruler running and kneeled to him, and asked him, Good Master, what shall I do that I may inherit eternal life?

And Jesus said unto him, *"Why callest thou me good?*

There is none good but one, that is, God: but if thou wilt enter into life, keep the commandments."

He saith unto him, Which?

Jesus said,

"Thou knowest the commandments, Thou shalt do no murder, do not kill, Thou shalt not commit adultery, Thou shalt not steal, Thou shalt not bear false witness, Defraud not, Honour thy father and thy mother: and Thou shalt love thy neighbor as thyself."

Part VI – From Third Passover to the Beginning of the Last Passover Week

Peter Contrasts the Disciples' Self Sacrifice

The young man saith unto Jesus, All these things have I kept from my youth up: what lack I yet?

Then Jesus beholding him loved him, and said unto him,

"One thing thou lackest: go thy way, sell whatsoever thou hast, and give to the poor, and thou shalt have treasure in heaven: and come, take up the cross, and come follow me."

And he was sad at the saying, and went away grieved: for he had great possessions.

And Jesus looked round about, and saith unto his disciples,

"How hardly shall they that have riches enter into the kingdom of God!"

And the disciples were astonished at his words. But Jesus answereth again, and saith unto you,

"Children, how hard is it for them that trust in riches to enter into the kingdom of God!

"It is easier for a camel to go through the eye of a needle, than for a rich man to enter into the kingdom of God."

And they were astonished out of measure, saying amongst themselves, Who then can be saved?

And Jesus looking upon them saith,

"With men it is impossible, but not with God: for with God all things are possible."

Then answered Peter and said unto him, Behold, we have left all and forsaken all and followed thee; what shall we have therefore?

Part VI – From Third Passover to the Beginning of the Last Passover Week

And Jesus said unto them,

"Verily I say unto you, That ye which have followed me, in the generation when the Son of man shall sit in the throne of his glory, ye also shall sit upon twelve thrones, judging the twelve tribes of Israel.

"And everyone that hath forsaken houses, or brethren, or sisters, or father, or mother, or wife, or children, or lands for my name's sake and the gospels, and for the kingdom of God's sake, shall receive an hundredfold now in this time, houses, and brethren, and sisters, and mothers, and children, and lands, with persecutions; and in the world to come eternal life, and shall inherit everlasting life.

"But many that are first shall be last; and the last shall be first."

Parable of the Laborers in the Vineyard to Warn Against Mercenary Service

"For the kingdom of heaven is like unto a man that is an householder, which went out early in the morning to hire labourers into his vineyard.

"And when he had agreed with the labourers for a penny a day, he sent them into his vineyard.

"And he went out about the third hour, and saw others standing idle in the marketplace.

"And said unto them: Go ye also into the vineyard, and whatsoever is right I will give you, And they went their way.

"Again he went out about the sixth and ninth hour, and did likewise.

"And about the eleventh hour he went out and found others standing idle, and saith unto them, Why stand ye here all the day idle?

"They say unto him, Because no man hath hired us. He saith unto them. Go ye also into the vineyard; and whatsoever is right, that ye shall receive. "So when even was come, the lord of the vineyard saith unto his steward, Call the labourers, and give them their hire, beginning from the last unto the first.

Part VI – From Third Passover to the Beginning of the Last Passover Week

"And when they came that were hired about the eleventh hour, they received every man a penny.

"But when the first came, they supposed that they should have received more; and they likewise received every man a penny.

"And when they had received it, they murmured against the good man of the house.

"Saying, These last have wrought but one hour, and thou hast made them equal to us, which have borne the burden and heat of the day.

"But he answered one of them, and said, Friend, I do thee no wrong: didst not thou agree with me for a penny?

"Take that thine is, and go thy way: I will give unto this last, even as unto thee.

"Is it not lawful for me to do what I will with mine own? Is thine eye evil, because I am good?

"So the last shall be first, and the first last: for many will be called, but few chosen."

NOTES: Scriptures of the Topics	Matt	Mark	Luke
- Jesus blesses little children	19:14	10:14,15	18:16,17
- Christ tells how to inherit Eternal Life	19:17-19	10:18,19	18:19,20
- Peter Contrasts the Disciples' Self-sacrifice	19:21,23, 24,25-30	10: 21,23 25,27, 29-31	18: 22, 25,27, 29,30
- Parable of the Labor in the vineyard to warn against mercenary service	20:1-16		

Part VI – From Third Passover to the Beginning of the Last Passover Week

Doctrines and Commandments

348. "Whosoever shall not receive the Kingdom of God as a little child, he shall not enter therein."

349. Jesus tells us how to inherit eternal life.

1.) If you enter into life, keep the commandments.

2.) Thou knows the commandments

3.) Thou shalt do no murder

4.) Do not kill

5.) Thou shalt not commit adultery

6.) Thou shalt not steal

7.) Thou shalt not bear false witness

8.) Defraud not

9.) Honor thy father and thy mother

10.) Thou shalt love thy neighbor as thyself

11.) If thou will be perfect, go thy way, sell whatsoever thou hast, and give to the poor, and thou shalt have treasure in heaven.

12.) And come take up the cross, and follow Me.

350. It is hard for them that trust in riches to enter into the kingdom of God. Christ says, *"It is easier for a camel to go through the eye of a needle, than for a rich man to enter into the kingdom of God." "With men it is impossible, but not with God: for with God all things are possible."*

351. Those who have followed Christ, in the generation when the Son of man shall sit in the throne of His glory, they also shall sit up twelve thrones, judging the twelve tribes of Israel.

352. Everyone that has forsaken houses, or brethren, or sisters, or father, or mother, or wife, or children, or lands, for Christ's name's sake, and the gospel's but he shall receive an hundredfold now in this time, houses, and brethren and sisters, and mothers, and children, and lands, with persecutions; and in the world to come eternal life; and shall inherit everlasting life.

353. Many that are first shall be last; and the last shall be first; many are called, but few chosen.

Part VI – From Third Passover to the Beginning of the Last Passover Week

Lessons We Should Learn

1.   Our little children are constant and continuous reminders of God's kingdom. As we become tempted unto worldliness and unrighteousness we must look deep into the eyes of our children and we shall see the glory of God, within.

2.   Christ is the way to life eternal. He reminds us that only God is good. In the Lord's prayer he teaches us that his name is hallowed. He states, *"If thou wilt enter into life, keep the commandments."* The statement is, 'If you will enter into life!' We are not in life yet! We must will ourselves to be reborn into life! Life eternal! How? Keep the Commandments!" He states twelve of them very emphatically and He says to know them all, and to keep them.

3.   Christ Jesus warns us about serving more than one Master in the temptation of the worldly rich. However, in His commandments is the key for the wealthy and worldly rich to overcome and to enter into His kingdom. Be perfect in all things, sell what you have and give to the poor; take up your cross and follow him.

4.   One must forsake all for the Lord in order to inherit His kingdom. Each of us should remember that Christ is the first and last, the beginning and the end. Living according to His words is the key to everlasting life.

Part VI – From Third Passover to the Beginning of the Last Passover Week

My Thoughts About the Lessons

_____

_____

_____

_____

_____

_____

_____

_____

_____

_____

_____

_____

_____

_____

_____

_____

_____

_____

_____

_____

_____

_____

_____

_____

_____

NOTES

Part VI – From Third Passover to the Beginning of the Last Passover Week

32

Jesus Again Foretells His Suffering, Death, and Resurrection; The Last Sabbath

On His Way to Jerusalem for the Last Time

A nd they were in the way going up to Jerusalem; and Jesus went before them: and they were amazed: and as they followed, they were afraid. And he took again the twelve, and began to tell them what things should happen unto him.

Saying, *"Behold, we go up to Jerusalem, and all things that are written by the prophets concerning the Son of man shall be accomplished."*

"And the Son of man shall be delivered unto the chief priests, and unto the scribes; and they shall condemn him to death, and shall deliver him to the Gentiles; and shall be mocked, and spitefully entreated, and spitted on:

"And they shall scourge him, and put him to death: and the third day he shall rise again."

James and John Desire Highest Places Next to Christ in the Temporal Kingdom

And James and John, the sons of Zebedee, come unto him, saying, Master, we would that thou shouldest do for us whatsoever we shall desire.

And he said unto them, *"What would ye that I should do for you?"*

They said unto him, Grant unto us that we may sit, one on thy right hand and the other on thy left hand, in thy glory.

Part VI – From Third Passover to the Beginning of the Last Passover Week

But Jesus said unto them,

"Ye know not what ye ask: can ye drink of the cup that I drink of? and be baptized with the baptism that I am baptized with?"

And they said unto him, We can. And Jesus said unto them,

"Ye shall indeed drink of the cup that I drink of; and with the baptism that I am baptized withal shall ye be baptized:

"But to sit on my right hand and on my left hand is not mine to give; but it shall be given to them for whom it is prepared of my Father."

And when the ten heard it, they began to be much displeased with James and John.

But Jesus called to him, and saith unto them,

"Ye know that they which are accounted to rule over the Gentiles exercise lordship over them; and their great ones exercise authority upon them.

"But so shall it not be among you: but whosoever will be great among you, shall be your minister:

And whosoever of you will be the chiefest shall be servant of all.

"For even the Son of man came not to be ministered unto, but to minister, and to give his life a ransom for many."

He Heals Two Blind Men Near Jericho

And as they departed from Jericho, a great multitude followed him. And behold, two blind men, one of them Bartimaers, the son of Timaeus, sitting by the wayside, when they heard that Jesus passed by, cried out, saying, Have mercy on us, O Lord, thou Son of David.

And Jesus stood still, and called them, and said,

"What will ye that I shall do unto you?"

They say unto him, Lord, that our eyes may be opened. And Jesus said unto him,

"Receive thy sight, go thy way: thy faith hath saved thee and hath made thee whole."

Part VI – From Third Passover to the Beginning of the Last Passover Week

And he touched their eyes: and immediately they received their sight, and followed him, glorifying God: and all the people, when they saw it, gave praise unto God.

Zaccheus is Called Down from Sycamore Tree by Jesus
Salvation Comes to His House

And Jesus entered and passed through Jericho. And there was a man named Zacchaeus, which was the chief among the publicans, and he was rich.

And he sought to see Jesus who he was; and could not for the press, because he was little of stature.

And he ran before, and climbed up into a Sycamore tree to see him; for Jesus was to pass that way.

And when Jesus came to the place, He looked up, and saw him, and he said unto him, *"Zacchaeus, make haste, and come down; for today I must abide at thy house."*

And he made haste, and came down, and received him joyfully.

And when they saw it, they all murmured, saying, that he was gone to be a guest with a man that is a sinner. And Zaccheus stood and said unto the Lord; Behold, Lord, the half of my goods I give to the poor: and if I have taken anything from any man by false accusation, I restore him fourfold.

And Jesus said unto him,

"This day is salvation come to this house, forsomuch as he also is a son of Abraham."

"For the Son of man is come to seek and to save that which was lost."

Part VI – From Third Passover to the Beginning of the Last Passover Week

Jesus Answers Those Who Think the Kingdom of God Shall Immediately Appear: With Parable of the Pound

And as they heard these things, he added and spake a parable, because he was nigh to Jerusalem, and because they thought that the kingdom of God should immediately appear.

He said therefore, *"A certain nobleman went into a far country to receive for himself a kingdom, and to return.*

"And he called his ten servants, and delivered them ten pounds, and said unto them, Occupy till I come.

"But his citizens hated him, and sent a message after him, saying, We will not have this man to reign over us.

"And it came to pass, that when he returned, having received the kingdom, then he commanded those servants to be called unto him, to whom he had given the money, that he might know how much every man had gained by trading.

"Then came the first, saying, Lord, thy pound hath gained ten pounds.

"And he said unto him, well, thou good servant: because thou hast been faithful in a very little, have thou authority over ten cities.

"And the second came, saying, Lord, thy pound hath gained five pounds.

"And he said likewise to him, Be thou also over five cities.

"And another came, saying, Lord, behold here is thy pound, which I have kept laid up in a napkin:

"For I fear thee, because thou art an austere man: thou takest up that thou layedst not down, and reapest that thou didst not sow.

"And he saith unto him, Out of thine own mouth will I judge thee, thou wicked servant. Thou knowest that I was an austere man, taking up that I laid not down, and reaping that I did not sow.

"Wherefore then gavest not thou my money into the bank, that at my coming I might have required mine own with usury?

"And he said unto them that stood by, Take from him the pound, and give it to him that hath ten pounds.

Part VI – From Third Passover to the Beginning of the Last Passover Week

"(And they said unto him, Lord, he hath ten pounds.) *"For I say unto you, that unto every one which hath shall be given; and from him that hath not, even that he hath shall be taken away from him.*

"But those mine enemies, which would not that I should reign over them, bring hither, and slay them before me."

And when he had thus spoken, he went before, ascending up to Jerusalem.

The Last Sabbath

Then Jesus six days before the Passover came to Bethany, where Lazarus was which had been dead, whom he raised from the dead.

There they made him a supper; and Martha served: but Lazarus was one of them that sat at the table with him.

Then took Mary a pound of ointment of spikenard, very costly, and anointed the feet of Jesus, and wiped his feet with her hair, and she brake a box of ointment and poured it on his head.

When his disciples saw it, some had indignation, and then Judas Iscariot, Simon's son, which should betray him, asked, Why was this ointment sold for three hundred pence, and given to the poor?

This he said, Not that he cared for the poor; but because he was a thief.

Then said Jesus, *"Let her alone: against the day of my burying hath she kept this. Why trouble ye her? she hath wrought a good work on me.*

"For ye have the poor with you always, and whensoever ye will ye may do them good; but me ye have not always.

"She hath done what she could; for in that she hath poured this ointment on my body; she is come aforehand to anoint my body to the burying; she did it for my burial.

"Verily I say unto you, Wheresoever this gospel shall be preached throughout the whole world, this also that she hath done shall be spoken of for a memorial of her."

Part VI – From Third Passover to the Beginning of the Last Passover Week

NOTES: Scriptures of the Topics	Matt	Mark	Luke	John
- On his way to Jerusalem for the last time	20:18,19	10:33,34	18:31-33	
- James and John desire the highest places next to Christ in the temporal kingdom	20:21-23 25-28	10:36,38- 40,42-45		
- He heals two blind men near Jericho	20:32	10:51,52	18:41,42	
- Zaccheus is called down from Sycamore tree by Jesus, salvation comes to his house			19:5,9-10	
- Jesus answers those who think the Kingdom of God shall immediately Appear: with parable of the pound			19:12-27	
- The last Sabbath	26:10-13	14:6-9		12:7,8

Doctrines and Commandments

354. God the Father chooses those, and prepares for them, who shall sit on the right and left hand of Christ Jesus in the Kingdom. It is not in Christ's authority to do so.

355. Whosoever that is greatest among you shall be your servant, and whosoever will be chiefest shall be servant of all.

356. The Son of man came not to be ministered unto, but to minister, and to give His life a ransom for many.

357. Christ Jesus, through one's faith, and his spoken word can restore sight and bring about all types of healings.

358. The Son of man is come to seek and to save that which was lost.

359. Unto everyone that has shall be given, and he shall have abundance: but from him that has nothing shall be taken away even that which he has.

360. Whosoever the gospel of Christ Jesus is preached to throughout the whole world a memorial will be spoken of Mary for anointing Christ Jesus

Part VI – From Third Passover to the Beginning of the Last Passover Week

Lessons We Should Learn

1.   Most true followers of Christ Jesus would want to be chosen to be with Christ in the kingdom, but one should be humble and place oneself in the hands of God only, for he chooses those for His will.

2.   We should learn to serve in whatever capacity that we are chosen by God—a difficult lesson for those of us that attain high positions in life. But to be in the true image and likeness of Christ, those of us who are in high positions should be servant of all. After all, Christ did minister unto all so completely that He gave His life for each of us.

3.   Through one's faith in His spoken word that manifests within us, glory shall be given to God for all types of healings.

4.   As one seeks to do the will of the Lord, salvation may come unto him. For Christ says, *"For the Son of man is come to seek and to save that which is lost."*

5.   Again the lord in the parable of the pounds as in the parable of the ten virgins we must learn to do that which God gives us to do, and to use the talents He gives us. For instance, if He gives us a beautiful and gifted voice and we sing to discover that within there is a beautiful voice, and then never use it. As time passes another attempt is made to use the voice and now it is gone, no longer beautiful and little to be trained once again. This is true in developing talents in musical instruments, athletic and physical development, and our own soul development. In the parable of the pounds, the Lord says, *"For I say unto you, that unto everyone which hath shall be given; and from him that hath not, even that he hath shall be taken away from him."*

In the parable of the traveling man, his servants and the talents, Jesus says, *"For unto everyone that hath shall be given, and he shall have abundance: but from him that hath not shall be taken away even that which he hath."*

6.   One of the only places in the word of God that Christ Jesus himself announces a memorial is to Mary, a woman; not to His disciples, but to Mary a sinner. Why? For she anointed Christ, and did the will of our Heavenly Father. She repented and sinned no more. She became a follower, a believer, and a doer of Christ Jesus' commandments. Women must notice those special scriptures and realize that when 'he', 'him' and 'his' are used it includes both genders as 'she', 'her' and 'hers' when other people, or people in general are indicated.

Part VI – From Third Passover to the Beginning of the Last Passover Week

My Thoughts About the Lessons

_____

_____

_____

_____

_____

_____

_____

_____

_____

_____

_____

_____

_____

_____

_____

_____

_____

_____

_____

_____

_____

_____

_____

_____

Part VII – Last Passover Week, Ending with the Crucifixion

33

Last Passover Week

Jesus Triumphantly Enters Jerusalem

And when they came nigh to Jerusalem, unto Bethphage and Bethany, at the mount of Olives, he sendeth forth two of his disciples,

And saith unto them, *"Go your way into the village over against you: and as soon as ye be entered into it, ye shall find a colt tied, whereon never man sat; loose him, and bring him.*

"And if any man say unto you, Why do ye this? Say ye that the Lord hath need of him; and straightway he will send him hither."

And they that were sent went their way, and found even as he had said unto them.

And as they were loosing the colt, the owners thereof said unto them, Why loose ye the colt?

And they said, The Lord hath need of him.

And they brought him to Jesus: and they cast their garments upon the colt, and they set Jesus thereon.

And as he went, they spread their clothes in the way.

And when he was come nigh, even now at the descent of the mount of Olives, the whole multitude of the disciples began to rejoice and praise God with a loud voice for all the mighty works they had seen;

Saying, Blessed be the King that cometh in the name of the Lord: peace in heaven, and glory in the highest.

Part VII – Last Passover Week, Ending with the Crucifixion

And some of the Pharisees from among the multitude said unto him, Master, rebuke thy disciples.

And he answered and said unto them, *"I tell you that, if these should hold their peace, the stones would immediately cry out.*

He Weeps Over Jerusalem as Doomed

And when he come near, he beheld the city, and wept over it Saying, *"If thou hadst known, even thou, at least in this thy day, the things which belong unto thy peace! but now they are hid from thine eyes.*

"For the days shall come upon thee, that thine enemies shall cast a trench about thee, and compass thee round, and keep thee in on every side.

"And shall lay thee even with the ground, and thy children within thee; and they shall not leave in thee one stone upon another; because thou knewest not the time of thy visitation."

Story of the Barren Fig Tree

And on the morrow, when they were come from Bethany, he was hungry: and seeing a fig tree afar off having leaves, he came, if haply he might find any thing thereon: and when he came to it, he found nothing but leaves; for the time of figs was not yet.

And Jesus answered and said unto it,

"Let no fruit grow on thee hence forward forever. And no man eat fruit of thee hereafter forever."

And his disciples heard it, and said, "How soon is the fig tree withered away?

Jesus answered and said, *"Verily I say unto you, If ye have faith and doubt not, ye shall not only do this which is done to the fig tree, but also if ye shall say unto this mountain, Be thou removed, and be thou cast into the sea; it shall be done.*

"And all things, whatsoever ye shall ask in prayer, believing, ye shall receive."

Part VII – Last Passover Week, Ending with the Crucifixion

He Again Purges the Temple at the Close of His Ministry

And they come to Jerusalem: and Jesus went into the temple, and began to cast out all them that sold and them that bought in the temple, and over threw the tables of the money changers, and the seats of them that sold doves:

And would not suffer that any man should carry any vessel through the temple.

And he taught saying unto them, *"Is it not written, My house shall be called of all nations the house of prayer? but ye have made it a den of thieves."*

And the blind and the lame came to him in the temple; and he healed them.

And when the chief priests and scribes saw the wonderful things that he did, and the children crying in the temple, and saying, Hosanna to the son of David: they were sore displeased, and they sought to destroy him. And said unto him, Hearest thou what these say?

And Jesus saith unto them,

"Yea; have ye never read, Out of the mouth of babes and sucklings thou hast perfected praise?"

And the scribes and chief priests heard it, and sought how they might destroy him: for they feared him, because all the people were astonished at his doctrine. And when even was come, he went out of the city.

NOTES: Scriptures of the Topics	Matt.	Mark	Luke
- Jesus triumphantly enters Jerusalem	21:2,3	11:2,3	19:30,31,40
- He weeps over Jerusalem as doomed			19:42-44
- Story of the Barren Fig Tree	21:19,21,22	11:14	
- He again purges the temple at the close of his ministry	21:13,16	11:17	19:46

Part VII – Last Passover Week, Ending with the Crucifixion

Doctrines and Commandments

361. Christ Jesus is the word; he makes all things known to us.

362. Christ Jesus performed works that no other man has done:

for this they have seen and hated Jesus and God.

363. Christ foretells the future; that we may know.

364. Jesus purges the temple, again, to return it to a house of prayer.

Lessons We Should Learn

1.   Christ Jesus knew where he could find the colt to take him into Jerusalem and he also knew that the chief Jewish priests would not accept his triumphal entry into Jerusalem and receive him as the Messiah. As he entered Jerusalem he saw the fateful future of the city and enemies on every side. As Jesus foresaw these things he makes all things known to us.

2.   Because of the works that he performed that no other man, chief priest, or prophet could have done, the Jews hated him and they failed to recognize him as the Messiah.

3.   In the story of the barren fig tree, one can see oneself in the story, being doubtful with lack of faith to remove mountains of worldly things and influences of the world which may keep us barren and unfruitful in the ways and path to our everlasting life with God.

4.   Jesus during his public ministry purged the Temple twice.

The first time, early during the first year after his baptism, he drove out those who were the moneychangers that made the temple "an house of merchandise" and cleared the temple of sellers. When the Jews asked Jesus to show them a sign for doing these things, He answered, *"Destroy this temple and in three days I will raise it up."*

From this one may realize that our body is in the image of God and should keep it from the indulging ways of the world and not desecrate it, but keep it as the temple to our soul.

The second time the temple was purged by Jesus, it was the last week just before his crucifixion when he again drove out those bought and sold and made the temple a den of thieves. Then he taught them saying, *"Is it not written, my house shall be called of all nations the house of prayer"* Therefore, if we know that our body is the temple to our soul, in the image of our Heavenly Father, then as we learn from Christ Jesus we should keep it a house of prayer, each day, in oneness with God.

Part VII – Last Passover Week, Ending with the Crucifixion

My Thoughts About the Lessons

_____

_____

_____

_____

_____

_____

_____

_____

_____

_____

_____

_____

_____

_____

_____

_____

_____

_____

_____

_____

_____

_____

_____

_____

NOTES

Part VII – Last Passover Week, Ending with the Crucifixion

34

Christ's Authority Challenged

Jesus Teaches That the Power of Prayer Can Move Mountains

And in the morning, as they passed by, they saw the fig tree dried up from the roots.

And Peter calling to remembrance saith unto him, Master, behold, the fig tree which thou cursedst is withered away.

And Jesus answering saith unto them, *"Have faith in God.*

"For verily I say unto you, That whosoever shall say untothis mountain, Be thou removed, and be thou cast into the sea; and shall not doubt in his heart, but shall believe that those things which he saith shall come to pass; he shall have whatsoever he saith.

"Therefore I say unto you, What things soever ye desire, when ye pray, believe that ye receive them, and ye shall have them"

"And when ye stand praying, forgive, if ye have ought against any: that your Father also which is in heaven may forgive you your trespasses."

"But if ye do not forgive, neither will your Father which is in heaven forgive your trespasses."

His Authority is Challenged

They came again to Jerusalem: and as he taught the people in the temple, and preached the gospel, the chief priests and the scribes and elders came to him, saying, Tell us by what authority doest thou these things? or who is he that gave thee this authority?

And he answered and said unto them, *"I will also ask you one question, and answer me, which if ye tell me, I in likewise will tell you by what authority I do these things."*

Part VII – Last Passover Week, Ending with the Crucifixion

"The baptism of John, whence was it? From heaven, or of men? answer me."

And they reasoned with themselves, saying, If we shall say, from heaven; he will say, Why then believe ye him not?

But if we say, Of men; all the people will stone us; for they believed that John was a prophet indeed.

And they answered and said unto Jesus, We cannot tell. And Jesus answering saith unto them, *"Neither do I tell you by what authority I do these things."*

Parable of Two Sons and the Vineyard

Then he began to speak to the people by parables,

"But what think ye? A certain man had two sons; and he came to the first, and said, Son, go work to day in my vineyard.

"He answered and said, I will not: but afterward he repented and went.
"And he came to the second, and said likewise. And he answered and said, I go, sir: and went not.

"Whether of them twain did the will of his father?"

They say unto him, The first. Jesus saith unto them,

"Verily I say unto you, That the publicans and the harlots go into the kingdom of God before you.

"For John came unto you in the way of righteousness, and ye believed him not: but the publicans and the harlots believed him: and ye when ye had seen it, repented not afterward, that ye might believe him.

"Hear another parable: There was a certain householder, which planted a vineyard, and hedged it round about, and digged a winepress in it, and built a tower, and let it out to husbandmen, and went into a far country for a long time:

Part VII – Last Passover Week, Ending with the Crucifixion

"And at the season and when the time of the fruit drew near, a servant, that he might receive from the husbandmen of the fruit of the vineyard.

"But the husbandmen beat him, and sent him away empty.

"And again he sent unto them another servant; and they beat him also, and entreated him shamefully, and sent him away empty.

"And again he sent a third; and they wounded him also, and cast him out.

"And again he sent another; and him they killed, and many others; beating some and killing some.

"Having yet therefore one son, his well beloved, he sent him also last unto them, saying, They will reverence my son, when they see him.

"But those husbandmen said among themselves, This is the heir; come let us kill him, and the inheritance shall be ours. "And they took him, and killed him, and cast him out of the vineyard.

"What shall therefore the lord of the vineyard do unto them? He shall come and destroy those husbandmen, and will give the vineyard unto others."

And when they heard it, they said, God forbid.

And he beheld them and said, *"What is this then that is written, Did ye never read in the scriptures, The stone which the builders rejected, the same is become the head of the corner: this is the Lord's doing, and it is marvelous in our eyes?*

"Therefore I say unto you, The kingdom of God shall be taken from you, and given to a nation bringing forth the fruits thereof, "And whosoever shall fall on this stone shall be broken: but on whomsoever it shall fall, it will grind him to powder."

And when the chief priests and Pharisees had heard his parables, they perceived that he spake of them.

But when they sought to lay hands on him, they feared the multitude, because they took him for a prophet and they left him, and went their way.

Part VII – Last Passover Week, Ending with the Crucifixion

<u>Parable of the Marriage Feast</u>

And Jesus answered and spake unto them again by parables and said, *"The kingdom of heaven is like unto a certain king, which made a marriage for his son,*

"And sent forth his servants to call them that were bidden to the wedding: and they would not come.

"Again, he sent forth other servants, saying, Tell them which are bidden, Behold, I have prepared my dinner: my oxen and my fatlings are killed, and all things are ready: come unto the marriage.

"But they made light of it, and went their ways, one to his farm, another to his merchandise:

"And the remnant took his servants, and entreated them spitefully, and slew them.

"But when the king heard thereof, he was wroth: and he sent forth his armies, and destroyed those murderers, and burned up their city.

"Then saith he to his servants, The wedding is ready, but they which were bidden were not worthy.

"Go ye therefore into the highways, and gathered together all as many as they found, both bad and good: and the wedding was furnished with guests.

"And when the king came in to see the guests, he saw there a man which had not on a wedding garment, And he saith unto him, Friend, how camest thou in hither not having a wedding garment? And he was speechless.

"Then said the king to the servants, Bind him hand and foot, and take him away, and cast him into outer darkness; there shall be weeping and gnashing of teeth. "For many are called, but few are chosen."

Part VII – Last Passover Week, Ending with the Crucifixion

Pharisees Ask Jesus About Caesar's Power

Then went the Pharisees, and took counsel how they might entangle him in his talk.

And they sent out unto him their disciples with the Herodians, saying, Master, we know that thou art true, and teachest the way of God in truth, neither carest thou for any man: for thou regardest not the person of men.

Tell us therefore, What thinkest thou? Is it lawful to give tribute unto Caesar, or not?

But Jesus perceived their wickedness, and said, *"Why tempt ye me, ye hypocrites?"*
"Shew me the tribute money: bring me a penny, that I may see it."

And he said unto them, *"Whose is this image and superscription?"*
They say unto him, Caesar's. Then he saith unto them,

"Render therefore unto Caesar the things which are Caesar's;
and unto God the things that are God's."

When they had heard these words, they marveled, and left him, and went their way.

Saducees Ask Jesus About Wives in the Resurrection

The same day came to him certain Sadducees, which deny that there is any resurrection; and they asked him, saying, Master, Moses wrote unto us, If any man's brother die, having a wife, and he die without children, that his brother should take his wife, and raise up seed unto his brother.

There were therefore seven brethren: and the first took a wife, and died without children.

And the second took her to wife, and he died childless. And third took her; and in like manner the seven also: and they left no children and died.

Part VII – Last Passover Week, Ending with the Crucifixion

Last of all the woman died also.

Therefore in the resurrection whose wife of them is she? for seven had her to wife.

And Jesus answering said unto them, *"Do ye not therefore err, because ye know not the scriptures, neither the power of God?*

"The children of this world marry, and are given in marriage.

"But they which shall be accounted worthy to obtain that world, and the resurrection from the dead, neither marry, nor are given in marriage:

"For when they shall rise from the dead, they neither marry, nor are given in marriage; but are as the angels which are in heaven.

"Neither can they die any more; for they are equal unto the angels; and are the children of God, being the children of the resurrection.

"But as touching the resurrection of the dead, that they rise; have ye not read in the book of Moses, how in the bush God spake unto him, saying, I am the God of Abraham, and the God of Isaac, and the God of Jacob?

"Now that the dead are raised, even Moses showed at the bush, when he calleth the Lord the God of Abraham, and the God of Isaac, and the God of Jacob.

"He is not the God of the dead, but the God of the living: for all live unto him: ye therefore do greatly err."

And when the multitude heard this, they were astonished at his doctrines.

Part VII – Last Passover Week, Ending with the Crucifixion

The Greatest Commandments

But when the Pharisees had heard that he had put the Sadducees to silence, they were gathered together.

Then one of them, which was a lawyer, asked him a question, tempting him, and saying, Master which is the great commandment in the law?

Jesus said unto them,

"The first of all the commandments is, Hear O Israel:

The Lord our God is one Lord: and Thou shalt love the Lord thy God with all thy heart, and with all thy soul, and with all thy mind and with all thy strength. This is the first commandment.

"And the second is like unto it, Thou shalt love thy neighbor as thyself."

"On these two commandments hang all the law and the prophets. "There is none other commandment greater than these."

And the scribe said unto him, Well, Master, thou hadst said the truth: for there is one God: and there is none other but he:

And to love Him with all the heart, and with all the understanding and with all the soul, and with all the strength, and to love his neighbour as himself, is more than all whole burnt offerings and sacrifices.

And when Jesus saw that he answered discreetly, he said unto him, *"Thou art not far from the kingdom of God."* And no man after that durst ask him any question.

Part VII – Last Passover Week, Ending with the Crucifixion

Jesus Asks How the People Say He is the Son of David

While the Pharisees were gathered together, Jesus asked them, saying, *"What think ye of Christ? whose son is he?"* They say unto him, The son of David.

He saith unto them, *"How say the scribes that Christ is the son of David?*

"For David himself said by the Holy Ghost, and David himself saith in the book of Psalms; How then doth David in spirit call him Lord, saying,

"The Lord said unto my Lord, Sit thou on my right hand, Till I make thine enemies thy footstool?

"If David therefore calleth him Lord, how is he then his son and whence is he then his son?"

And no man was able to answer him a word, neither durst any man from that day forth ask him anymore questions. And the common people heard him gladly.

Jesus Gives Warnings to Jerusalem and Hypocrites

Then spake Jesus to the multitude and to his disciples, and he said unto them in his doctrine, *"The scribes and the Pharisees sit in Moses' seat:*

"All therefore whatsoever they bid you observe, that observe and do; but do not ye after their works: for they say, and do not.

"For they bind heavy burdens and grievous to be borne, and lay them on men's shoulders; but they themselves will not move them with one of their fingers.

"But all their works they do for to be seen of men: they make broad their phylacteries, and enlarge the borders of their garments,

"And love the uppermost rooms at feasts, and the chief seats in the synagogues,

Part VII – Last Passover Week, Ending with the Crucifixion

"And greetings in the markets, and to be called of men, Rabbi, Rabbi.

"Beware of scribes, which love to go in long clothing, and love salutations in the marketplaces.

"But be not ye called Rabbi: for one is your Master, even Christ; and all ye are brethren.

"And call no man your father upon the earth: for one is your Father, which is in heaven.

"Neither be ye called masters: for one is your Master, even Christ.

"But he that is greatest among you shall be your servant. "And whosoever shall exalt himself shall be abased; and he that shall humble himself shall be exalted.

"But woe unto you, scribes and Pharisees, hypocrites! for ye shut up the kingdom of heaven against men: for ye neither go in yourselves neither suffer ye them that are entering to go in.

"Woe unto you, scribes and Pharisees, hypocrites! for ye devour widows' houses, and for a pretense make long prayer: therefore ye shall receive the greater damnation.

"Woe unto you, scribes and Pharisees, hypocrites! for ye compass sea and land to make one proselyte, and when he is made, ye make him twofold more the child of hell than yourselves.

"Woe unto you, ye blind guides, which say, Whosoever shall swear by the temple, it is nothing; but whosoever shall swear by the gold of the temple, he is a debtor!

"Ye fools and blind: for whether is greater, the gold, or the temple that sanctifieth the gold?

" And, Whosoever shall swear by the altar, it is nothing; but whosoever sweareth by the gift that is upon it, he is guilty. "Ye fools and blind: for whether is greater, the gift, or the altar that sanctifieth the gift?

Part VII – Last Passover Week, Ending with the Crucifixion

"Whoso shall swear by the altar, sweareth by it, and by all things thereon.

"And whoso shall swear by the temple, sweareth by it, and by him that dwelleth therein.

"And he that shall swear by heaven, sweareth by the throne of God, and by him that sitteth thereon.

"Woe unto you, scribes and Pharisees, hypocrites! for ye pay tithe of mint and anise and cummin, and have omitted the weightier matters of the law, judgment, mercy, and faith: these ought ye to have done, and not to leave the other undone.

"Ye blind guides, which strain at a gnat, and swallow a camel.

"Woe unto you, scribes and Pharisees, hypocrites! for ye make clean the outside of the cup and of the platter, but within they are full of extortion and excess.

"Thou blind Pharisee, cleanse first that which is within the cup and platter, that the outside of them may be clean also,

"Woe unto you scribes and Pharisees, hypocrites! for ye are like unto whited sepulchers, which indeed appear beautiful outward, but are within full of dead men's bones, and of all uncleanness.

"Even so ye also outwardly appear righteous unto men, but within ye are full of hypocrisy and iniquity.

"Woe unto you, scribes and Pharisees, hypocrites! because ye build the tombs of the prophets, and garnish the sepulchers of the righteous.

"And say, If we had been in the days of our fathers, we would not have been partakers with them in the blood of the prophets.

"Wherefore ye be witnesses unto yourselves, that ye are the children of them which killed the prophets.

"Fill ye up then the measure of your fathers.

Part VII – Last Passover Week, Ending with the Crucifixion

"Ye serpents, ye generation of vipers, how can ye escape the damnation of hell?

"Wherefore, behold, I send unto you prophets, and wise men, and scribes: and some of them ye shall kill and crucify: and some of them shall ye scourge in your synagogues, and persecute them from city to city:

"That upon you may come all the righteous blood shed upon the earth, from the blood of righteous Abel unto the blood of Zacharias son of Barachias, whom ye slew between the temple and the altar.

"Verily I say unto you, all these things shall come upon this generation.

"O Jerusalem, Jerusalem, thou that killest the prophets, and stonest them which are sent unto thee, how often would I have gathered thy children together, even as a hen gathereth her chickens under her wings, and ye would not!
"Behold your house is left unto you desolate.

"For I say unto you, Ye shall not see me henceforth, till ye shall say, Blessed is he that cometh in the name of the Lord."

He Commends the Widow's Offering to God's Treasury

And Jesus sat over against the treasury, and beheld how the people cast money into the treasury: and many that were rich cast in much.

And there came a certain poor widow, and she threw in two mites, which make a farthing.

And he called unto his disciples and said, *"Verily I say unto you, That this poor widow hath cast more in, than all they which have cast into the treasury:*

"For all these have of their abundance cast in unto the offerings of God: but she of her want and penury hath cast in all the living that she had; even all her living."

Part VII – Last Passover Week, Ending with the Crucifixion

NOTES: Scriptures of the Topics	Matt.	Mark	Luke
- Jesus teaches that the power of prayer can move mountains	21:21,22	11:21-26	
- His authority is challenged	21:24,25,27	11:29,30,33	20:3,4,8
- Parable of two sons and the vineyard	21:28-40, 42-44	12:1-11	20:9-18
- Parable of the marriage feast	22:2-14		
- Pharisees ask Jesus about Caesar's power	22:18-21	12:15-17	20:24,25
- Sadducees ask Jesus about wives and marriage in resurrection	22:29-32	12:24-27	20:28-38
- The greatest commandments	22:37-40	12:29-31,34	
- Jesus asks how the people say that he is the son of David	22:42-45	12:35-37	20:41-44
- Jesus gives warnings to Jerusalem and hypocrites	23:2-39	12:38-40	20:46,47
- He commends the widow's offering to God's treasury		12:41-44	21:3,4

Doctrines and Commandments

364. Jesus teaches that the power of prayer can move mountains and he teaches how to bring things into manifestation.

1.) To have whatsoever one says; have faith in God and don't doubt in your heart and these things shall come to pass and shall be done.

2.) Jesus says, *"Therefore I say unto you, what things soever ye desire, when ye pray, believe that ye receive them, and ye shall have them." "And all things, whatsoever ye shall ask in prayer, believing, shall receive."*

3.) *"When you stand praying, forgive, if ye have ought against any: that your Father also which is in heaven may forgive you your trespasses." "But if ye do not forgive, neither will your Father which is in heaven forgive your trespasses.*

365. Many are called, but few are chosen.

Part VII – Last Passover Week, Ending with the Crucifixion

366. Children of God, being the children of the resurrection, neither can they die anymore: for they are equal unto the angels for whom they shall rise from the dead, they neither marry, nor are given in marriage; but are as the angels which are in heaven *"But they which shall be accounted worthy to obtain that world and the resurrection from the dead, neither marry, nor are given in marriage,"* Christ teaches.

367. God is God of the living, for all live unto him; for He is not a God of the dead.

368. The greatest commandments:

1st: Thou shalt love the Lord thy God with all thy heart and with all thy soul and with all thy mind, and with all thy strength.

2nd: Thou shalt love thy neighbor as thyself.

"On these two commandments hang all the laws and the prophets." "There is none other commandment greater than those."

369. Do not copy and do the things that hypocrites do. Jesus says; *"For they say and do not." "All their works they do for to be seen of men." "And love the uppermost rooms at feasts and the chief seats in the synagogues."*

370. Call no man your father upon the earth: for one is your Father which is in heaven.

371. Neither call yourselves masters: for one is your Master, even Christ.

372. He that is greatest among you shall be your servant.

373. Whosoever shall exalt himself shall be abased: and he that shall humble himself shall be exalted.

374. Whoso shall swear by the altar, swears by it, and by all things on it.

375. Whoso shall swear by the temple, swears by it, and by all things on it.

376. He that shall swear by heaven, swears by the throne of God, and by Him that sits upon it.

377. Jesus warns hypocrites who pay tithe in great gifts and sums and have omitted the weightier matters of the law, judgment, mercy and faith.

378. One should not be a hypocrite that goes to great length to appear beautiful outwardly but is blind to be clean within of all uncleanness, extortion, and excess.

Part VII – Last Passover Week, Ending with the Crucifixion

Lessons We Should Learn

1.   Jesus teaches us how to pray and to bring things into manifestation. He promises that all things, whatsoever you shall ask in prayer, believing, you shall receive. He says that one should pray believing—believing in God, having faith in Him. Don't allow any doubt slip into your heart and have complete faith and all things shall come to pass and it shall be done. Ask God to forgive your sins and sin no more by forgiving those who trespass against you. God will not forgive your sins until you forgive others. And when you pray, always forgive others.

2.   Those who engage in sinful and unrighteous deeds shall have the kingdom of God taken from them and given to those who are fruitful. Many are called but few are chosen for they are not fruitful.

3.   The children of this world marry and are given in marriage.

But they that shall be accounted worthy to obtain that world and the resurrection from the dead neither marry nor are given in marriage but are as angels that are in heaven. For God is God of the living, for all live unto him: for He is not a God of the dead.

4.   Christ Jesus makes specific reference to His greatest commandments: (1) Thou shalt love the Lord thy God with all thy heart and with all thy soul, and with all thy mind, and with all thy strength. (2) Thou shalt love thy neighbor as thyself. There are no greater commandments than those.

5.   One must follow Christ's example and not those church leaders who may be hypocrites to His word, as those scribes and Pharisees were during Christ's time. For Christ says he that shall swear by heaven, swears by the throne of God and Him that sits upon it. Also, He says the weightier matter than paying tithe is matter of the law, judgment, mercy and faith.

6.   One should look within to be cleansed of all uncleanness, extortion and excess and not to be blind to this need and beauty as well as outward appearance and beauty.

Part VII – Last Passover Week, Ending with the Crucifixion

My Thoughts About the Lessons

_____

_____

_____

_____

_____

_____

_____

_____

_____

_____

_____

_____

_____

_____

_____

_____

_____

_____

_____

_____

_____

NOTES

Part VII – Last Passover Week, Ending with the Crucifixion

35

The Son of Man Prays to His Father:
Ye May Be Children of Light

There were certain Greeks among them that came up to worship at the feast:

The same came to Philip which was of Bethsaida of Galilee and desired him, saying, Sir, we would see Jesus. Philip cometh and telleth Andrew: and again Andrew and Philip tell Jesus.

And Jesus answered them saying,

"The hour is come, that the Son of man should be glorified.

"Verily, verily, I say unto you, Except a corn of wheat fall into the ground and die, it abideth alone: but if it die, it bringeth forth much fruit.

"He that loveth his life, shall lose it; and he that hateth his life in this world shall keep it unto life eternal.

"If any man serve me, let him follow me; and where I am, there shall also my servant be: if any man serve me, him will my Father honour.

"Now is my soul troubled: and what shall I say? Father, save me from this hour: but for this cause came I unto this hour.

"Father, glorify thy name." Then came there a voice from heaven, saying, 'I have both glorified it, and will glorify it again.'

The people therefore, that stood by, and heard it, said that it thundered: others said, An angel spake to him.

Jesus answered and said, *"This voice came not because of me, but for your sakes.*

Part VII – Last Passover Week, Ending with the Crucifixion

"Now is the judgment of this world: now shall the prince of this world be cast out.

"And I, if I be lifted up from the earth, will draw all men unto me."

This he said, signifying what death he should die.

Walk While You Have The Light

The people answered him, We have heard out of the law that Christ abideth for ever: and how sayest thou,
"The Son of man must be lifted up?" Who is this Son of man?

Then Jesus said unto them, *"Yet a little while is the light with you. Walk while ye have the light, lest darkness come upon you: for he that walketh in darkness knoweth not whither he goeth.*

"While ye have light, believe in the light, that ye may be the children of light."
These things spake Jesus, and departed, and did hide himself from them.

NOTES: Scriptures of the Topics   John

- The Son of Man prays to His Father   12:23-28
- A voice from Heaven comes to the people 12:30-32
- Ye may be children of Light   12:34-36

Doctrines and Commandments

379. He that loves his life shall lose it; and he that hates his life in this world shall keep it unto life eternal.

380. If any person serves Christ Jesus, let him follow Jesus.

381. Where Christ Jesus is, his servant will be there, also.

382. God the Father will honor any person who serves Jesus.

383. Now is the judgment of this world: now shall the prince of this world, Satan, be cast out.

Part VII – Last Passover Week, Ending with the Crucifixion

384. As Jesus the Christ is lifted up from the earth, he will draw all persons unto him.

385. While you have the Light, walk in the Light to avoid darkness to come upon you.

386. He that walks in darkness does not know where he is going.

387. You may be children of Light; while you have the Light, believe in the Light.

Lessons We Should Learn

1. *"Father, glorify thy name."* Christ says these words to his Father in prayer. He gives himself upon the altar of the world to his Father in Heaven. *"The hour is come that the Son of man should be glorified."* Even at that hour Jesus is thinking of all men and he tells us to follow him and receive honor from God the Father. Jesus tells each of us how to keep one's life unto Life Eternal.

2. God the Father speaks to the people of the world. Jesus says, *"This voice came not because of me, but for your sakes."* What is God saying to us?

Jesus, help us to understand what God was and is telling us. There are two concepts in the following doctrines which are Christ's own words:

1.) *"Now is the judgment of this world: now shall the prince of this world be cast out."* Here Jesus is victorious for he will give himself to glorify the Father. Therefore, Satan has lost the battle with Christ. He Satan was not successful in tempting Christ. Jesus endured unto the end and now Satan will be cast out.

2.) *"And I, if I be lifted up from the earth, will draw all persons unto me."* What a promise Christ has for all persons. At last, a promise of life eternal. This is the promise to all persons from God.

3. You may be children of Light. How? Jesus says, *"Believe in the light and work in the light to avoid darkness to come upon you."* One must do these things of Light not darkness, and as one does these things of Light, darkness cannot come upon him. This is the key to breaking the shackles of darkness. Also, by doing this we are children of Light; children of God.

Part VII – Last Passover Week, Ending with the Crucifixion

My Thoughts About the Lessons

_____

_____

_____

_____

_____

_____

_____

_____

_____

_____

_____

_____

_____

_____

_____

_____

_____

_____

_____

_____

_____

_____

_____

_____

_____

Part VII – Last Passover Week, Ending with the Crucifixion

36

Jesus Foretells The Last Days

He Tells of Temple Destruction

And as he went out of the temple, one of his disciples saith unto him, Master, see what manner of stones and what buildings are here! And Jesus answering said unto him,

"See ye not all these things?; Seest thou those great buildings? As for these things which ye behold, the days will come, in which there shall not be left one stone upon another, that shall not be thrown down."

And as he sat upon the mount of Olives over against the temple, Peter, James, John and Andrew asked him privately, Tell us, when shall these things be? And what shall be the sign when all these things shall be fulfilled? And what shall be the sign of thy coming, and the end of the world?

He Foretells of False Christs and Deception

And Jesus answered and said unto them,

"Take heed that no man deceive you.

"For many shall come in my name, saying, I am Christ; and shall deceive many: and the time draweth near: go ye not therefore after them."

He Foretells of War and Earthquakes

"And ye shall hear of wars and rumours of wars: but when ye shall hear of wars and commotions, be not terrified; for these things must first come to pass: see that ye be not troubled: for all these things must come to pass, but the end is not by and by and shall not be yet.

"Nation shall rise against nation, and kingdom against kingdom: famines, and pestilences, and troubles; and fearful sights and great signs shall there be from heaven; All these are the beginnings of sorrows.

Part VII – Last Passover Week, Ending with the Crucifixion

Jesus Foretells the Persecution of His Followers and Great Tribulations

"But before all these, they shall lay their hands on you, and persecute you, delivering you up to councils and in the synagogues ye shall be beaten, and into prisons, being brought before kings and rulers for My Name's sake. But take heed to yourselves; for they shall deliver you up to be afflicted, and shall kill you: and ye shall be hated of all nations for My Name's sake, for testimony against them.

"Settle it therefore in your hearts, not to mediate before what ye shall answer.

"For I will give you a mouth and wisdom, which all your adversaries shall not be able to gainsay nor resist.

"But when they shall lead you, and deliver you up, take no thought before hand what ye shall speak, neither do ye premeditate: but whatsoever shall be given you in that hour, that speak ye: for it is not ye that speak, but the Holy Ghost.

"And then shall many be offended, and shall betray one another, and shall hate one another.

"And many false prophets shall rise, and shall deceive many.

"And ye shall be betrayed both by parents, and brethren, and kinsfolks, and friends; and some of you shall they cause to put to death.

"And ye shall be hated of all men for my name's sake. "Now the brother shall betray the brother to death, and the father the son; and children shall rise up against their parents, and shall cause them to be put to death. "And because iniquity shall abound, the love of many shall wax cold. "But there shall not an hair of your head perish.

"In your patience possess ye your souls."

"But he that shall endure unto the end, the same shall be saved."

Part VII – Last Passover Week, Ending with the Crucifixion

"When ye therefore, shall see the abomination of desolation, spoken of by Daniel the prophet, stand in the holy place, stand where it ought not," (whoso readeth, let him understand:)

"And when ye shall see Jerusalem compassed with armies, then know that the desolation thereof is nigh.

"Then let them which are in Judea flee to the mountains; and let them which are in the midst of it depart out; and let not them that are in the countries enter thereinto.

"For these be the days of vengeance, that all things which are written may be fulfilled.

"Let him which is on the housetop not come down to take anything out of his house:
"Neither let him which is in the field return back to take his clothes.

"And woe unto them that are with child, and to them that give suck, in those days! for there shall be great distress in the land, and wrath upon this people.

"But pray ye that your flight be not in the winter, neither on the Sabbath day:

"For in those days shall be affliction, such as was not from the beginning of the creation which God created unto this time, neither shall be.

"For then shall be great tribulation, such as was not since the beginning of the world to this time, no, nor ever shall be.

"And except that the Lord had shortened those days, there should no flesh be saved: but for the elect's sake whom he hath chosen, he hath shortened the days.

"And they shall fall by the edge of the sword, and shall be led away captive unto all nations: and Jerusalem shall be trodden down of the Gentiles, until the times of the Gentiles be fulfilled.

Part VII – Last Passover Week, Ending with the Crucifixion

"Then if any man shall say unto you, Lo, here is Christ, or there; believe it not.

"For there shall arise false Christs, and false prophets, and shall shew great signs and wonders to seduce: insomuch that if it were possible, they shall deceive the very elect.

"Behold, I have told you before.

"Wherefore if they shall say unto you, Behold, he is in the desert; go not forth: behold, he is in the secret chambers; believe it not.

"For as the lightning cometh out of the east, and shineth even unto the west; so shall also the coming of the Son of man be.

"For wheresoever the carcass is, there will the eagles be gathered together.
"But take ye heed: behold, I have foretold you all things."

There Will Be Signs from Galaxies: Then They Shall See the Son of Man Coming in a Cloud

"And there shall be signs in the sun, and in the moon, and in the stars; and upon the earth distress of nations, with perplexity; the sea and the waves roaring;

"Mens' hearts failing them for fear, and for looking after those things which are coming on the earth: for the powers of heaven shall be shaken.

"Immediately after the tribulation of those days shall the sun be darkened, and the moon shall not give her light, and the stars shall fall from heaven, and the powers of the heavens shall be shaken:

"And then shall appear the sign of the Son of man in heaven: and then shall all the tribes of the earth mourn, and they shall see the Son of man coming in the clouds of heaven with power and great glory.

Part VII – Last Passover Week, Ending with the Crucifixion

"And he shall send his angels with a great sound of a trumpet, and they shall gather together his elect from the four winds, from the uttermost part of the earth to the uttermost part of heaven, from one end of heaven to the other.

"And when these things begin to come to pass, then look up, and lift up your heads; for your redemption draweth nigh."

This Generation Shall Not Pass Until All is Fullfilled

And he spake unto them a parable:

"Behold the fig tree, and all trees; when her branch is yet tender, and putteth forth leaves, ye know that summer is near; when they now shoot forth, ye see and know of your ownselves that summer is now nigh at hand."

"So ye in like manner, when ye shall see these things come to pass, know that it is nigh, even at the doors; know ye that the kingdom of God is nigh at hand.

"Verily I say unto you, This generation shall not pass away, till all things are done, till all things be fulfilled.

Heaven and Earth Shall Pass Away, But My Words Shall Not Pass Away

"Heaven and earth shall pass away, but my words shall not pass away."

The Gospel of the Kingdom Shall be Preached in All the World

"And the gospel must first be published among all nations: and this gospel of the kingdom shall be preached in all the world for a witness unto all nations; and then shall the end come.

Part VII – Last Passover Week, Ending with the Crucifixion

Take Heed Each Day; No Man Knowest the Day and Hour Your Lord Doth Come

"And take heed to yourselves, lest at any time your hearts be overcharged with surfeiting, and drunkenness, and cares of this life, and so that day come upon you unawares.

"For as a snare shall it come on all them that dwell on the face of the whole earth.

"But of that day and that hour knoweth no man, no, not the angels which are in heaven, neither the Son, but my Father, only.

"But as the days of Noe were, so shall also the coming of the Son of man be.

"For as in the days that were before the flood they were eating and drinking, marrying and given in marriage, until the day that Noe entered into the ark,

"And knew not until the flood came, and took them all away; so shall also the coming of the Son of man be.

"Then shall two be in the field; the one shall be taken , and the other left.

"Two women shall be grinding at the mill; the one shall be taken, and the other left.

"Watch therefore: for ye know not what hour your Lord doth come.

"Take ye heed, watch and pray: for ye know not when the time is.

"Watch ye therefore, and pray always, that ye may be accounted worthy to escape all these things that shall come to pass, and to stand before the Son of man."

Part VII – Last Passover Week, Ending with the Crucifixion

<u>Parable of the Good Man of the House, the Wise and Evil Servant</u>

"For the Son of man is as a man taking a far journey, who left his house, and gave authority to his servants, and to every man his work, and commanded the porter to watch.

"Watch ye therefore; for ye know not when the master of the house cometh, at even, or at midnight, or at the cockcrowing, or in the morning:

"Lest coming suddenly he find you sleeping. "And what I say unto you, I say unto all, watch.

"But know this, that if the Goodman of the house had known in that watch the thief would come, he would have watched, and would not have suffered his house to be broken up.

"Therefore be ye also ready; for in such an hour as ye think not the Son of man cometh.

"Who then is a faithful and wise servant, whom his Lord hath made ruler over his household, to give them meat in due season?

"Blessed is that servant, whom his lord when he cometh shall find so doing.
"Verily I say unto you, that he shall make him ruler over all his goods.

"But and if that evil servant shall say in his heart, my Lord delayeth his coming;

"And shall begin to smite his fellow servants, and to eat and drink with the drunken;

"The lord of that servant shall come in a day when he looketh not for him, and in an hour that he is not aware of,

"And shall cut him asunder, and appoint him his portion with the hypocrites: There shall be weeping and gnashing of teeth."

Part VII – Last Passover Week, Ending with the Crucifixion

Parable of the Ten Virgins

"Then shall the kingdom of heaven be likened unto ten virgins, which took their lamps, and went forth to meet the bridegroom.

"And five of them were wise, and five were foolish.

"They that were foolish took their lamps, and took no oil with them:

"But the wise took oil in their vessels with their lamps. "While the bridegroom tarried, they all slumbered and slept.

"And at midnight there was a cry made, Behold, the bridegroom cometh; go ye out to meet him.

"Then all those virgins arose, and trimmed their lamps. "And the foolish said unto the wise, Give us of your oil; for our lamps are gone out.

"But the wise answered, saying, Not so; lest there be not enough for us and you: but go ye rather to them that sell, and buy for yourselves.

"And while they went to buy, the bridegroom came; and they that were ready went in with him to the marriage: and the door was shut.

"Afterward came also the other virgins, saying, Lord, Lord, open to us.
"But he answered and said, Verily I say unto you, I know you not.

"Watch therefore, for ye know neither the day nor the hour wherein the Son of man cometh.

Part VII – Last Passover Week, Ending with the Crucifixion

Parable of the Traveling Man, His Servants and the Talents

"For the kingdom of heaven is as a man traveling into a far country, who called his own servants and delivered unto them his goods.

"And unto one he gave five talents, to another two, and to another one; to every man according to his several ability; and straightway took his journey.

"Then he that had received the five talents went and traded with the same, and made them other five talents.

"And likewise he that had received two, he also gained other two.

"But he that had received one went and digged in the earth, and hid his lord's money.

"After a long time the lord of those servants cometh, and reckoneth with them.

"And so he that had received five talents came and brought other five talents, saying, Lord, thou deliveredst unto me five talents: behold, I have gained beside them five talents more. "His lord said unto him, well done, thou good and faithful servant: thou hast been faithful over a few things, I will make thee ruler over many things: enter thou into the joy of the lord.

"He also that had received two talents came and said, Lord, thou deliveredst unto me two talents: behold, I have gained two other talents beside them.

"His lord said unto him, Well done, good and faithful servant; thou hast been faithful over a few things, I will make thee ruler over many things: enter thou into the joy of the lord.

"Then he which had received the one talent came and said, Lord, I knew thee that thou art an hard man, reaping where thou has not sown, and gathering where thou hast not strawed:

"And I was afraid, and went and hid thy talents in the earth: lo, there thou hast that is thine.

Part VII – Last Passover Week, Ending with the Crucifixion

"His lord answered and said unto him, Thou wicked and slothful servant, thou knewest that I reap where I sowed not, and gather where I have not strawed:

"Thou oughtest therefore to have put my money to the exchangers, lent then at my coming I should have received mine own with usury.

"Take therefore the talent from him, and give it unto him which hath ten talents.

"For unto every one that hath shall be given, and he shall have abundance: but from him that hath not shall be taken away even that which he hath.

"And cast ye the unprofitable servant into outer darkness; there shall be weeping and gnashing of teeth.

The Parable of the Sheep and the Goats

"When the Son of man shall come in his glory, and all the holy angels with him, then shall he sit upon the throne of his glory:

"And before him shall be gathered all nations: and he shall separate them one from another, as a shepherd divideth his sheep from the goats:

"And he shall set the sheep on his right hand, but the goats on the left.

"Then shall the king say unto them on his right hand, Come, ye blessed of my Father, inherit the kingdom prepared for you from the foundation of the world.

"For I was an hungered, and ye gave me meat: I was thirsty, and ye gave me drink: I was a stranger, and ye took me in:

"Naked, and ye clothed me: I was sick, and ye visited me: and ye came unto me.

"Then shall the righteous answer him, saying, Lord, when saw we thee an hungered, and fed thee? or thirsty, and gave thee drink?

Part VII – Last Passover Week, Ending with the Crucifixion

"When saw we thee a stranger, and took thee in? or naked, and clothed thee?"?

"Or when saw we thee sick , or in prison, and came unto thee?"

"And the king shall answer and say unto them, Verily I say unto you, Inasmuch as ye have done it unto one of the least of these my brethren, ye have done it unto me.
"Then shall he say also unto them on the left hand,

Depart from me, ye cursed, into everlasting fire, prepared for the devil and his angels:

"For I was hungered, and ye gave me no meat: I was thirsty, and ye gave me no drink:

"I was a stranger, and ye took me not in: naked and ye clothed me not: sick, and in prison, and ye visited me not.

"Then shall they also answer him, saying, Lord, when
saw we thee an hungered, or at thirst, or a stranger, or naked, or sick, or in prison, and did not minister unto thee?

"Then shall he answer them saying, Verily I say unto you, Inasmuch as ye did it not to one of the least of these, ye did it not to me.
"And these shall go away into everlasting punishment: but the righteous into life eternal."

Part VII – Last Passover Week, Ending with the Crucifixion

NOTES: Scriptures of the Topics	Matt	Mark	Luke
- He tells of temple destruction	24:2	13:2	21:6
- He foretells of false Christs and deception	24:4,5,11 23-28	13:5,6	21:8
- He foretells of war and earthquakes	24:6-8	13:7,8	21:9-11
- Jesus foretells the persecution of His followers and great tribulation	24:9-28	13:9, 14-23	21:12-24
- There will be signs from galaxies then they shall see the Son of man coming in a cloud	24:29-31	13:24-27	21:25,26, 27-31
- This generation shall not pass until all is fulfilled	24:32-34		21:29-32
- Heaven and Earth shall pass away but my words shall not	24:35	13:31	21:33
- The Gospel of the kingdom shall be preached in all the world	24:14	13:10	
- Take heed each day; no man knowest the day and hour the Lord doth come	24:36-44	13:32-33	21:34-36
- Parable of the Goodman of the house, the wise and evil servant	24:43-51	13:34-37	
- Parable of the Ten Virgins	25:1-13		
- Parable of traveling man, his servants and the talents	25:14-30		
- The parable of the sheep and the goats	25:31-46		

Part VII – Last Passover Week, Ending with the Crucifixion

Doctrines and Commandments

388. Christ Jesus foretells great affliction and tribulations that will come to pass:

1.) Temple destruction

2.) False Christs—take heed that no man deceive you, many shall come in my name, saying I am Christ.

3.) War and earthquakes—famine and pestilences and troubles.

4.) Fearful sights and great signs from heaven. These are the beginnings of sorrows.

5.) The persecution of His followers: you shall be hated of all nations for My name's sake, for a testimony against them settle it therefore in your hearts, not to mediate before what you answer. For I will give you mouth and wisdom, which all your adversaries shall not be able gainsay nor resist; for it is not you that speaks, but the Holy Ghost.

6.) Many shall be offended, and shall betray one another— you shall be betrayed both by parents, and brethren and kinsfolk and friends and some shall they cause to be put to death.

7.) Great affliction and tribulation: for in those days there shall be affliction such as was not from the beginning of the creation which God created unto this time, neither shall be: For them shall be great tribulation, such as was not since the beginning of the world to this time, no, nor, ever shall be.

389. He that shall endure to the end, the same shall be saved.

390. In your patience possess you your souls.

391. All the tribes of the earth shall see Christ Jesus coming in the clouds of heaven with power and great glory. There will be signs from galaxies and the powers of the heavens shall be shaken. He shall send His angels with a great sound of a trumpet to gather His elect from the uttermost part of the earth to the uttermost part of heaven, from one end of heaven to the other. And when these things begin to come to pass, then look up, and lift up your heads; for your redemption draweth nigh.

392. The Gospel of the kingdom shall be published and preached in all the world and then shall the end come.

393. Take heed each day; no man knowest the day and hour your Lord doth come, no, not the angels, neither the Son, but the Father only.

394. Heaven and earth shall pass away; but My words shall not pass away.

Part VII – Last Passover Week, Ending with the Crucifixion

395. Unto everyone that has shall be given, and he shall have abundance: but from him that has nothing shall be taken away even that which he has.

396. You the unprofitable servant shall be cast into outer darkness.

397. All the holy angels shall come with Christ Jesus when He comes in His glory.

398. Christ Jesus shall separate one nation from another when all nations are gathered before Him.

399. The Kingdom of God has been prepared for you from the foundation of the world.

400. The righteous blessed of God shall inherit His Kingdom.

401. The righteous are those who do good unto strangers, to take them in to minister to their thirst, hunger and ills. In as much as you have done it unto one of the least of these, His brethren, you have done it unto God.

402. The unrighteous are those who ignore the stranger and do nothing to minister unto their thirst, hunger and ills. In as much as you have not done it unto one of the least of these His brethren, you have not done it unto God.

403. The righteous shall go into life eternal.

404. The unrighteous shall go into everlasting punishment.

405. The unrighteous are preparing for the devil and his angels and are depart from Christ, into everlasting fire.

Lessons We Should Learn

1.   Jesus foretells the future to several disciples and one of the first topics to question is the Jewish Temple. Jesus explains that there shall not be left one stone upon another. The Jewish temple encompasses all of the Jewish theocracy and beliefs. Jesus knew that Jewish theocracy could not be used to preach the gospel in all the world. Christianity, His word, is the gospel which shall be published and preached in all the world. Therefore, Christ is foretelling the beginning of Christianity the spreading of His word and the fulfillment of the will of His Heavenly Father.

2.   Jesus foretells of deception and false Christs and of war and earthquakes and He tells us that the time draws near and that all these things must come to pass, but the end shall not be yet. Actually Christ cannot tell us when the end shall be, for in the scripture of St. Mark 13:32 He says; take heed each day; no man knowest the day and hour your Lord doth come, no, not the angels, neither the Son, but the Father only. Therefore, Christ can comfort us with how to conduct one's self through these commotions. He says, "Take heed that no man deceive you," "Go ye not therefore after them:"" Also, "Be not terrified, see that ye be not troubled."

Part VII – Last Passover Week, Ending with the Crucifixion

3.   Christ Jesus warns His followers that great affliction and tribulation is to come, such as was not from the beginnings of the creation which God created unto this time, neither shall be. "For these be the days of vengeance, that all things which are written may be fulfilled," he tells us. Also, some of his disciples will be in prison and put to death. And the brother shall betray the brother to death, and the father and the son; and children shall rise up against their parents and shall cause them to be put to death, He warns. For those that shall endure unto the end, the same shall be saved. And Christ makes other promises and statements:

"In your patience posses ye your souls."

"There shall not an hair of head perish."

"There should no flesh be saved: but for the elect sake whom He hath chosen, He hath shortened the days."

"But take ye heed: behold, I have foretold you all things."

One must take refuge in His word: that He lets all things be known, even those things that are yet to come. We must be patient and prepare to endure unto the end.

4.   The elect shall be gathered from the uttermost part of the earth to the uttermost part of heaven. Jesus tells us what to look for in the galaxies in tribulation of those days. And all tribes of the earth shall see Him coming in the clouds of heaven with power and great glory. He tells us that our redemption is near when these things begin to come to pass.

5.   The end shall come when His gospel is published and preached among all nations in all the world. Each must take heed unto oneself not to be overcharged with the cares of this life, surfeiting and drunkenness. For no one knows the day and that hour but the Father.

Christ's commandment is the lesson:

"Watch ye therefore, and pray always, that ye may be accounted worthy to escape all these things that shall come to pass, and to stand before the Son of man.

"Heaven and earth shall pass away, but my words shall not pass away."

Part VII – Last Passover Week, Ending with the Crucifixion

6.   In the parable of the traveling man, his servants and the talents, Jesus says, *"For unto everyone that hath shall be given, and he shall have abundance: but from him that hath not shall be taken away even that which he hath."* As here in one's life, if a talent is achieved, growth and abundance shall follow if that talent is used. If the talent is put aside it will be lost, taken away. Such as developing a beautiful voice or playing a musical instrument. If it is not used the skill will be lost and taken away.

7.   The lesson in the parable of the sheep and the goats is the development and living a life of righteousness, and or unrighteousness. The consequences are plain and obvious.

For the righteous—inheritance of our Father's kingdom and life eternal.

For the unrighteous everlasting fire, prepared for the devil and his angels, and into everlasting punishment.

Part VII – Last Passover Week, Ending with the Crucifixion

My Thoughts About the Lessons

_____

_____

_____

_____

_____

_____

_____

_____

_____

_____

_____

_____

_____

_____

_____

_____

_____

_____

_____

_____

_____

_____

_____

NOTES

Part VII – Last Passover Week, Ending with the Crucifixion

37

Jesus Publicly Announces His Betrayal and Crucifixion

Fourth Day of the Passover Week

Judas Avails Himself

And it came to pass, when Jesus had finished all those sayings, he said unto his disciples, *"Ye know that after two day is the feast of the Passover, and the Son of man is betrayed to be crucified."*

Then assembled together the chief priests, and the scribes, and the elders of the people, unto the palace of the high priest, who was called Caiaphas.

And consulted that they might take Jesus by subtilty, and kill him.

But they said, Not on the feast day, lest there be an uproar among the people.

Then one of the twelve, called Judas Iscariot went unto the chief priests.

And said unto them, What will ye give me, and I will deliver him unto you? And they covenanted with him for thirty pieces of silver.

And from that time he sought opportunity to betray him.

Christ the Light of the World: You May Be the Children of Light

Then Jesus said unto them, *"Yet a little while is the light with you. Walk while ye have the light, lest darkness come upon you: for he that walketh in darkness knoweth not whither he goeth."*

Part VII – Last Passover Week, Ending with the Crucifixion

"While ye have light, believe in the light, that ye may be the children of light,"
These things spake Jesus, and departed, and did hide himself from them.

But though he had done so many miracles before them, yet they believed not on him:

That the saying of Esaias the prophet might be fulfilled, which he spake, Lord, who hath believed our report? and to whom hath the arm of the Lord been revealed?

Therefore they could not believe, because that Esaias said again.

He hath blinded their eyes, and hardened their heart; that they should not see with their eyes, nor understand with their heart, and be converted, and I should heal them.

These things said Esaias, when he saw his glory, and spoke of him.

Nevertheless among the chief rulers also many believed on him; but because of the Pharisees they did not confess him, lest they should be put out of the synagogue:

For they loved the praise of men more than the praise of God.

How to Believe in God and See God

Jesus cried and said, *"He that believeth on me, believeth not on me, but on him that sent me.*

"And he that seeth me seeth him that sent me.

"I am come a light into the world, that whosoever believeth on me should not abide in darkness."

Part VII – Last Passover Week, Ending with the Crucifixion

Jesus Came Not to Judge the World But to Save the World

"And if any man hear my words, and believe not, I judge him not: for I came not to judge the world, but to save the world.

"He that rejecteth me, and receiveth not my words, hath one that judgeth him: the word that I have spoken, the same shall judge him in the last day."

God's Commandments—Life Everlasting

"For I have not spoken of myself; but the Father which sent me, he gave me a commandment, what I should say, and what I should speak.

"And I know that his commandment is life everlasting: whatsoever I speak therefore, even as the Father said unto me, so I speak."

NOTES: Scriptures of the Topics	Matt	John
- Jesus publicly announces his betrayal and crucifixion	26:2	
- Christ the light of the world: you may be children of light		12:35,36,46
- How to believe in God and see God.		12:44-46
- Jesus came not to judge the world but to save the world		12:47,48
- God's commandment—life everlasting		12:49,50

Doctrines and Commandments

406. The Son of man is betrayed to be crucified.

407. Christ is the light of the world and you may be the children of light. *"I am come a light into the world, that whosoever believeth on me should not abide in darkness." "Yet a little while is the light with you. Walk while ye have the light, lest darkness come upon you: for he that walketh in darkness knoweth not whither he goeth." "While ye have the light, believe in the light, that ye may be the children of light."*

408. How to believe in God and see God. (Jn. 12:44-46)

24. Jesus came not to judge the world but to save the world.

47. God's commandment—life everlasting. *"For I have not spoken of myself; but the Father which sent me, he gave me a commandment, what I should say, and what I should speak." "And I know that his commandment is life everlasting: whatsoever I speak therefore, even as the Father unto me, so I speak."*

Part VII – Last Passover Week, Ending with the Crucifixion

Lessons We Should Learn

1.   Christ's disciples could not understand only two days before the crucifixion that it would happen nor why it would happen because their mission with the Lord was going well and reaching great multitudes. They didn't realize that God's commandment was life everlasting and all the laws and scriptures would be fulfilled with the crucifixion of Christ Jesus. One must ask, "Could I be one of the children of light if Jesus was not crucified? Was he crucified for me? For each of us?"

2.   Christ Jesus shares all things with us. He is come as a light into the world and we may be the children of light Christ Jesus spoke openly about His doctrines to the world and in secret He said nothing. You may eat and drink at my table in my kingdom and sit on thrones judging the twelve tribes of Israel.

I appointed unto you a kingdom, as My Father hath appointed unto me. These doctrines and others indicates that what Christ has is ours, that He is the bread of life, the light of the world and all of these are for each of us that we may indeed be children of light and His light, and understanding of His words may be known unto us.

3.   These are Christ's words:

"He that believeth on me, believeth not on me, but on him that sent me."

"And he that seeth me seeth him that sent me." One must believe in Christ and His words as the truth for it is of God and believe therein in God and His word, and that word is Christ Jesus. For Christ is one with God and God is one with Christ. Therefore, those who see Christ see God. Those who believe on Christ believe on God who sent Christ Jesus to us.

4.   Christ says, *"If any man hear my words, and believe not, I judge him not; for I came not to judge the world, but to save the world."*

Man is of his own free will—that is the way that our Heavenly Father created us. If we are sincere and truthful about our being and our true relationship with God then we bring Christ Jesus into our lives. When this happens His words become known to us and God reveals to us all truth and light in Jesus the Christ. Jesus the Christ is to say Jesus the Messiah, Jesus the Savior; for He claims His Godhead with our Heavenly Father. Jesus the Christ is the perfect manifestation of God. In Christ we see God in man, God in oneself. As Jesus the Savior, He can save us from what? Can He save us from sin?

Part VII – Last Passover Week, Ending with the Crucifixion

Can He save us from temptation? Can He save us from darkness? Christ Jesus says that He can, but He is not going to judge us if we don't believe Him. Again to repeat His words, *"I came not to judge the world but to save the world."*

If we do not believe on Him He cannot save us. And one's beliefs on Him, Christ Jesus, should be of love of Him, not fear. For He came into the world to show us the way, to overcome the world to save the world because He loves us! His love is expressed in this new commandment that He gave us.

"A new commandment I give unto you, that ye love one another; as I have loved you, that ye also love one another. Believe in God, believe also in me, let not your heart be troubled.

"If ye love me: keep my commandments.

"He that hath my commandments and keepeth them, he is that loveth me: and he that loveth me shall be loved of my Father, and I will love him; and will manifest myself to him."

5.   Christ Jesus says, *"I know that His commandment is life everlasting."* In this doctrine of everlasting and eternal life one can see that Christ is the fulfillment of this promise and the word of God. This is God's commandment—life everlasting. Who did He command it? To each of us, His creation, His children. Who did He send to show us how this commandment could be achieved? His Son, Christ Jesus.

Jesus claims this to be in His own words from God,

"Whatsoever I speak therefore, even as the Father said unto me, so I speak."

One could say that everlasting life is Christ's word; for He says,

"Heaven and earth shall pass away, but my words shall not pass away."

Part VII – Last Passover Week, Ending with the Crucifixion

My Thoughts About the Lessons

_____

_____

_____

_____

_____

_____

_____

_____

_____

_____

_____

_____

_____

_____

_____

_____

_____

_____

_____

_____

_____

_____

_____

Part VIII – The Lord's Supper: Farewell Address: Crucifixion and Resurrection

38

Jesus Celebrates His Last Passover

The Fifth Day

Jesus Sends Two Disciples in to the City to Prepare for the Passover

Then came the day of unleavened bread, when the Passover must be killed.

And he sent Peter and John, saying, *"Go and prepare us the Passover, that we may eat."*

And they said unto him, Where wilt thou that we prepare?

And he said unto them, *"Go ye into the city, and there shall meet you a man bearing a pitcher of water: follow him.*

"And wheresoever he shall go in, say ye to the goodman of the house, The Master saith, My time is at hand: Where is the guest chamber, where I shall keep the Passover at thy house and eat the Passover with my disciples?

"And he will show you a large upper room furnished and prepared: there make ready for us."

And they went and found as he had said unto them: and they made ready the Passover.

Part VIII – The Lord's Supper: Farewell Address: Crucifixion and Resurrection

Jesus Ordains the Lord's Supper

And when the hour was come, he said unto them, *"With desire I have desired to eat this Passover with you before I suffer:*

"For I say unto you, I will not any more eat thereof, until it be fulfilled in the kingdom of God."

And as he took the cup, and gave thanks, he said, *"Take this, and divide it among yourselves:*

"For I say unto you, I will not drink of the fruit of vine until the kingdom of God shall come."

And he took bread and gave thanks, and brake it and gave unto them, saying, *"Take, eat: This is my body, which is broken and given for you: this do in remembrance of me."*

Likewise also the cup after supper, saying, *"Drink ye all of it; This cup is the new testament in my blood, which is shed for you, for many, for the remission of sins, this do ye, as oft as ye drink it, in remembrance of me.*

"Verily I say unto you, I will drink no more of the fruit of the vine, until that day that I drink it new with you in my Father's kingdom, in the kingdom of God."

Jesus Promises the Kingdom and Reproves the Ambition of His Disciples

And when the hour was come in the evening he sat down, and the twelve apostles with him.

And there was a strife among them, which of them should be accounted the greatest.

And he said unto them, *"The Kings of the gentiles exercise Lordship over them; and they that exercise authority upon them are called benefactors.*

"But ye shall not be so: but he that is greatest among you, let him be as the younger; and he that is chief, as he that doth serve.

Part VIII – The Lord's Supper: Farewell Address: Crucifixion and Resurrection

"For whether is greater, he that sitteth at meat, or he that serveth? is not he that sitteth at meat? but I am among you as he that serveth.

"Ye are they which have continued with me in my temptations.
"And I appoint unto you a kingdom, as my Father hath appointed unto me:

"That ye may eat and drink at my table in my kingdom, and sit on thrones judging the twelve tribes of Israel.

He Teaches Love and Humility by Washing Disciples' Feet

And the supper being ended, Jesus knowing that the Father had given all things into his hands, and that he was come from God, and went to God;

He riseth from supper, and laid aside his garments: and took a towel, and girded himself.

After that, he poured water into a basin, and began to wash the disciples' feet, and to wipe them with the towel wherewith he was girded.

Then cometh he to Simon Peter: and Peter saith unto him, "Lord, doest thou wash my feet."

Jesus answered, *"What I do thou knowest not now; but thou shalt know hereafter."*

Peter said unto him, "Thou shalt never wash my feet." Jesus answered him, *"If I wash thee not, thou hast no part with me."*

Simon Peter saith unto him, "Lord, not my feet only, but also my hands and my head."

Part VIII – The Lord's Supper: Farewell Address: Crucifixion and Resurrection

Jesus saith to him, *"He that is washed needeth not save to wash his feet, but is clean every whit: and ye are clean, but not all."*

For he knew who should betray him; therefore said he, *Ye are not all clean."*

So after he had washed their feet and had taken his garments, and was set down again, he said unto them,

"Know ye what I have done to you?

"Ye call me Master and Lord: and ye say well: for so I am.

"If I then, your Lord and Master, have washed your feet; ye also ought to wash one another's feet.

"For I have given you an example, that ye should do as I have done to you.

"Verily, verily, I say unto you, The servant is not greater than his lord; neither he that is sent greater than he that sent him.

"If ye know these things, happy are ye if ye do them.

"I speak not of you all: I know whom I have chosen: but that the scripture may be fulfilled, He that eateth bread with me hath lifted up his heel against me.

"Now I tell you before it come, that, when it is come to pass, ye may believe that I am he.

"Verily, verily, I say unto you, He that receiveth whomsoever I sent receiveth me; and he that receiveth me receiveth him that sent me."

Part VIII – The Lord's Supper: Farewell Address: Crucifixion and Resurrection

He Indicates His Betrayer

Jesus was troubled in spirit, and testified, and said,

"Verily, verily, I say unto you, that one of you shall betray me. "But, behold, the hand of him that betrayeth me is with me on the table. One of you which eateth with me shall betray me.

"And truly the Son of man goeth, as it is written of him: and as it was determined: but woe to that man by whom the Son of man is betrayed! it had been good for that man if he had not been born."

Simon Peter therefore beckoned to him, that he should ask who it should be of whom he spake.

He then lying on Jesus' breast saith unto him, Lord, who is it?

Jesus answered, *"It is one of the twelve, that dippeth with me in the dish, the same shall betray me. He it is, to whom I shall give a sop, when I have dipped it."*
Then Judas betrayed him, answered and said, Master, is it I? He said unto him, *"Thou hast said."*

And when Jesus dipped the sop, he gave it to Judas Iscariot, the son of Simon.

And after the sop Satan entered into him. Then said Jesus unto him, *"That thou doest, do quickly."*

Now no man at the table knew for what intent he spake this unto him.

For some of them thought, because Judas had the bag, that Jesus had said unto him, Buy those things that we have need of against the feast; or, that he should give something to the poor.

He then having received the sop went immediately out: and it was night.

Part VIII – The Lord's Supper: Farewell Address: Crucifixion and Resurrection

He Tells of Satan Desiring to Have Peter

And the Lord said, *"Simon, Simon, behold, Satan hath desired to have you, that he may sift you as wheat:*

"But I have prayed for thee, that thy faith fail not: and when thou art converted, strengthen thy brethren."

And he said unto him, Lord, I am ready to go with thee, both into prison, and to death.

And he said, *"I tell thee, Peter, the cock shall not crow this day, before that thou shalt thrice deny that thou knowest me."*

NOTES: Scriptures of the Topics	Matt.	Mark	Luke	John
- Jesus sends two disciples into the city to prepare for the Passover	26:18	14:13-15	22:8, 10-12	
- Jesus ordains the Lord's Supper	26:26-29	14:22, 24,25	22:15-20	

** see also I Cor. 11:24,25

	Matt.	Mark	Luke	John
- Jesus promises the kingdom and reproves the ambition of his disciples			22:25-30	
- He teaches love and humility by washing disciples' feet				13:7,8 10,11-20
- He indicates His betrayer	26:21, 23-25	4:18, 20,21	22:21,22	13:21, 26,27-30
- He tells of Satan desiring to have Peter			22:31, 32,34	

Part VIII – The Lord's Supper: Farewell Address: Crucifixion and Resurrection

Doctrines and Commandments

409. He that is greatest among you, let him be as the younger; and he that is chief be as he that doth serve.

410. Christ is among you as he that serves.

411. I appointed unto you a kingdom, as my Father hath appointed unto me.

412. Ye may eat and drink at my table in my kingdom and sit on thrones judging the twelve tribes of Israel.

413. Simon, behold, Satan hath desired to have you, that he may sift you as wheat.

414. The Lord's Supper: Jesus, taking bread and giving thanks and gave unto them saying, *"Take, eat; this is my body, which is broken and given for you: This do in remembrance of me." "This cup is the new Testament in my blood, which is shed for you, for many, this do ye, as oft as ye drink it, in remembrance of me." "Verily I say unto you, I will drink no more of the fruit of the vine, until that day that I drink it new in the kingdom of God."*

415. Jesus teaches love and humility by washing disciples' feet.

"What I do thou knowest not now, but shall know hereafter."

416. The Son of man is betrayed. *"The Son of man indeed goeth as it is written of him: but woe to that man by whom the Son of man is betrayed."*

Part VIII – The Lord's Supper: Farewell Address: Crucifixion and Resurrection

Lessons We Should Learn

1.   Which is greatest among you, the chief being served, or he that does the serving? Christ Jesus washing the disciples' feet shows that we need practice in loving one another, serving one another, being humble to one another: for how came we to love God the Father and serve Him, and do his will, when we don't know how to be humble and serve one another and to love one another.

2.   As God the Father has appointed unto Christ Jesus, Christ Jesus appoints unto you a kingdom.

3.   Satan desires to have you as he did Peter. Even after Peter had a fair warning he could not be strengthened and resist Satan for he did just as the Lord said, *"I tell thee Peter, the cock shall not crow this day, before that thou shalt thrice deny that thou knowest me."* How often do we deny Christ and give in to Satan's desires to have us. We must stay strong and steadfast in his righteousness and pray daily that God our Father will lead us not into temptation but deliver us from evil!

4.   Partaking of the Lord's Supper is a symbol of our remembrance of him and the kingdom of God. He is the word, the bread of life; he is the cup of life and the new testament unto the kingdom of God.

5.   Christ warns mankind by whom the Son of man is betrayed.

How many times does this man betray him, with lack of love, faith, righteousness, doing our Father's will or even a regular period of prayer. Out of 16 hours of awakeness do we give him 1/16th? One hour each day devoted to study and to learn his word? Are we all hypocrites with our sensuous worldly lusts after our own desires and waste and rationalizing that in my twilight years I will repent unto the Lord and do his will but for now I am having fun, doing my thing. We are in darkness, dead and not alive. Luke warm at the best!

Part VIII – The Lord's Supper: Farewell Address: Crucifixion and Resurrection

My Thoughts About the Lessons

_____

_____

_____

_____

_____

_____

_____

_____

_____

_____

_____

_____

_____

_____

_____

_____

_____

_____

_____

_____

_____

_____

_____

_____

_____

_____

_____

NOTES

Part VIII – The Lord's Supper: Farewell Address: Crucifixion and Resurrection

39

Farewell Address: Commandment and Promises: Intercessory Prayer

Christ is Glorified, and God is Glorified in Him

Therefore, when he was gone out, Jesus said, *"Now is the Son of man glorified, and God is glorified in him.*

"If God be glorified in him, God shall also glorify him in himself, and shall straightway glorify him."

Christ Addresses His Disciples as Little Children

"Little Children, yet a little while I am with you. Ye shall seek me: and as I said unto the Jews, Whither I go, ye cannot come; so now I say to you."

A New Commandment: Love One Another As I Loved You

"A new commandment I give unto you, That ye love one another; as I have loved you, that ye also love one another.

"By this shall all men know that ye are my disciples, if you have love one to another."

Peter Desires to Follow Christ: Jesus sees Peter's Denial

Simon Peter said unto him, Lord, whither goest thou? Jesus answered him, *"Whither I go, thou canst not follow me now; but thou shalt follow me afterwards."*

Peter said unto him, Lord, why cannot I follow thee now? I will lay down my life for thy sake. I am ready to go with thee, both into prison and to death.

Part VIII – The Lord's Supper: Farewell Address: Crucifixion and Resurrection

Jesus answered him, *"Wilt thou lay down thy life for my sake? Verily, verily, I say unto thee, The cock shall not crow till thou hast denied me thrice, and that thou shalt thrice deny that thou knowest me."*

And he said unto them, *"When I sent you without purse, and scrip, and shoes, lack ye any thing?"* And they said, Nothing.

Then said he unto them, *"But now he that hath a purse, let him take it, and likewise his scrip: and he that hath no sword, let him sell his garment, and buy one.*

"For I say unto you, that this that is written must yet be accomplished in me, And he was reckoned among the transgressors: for the things concerning me have an end."

And they said, Lord, behold, here are two swords. And he said unto him, *"It is enough."*

In My Father's House Are Many Mansions; Christ Jesus Goes to Prepare a Place for Us

"Let not your heart be troubled: ye believe in God, believe also in me. "In my Father's house are many mansions: if it were not so, I would have told you. I go to prepare a place for you."

I Will Come Again, and Receive You unto Myself; Where I Am, There Ye May Be Also

"And if I go and prepare a place for you, I will come again, and receive you unto myself: that where I am, there ye may be also.
"And whither I go ye know, and the way ye know."

Christ Is the Way, the Truth, and the Life

Thomas saith unto him, Lord we know not whither thou goest; and how can we know the way?

Jesus saith unto him, *"I am the way, the truth, and the life: no man cometh unto the Father, but by me."*

Part VIII – The Lord's Supper: Farewell Address: Crucifixion and Resurrection

Christ is in the Father: To See Christ is to See God

"If ye had known me, ye should have known my Father also: and from heneceforth ye know him, and have seen him."

Philip saith unto him, Lord, shew us the Father, and it sufficeth us.

Jesus saith unto him, *"Have I been so long time with you, and yet hast thou not known me, Philip? He that hath seen me hath seen the Father; and how sayest thou then, Shew us the Father?*

"Believest thou not that I am in the Father, and the Father in me? the words that I speak unto you I speak not of myself: but the Father that welleth in me, he doeth the works.

"Believe me that I am in the Father, and the Father in me: or else believe me for the very works' sake.

"Verily, verily, I say unto you, He that believeth on me, the works that I do shall he do also; and greater works than these shall he do; because I go unto my Father."

If You Will Ask Anything in My Name, I Will Do It

"And whatsoever ye shall ask in my name, that will I do, that the Father may be glorified in the son.

"If ye shall ask anything in my name, I will do it."

Part VIII – The Lord's Supper: Farewell Address: Crucifixion and Resurrection

If You Love Me, Keep My Commandments

"If ye love me, keep my commandments.

"He that hath my commandments; and keepeth them, he it is that loveth me: and he that loveth me shall be loved of my Father, and I will love him, and will manifest myself to him."

Judas saith unto him, not Iscariot, Lord, how is it that thou wilt manifest thyself unto us, and not unto the world?

Jesus answered and said unto him, *"If a man love me, he will keep my words: and my Father will love him, and we will come unto him, and make our abode with him.*

"He that loveth me not keepeth not my sayings: and the word which ye hear is not mine, but the Father's which sent me."

God Will Give Us Another Comforter, The Spirit of Truth, He Dwells With You and Shall Be in You

"And I will pray the Father, and he shall give you another Comforter, that he may abide with you for ever;

"Even the spirit of truth; whom the world cannot receive, because it seeth him not, neither knoweth him: but ye know him; for he dwelleth with you, and shall be in you.

"I will not leave you comfortless: I will come to you. "Yet a little while, and the world seeth me no more; but ye see me: because I live, ye shall live also.

Part VIII – The Lord's Supper: Farewell Address: Crucifixion and Resurrection

I Am in My Father and You in Me and I in You

"At that day ye shall know that I am in my Father, and ye in me, and I in you.
"These things have I spoken unto you, being yet present with you.

"But the Comforter, which is the Holy Ghost, whom the Father will send in my name, he shall teach you all things, and bring all things to your remembrance, whatsoever I have said unto you.

Peace I Leave With You

"Peace I leave with you, my peace I give unto you: not as the world giveth, give I unto you, let not your heart be troubled, neither let it be afraid."

I Go Unto the Father: The Father is Greater Than I

"Ye have heard how I said unto you, I go away, and come again unto you. If ye loved me, ye would rejoice, because I said, I go unto the Father: for my Father is greater than I."

As the Father Gave Me Commandments Even So I Do

"And now I have told you before it come to pass, that, when it is come to pass, ye might believe.

"Hereafter I will not talk much with you: for the prince of this world cometh, and hath nothing in me.

"But that the world may know that I love the Father; and as the Father gave me commandment, even so I do. Arise, let us go hence."

Part VIII – The Lord's Supper: Farewell Address: Crucifixion and Resurrection

Abide in Me and I in You

"I am the true vine, and my Father is the husbandman. "Every branch in me that beareth not fruit, he taketh away: and every branch that beareth fruit, he purgeth it, that it may bring forth more fruit.

"Now ye are clean through the word which I have spoken unto you.

"Abide in me, and I in you. As the branch cannot bear fruit of itself, except it abide in the vine: no more can ye, except ye abide in me.

"I am the vine, ye are the branches: He that abideth in me, and I in him, the same bringeth forth much more fruit: for without me ye can do nothing.

"If a man abide not in me, he is cast forth as a branch, and is withered; and men gather them, and cast them into the fire, and they are burned.

"If ye abide in me, and my words abide in you, ye shall ask what ye will, and it shall be done unto you."

You Shall Be My Disciples—That You Bear Much Fruit Herein Is My Father Glorified

"Herein is my Father glorified, that ye bear much fruit; so ye shall be my disciples."

Part VIII – The Lord's Supper: Farewell Address: Crucifixion and Resurrection

<u>If You Keep My Commandments You Shall Abide in My Love</u>

"As the Father hath loved me, so have I loved you: continue ye in my love.

"If ye keep my commandments, ye shall abide in my love; even as I have kept my Father's commandments, and abide in his love.

"These things have I spoken unto you, that my joy might remain in you, and that your joy might be full.

"This is my commandment, That ye love one another, as I have loved you.

"Greater love hath no man than this, that a man lay down his life for his friends.

"Ye are my friends, if ye do whatsoever I command you."

<u>All Things That I Have Heard of My Father I Have Made Known Unto You</u>

"Hence forth I call you not servants; for the servant knoweth not what his Lord doeth: but I have called you friends; for all things that I have heard of my Father I have made known unto you."

<u>Christ Has Chosen His Disciples and Ordains Them</u>

"Ye have not chosen me, but I have chosen you, and ordained you, that ye should go and bring forth fruit, and that your fruit should remain: that whatsoever ye shall ask of the Father in my name, he may give it you.

"These things I command you, that ye love one another."

Part VIII – The Lord's Supper: Farewell Address: Crucifixion and Resurrection

You Are Not of This World

"If the world hate you, ye know that it hated me before it hated you.

"If ye were of the world, the world would love his own: but because ye are not of the world, but I have chosen you out of the world, therefore the world hateth you."

The Servant is Not Greater Than His Lord

"Remember the word that I said unto you, The servant is not greater than his lord. If they have persecuted me, they will also persecute you; if they have kept my saying, they will keep your's also.

"But all these things will they do unto you for my name's sake, because they know not him that sent me,

"If I had not come and spoken unto them, they had not had sin: but now they have no cloke for their sin.

He That Hates Me Hates The Father

"He that hateth me hateth my Father also.

"If I had not done among them the works which none other man did, they had not had sin: but now have they both seen and hated both me and my Father.

"But this cometh to pass, that the word might be fulfilled that is written in their law, They hated me without a cause."

You Have Been with Jesus from the Beginning You Also Shall Bear Witness

"But when the Comforter is come, whom I will send unto you from the Father, even the Spirit of truth, which proceedeth from the Father, he shall testify of me:

"And ye also shall bear witness, because ye have been with me from the beginning.

Part VIII – The Lord's Supper: Farewell Address: Crucifixion and Resurrection

People Will Do Things unto You for They Have Not Known the Father Nor Me

"These things have I spoken unto you, that ye should not be offended.

"They shall put you out of the synagogues: yea, the time cometh, that whosoever killeth you will think that he doeth God service.

"And these things will they do unto you, because they have not known the Father, nor me."

These Things I Said Not unto You at the Beginning Because I Was with You

"But these things have I told you, that when the time shall come, ye may remember that I told you of them. And these things

I said not unto you at the beginning, because I was with you. "But now I go my way to him that sent me; and none of you asketh me, Whither goest thou?

"But because I have said these things unto you, sorrow hath filled your heart.

"Nevertheless I tell you the truth; It is expedient for you that I go away: for if I go not away, the Comforter will not come unto you; but if I depart, I will send him unto you.

"And when he is come, he will reprove the world of sin, and of righteousness, and of judgment.

"Of sin, because they believe not on me;
"Of righteousness, because I go to my Father, and ye see me no more;
"Of judgment, because the prince of this world is judged. "I have yet many things to say unto you, but ye cannot bear them now.

Part VIII – The Lord's Supper: Farewell Address: Crucifixion and Resurrection

"Howbeit when he, the Spirit of truth is come, he will guide you into all truth; for he shall not speak of himself; but whatsoever he shall hear; that shall he speak: and he will show you things to come.

"He shall glorify me: for he shall receive of mine, and shall shew it unto you."

All Things That the Father Has Are Mine

"All things that the Father hath are mine: therefore said I, that he shall take of mine, and shall shew it unto you."

I Came from the Father and Go to the Father

"A little while and ye shall not see me: and again, a little while, and ye shall see me, because I go to the Father."

Then said some of his disciples among themselves, What is this that he saith unto us, "A little while, and ye shall not see me: and again, a little while, and ye shall see me: and, because I go to the Father?"

They said therefore, What is this that he saith, A little while? We cannot tell what he saith.

Now Jesus knew that they were desirous to ask him, and said unto them, *"Do ye enquire among yourselves of that I said,*

A little while, and ye shall not see me: and again, a little while, and ye shall see me?

"Verily, verily, I say unto you, That ye shall weep and lament, but the world shall rejoice: and ye shall be sorrowful, but your sorrow shall be turned into joy.

Part VIII – The Lord's Supper: Farewell Address: Crucifixion and Resurrection

"A woman when she is in travail hath sorrow, because her hour is come: but as soon as she is delivered of the child, she remembereth no more the anguish, for joy that a man is born into the world.

"And ye now therefore have sorrow: but I will see you again, and your heart shall rejoice, and your joy no man taketh from you.

"And in that day ye shall ask me nothing. Verily, verily, I say unto you, Whatsoever ye shall ask the Father in my name, he will give it you.

"Hitherto have ye asked nothing in my name: ask, and ye shall receive, that your joy may be full.

"These things have I spoken unto you in proverbs: but the time cometh, when I shall no more speak unto you in proverbs, but I shall shew you plainly of the Father.

"At that day ye shall ask in my name: and I say not unto you, that I will pray the Father for you:

"For the Father himself loveth you, because ye have loved me, and have believed that I came out from God.

"I came forth from the Father, and am come into the world: again, I leave the world, and go to the Father."

Part VIII – The Lord's Supper: Farewell Address: Crucifixion and Resurrection

I am Not Alone Because the Father Is With Me

His disciples said unto him, Lo, now speakest thou plainly, and speakest no proverb.

Now are we sure that thou knowest all things, and needest not that any man should ask thee: by this we believe that thou camest forth from God.

Jesus answered them, *"Do ye now believe?*

"Behold; the hour cometh, yea, is now come, that ye shall be scattered, every man to his own, and shall leave me alone: and yet I am not alone, because the Father is with me.

"These things I have spoken unto you, that in me ye might have peace. In the world ye shall have tribulation: but be of good cheer, I have overcome the world."

"Father, Glorify Thy Son, The Hour is Come"

These words spake Jesus, and lifted up his eyes to heaven, and said,
"Father, the hour is come; glorify thy Son, that thy son also may glorify thee:"

Christ Has Power Over All Flesh: Given by His Father

"As thou has given him power over all flesh, that he should give eternal life to as many as thou hast given him."

This is Eternal Life, That They Know the Father the Only True God

"And this is life eternal, that they might know thee the only true God, and Jesus Christ, whom thou hast sent."

Part VIII – The Lord's Supper: Farewell Address: Crucifixion and Resurrection

Christ Finishes the Work Given Him on Earth

"I have glorified thee on the earth: I have finished the work which thou gavest me to do."

Christ Asks God for the Glory He Had with Him before the World Was

"And now, O Father, glorify thou me with thine own self with the glory which I had with thee before the world was.

"I have manifested thy name unto the men which thou gavest me out of the world: thine they were, and thou gavest them me; and they have kept thy word."

"Now they have known that all things whatsoever thou hast given me are of thee."

Christ Gave Us the Words that God Gave to Him

"For I have given unto them the words which thou gavest me; and they have received them, and have known surely that I came out from thee, and they have believed that thou didst send me."

Jesus' Prayer For His Disciples

Christ Prays for Those Given to Him by God that They Too Might Be Sanctified through the Truth

"I pray for them: I pray not for the world, but for them which thou hast given me; for they are thine.

"And all mine are thine, and thine are mine: and I am glorified in them.

"And now I am no more in the world, but these are in the world, and I come to thee. Holy Father, keep through thine own name those whom thou hast given me, that they may be one, as we are.

Part VIII – The Lord's Supper: Farewell Address: Crucifixion and Resurrection

"While I was with them in the world, I kept them in thy name; those that thou gavest me I have kept, and none of them is lost, but the son of perdition; that the scripture might be fulfilled.

"And now come I to thee; and these things I speak in the world, that they might have my joy fulfilled in themselves.

"I have given them thy word; and the world hath hated them, because they are not of the world, even as I am not of the

world,

"I pray not that thou shouldest take them out of the world, but that thou shouldest keep them from the evil.

"They are not of the world, even as I am not of the world. "Sanctify them through thy truth. Thy word is truth.

"As thou hast sent me into the world, even so have I also sent them into the world.

"And for their sakes I sanctify myself, that they also might be sanctified through the truth.

Jesus Prays for Those that Believe on Him Through Their Word: That They May Be One with God and Christ

"Neither pray I for these alone, but for them also which shall believe on me through their word;

"That they all may be one; as thou, Father, art in me, and I in thee, that they also may be one in us: that the world may believe that thou hast sent me.

"And the glory which thou gavest me I have given them; that they may be one, even as we are one:

Part VIII – The Lord's Supper: Farewell Address: Crucifixion and Resurrection

"I in them, and thou in me, that they may be made perfect in one; and that the world may know that thou hast sent me and hast loved them, as thou hast loved me.

"Father, I will that they also, whom thou hast given me, be with me where I am; that they may behold my glory, which thou hast given me: for thou lovedst me before the foundation of the world."

"O righteous Father, the world hath not know thee: but I have known thee, and these have known that thou hast sent me. "And I have declared unto them thy name, and will declare it: that the love wherewith thou hast loved me may be in them, and I in them."

When Jesus had spoken these words and they had sung an hymn he went forth with his disciples over the brook Cedron, where was a garden, into the which he entered, and his disciples.

NOTES: Scriptures of the Topics	Luke	John
- Christ is glorified, and God is glorified in Him		13:31,32
- Christ addresses his disciples as little children		13:33
- A new commandment: love one another as I loved you		13:34,35
- Peter desires to follow Christ: Jesus sees Peter's denial	22:34-38	13:36,38
- In My Father's house there are many mansions; Christ Jesus goes to prepare a place for you		14:1,2
- I will come again, and receive you unto Myself where I am, there ye may be also		14:3,4
- Christ is the way, the Truth, and the Life		14:6

Part VIII – The Lord's Supper: Farewell Address: Crucifixion and Resurrection

	John
- Christ is in the Father: to see Christ is to see God	14:7,9-12
- If you will ask anything in My name, I will do it	14:13,14
- If you love me, keep My commandments	14:15,21,23,24
- God will give us another Comforter, the Spirit of Truth; he dwells with you and shall be in you	14:16-19,26
- I am in My Father and you in Me and I in you	14:20,25,26
- Peace I leave with you	14:27
- I go unto the Father: the Father is greater than I	14:28
- As the Father gave Me commandments even so I do	14:29-31
- Abide in me and I in you	15:1-7
- You shall be My disciples—that you bear much fruit herein is My Father glorified	15:8
- If you keep my commandments you shall abide in my love	15:9,10-14,17
- All things that I have heard of My Father I have made known unto you	1 5:15
- Christ has chosen His disciples and ordains them	15:15,16
- You are not of this world	15:18,19
- The servant is not greater than his Lord	15:20-22
- He that hates Me hates the Father	15:23-25
- When the Comforter is come He shall testify of Me	15:26
- You have been with Jesus from the beginning, you also shall bear witness	15:27
- People will do things unto you for they have not known the Father nor Me	16:1-3
- These things I said not unto you at the beginning because I was with you	16:4

Part VIII – The Lord's Supper: Farewell Address: Crucifixion and Resurrection

	<u>John</u>
- I go My way to Him that sent Me	16:5-12
- When the Spirit of truth comes He will guide you into all truth	16:13,14
- All things that the Father has are Mine	16:15
- I came from the Father and go to the Father	16:16-28
- I am not alone because the Father is with me	16:31,32,33
- Father, glorify thy Son, the hour is come	17:1
- Christ has power over all flesh; given by His Father	17:2
- This is eternal life, that they know the Father, the only true God	17:3
- Christ finishes the work given him on Earth	17:4
- Christ asks God for the glory He had with Him before the world was	17:5-7
- Christ gave us the words that God gave to Him	17:8
Jesus' Prayer For His Disciples:	
- Christ prays for those given to Him by God	17:9-19
- Jesus prays for those that believe on Him through their word: that they may be one with God and Christ	17:20-26

Part VIII – The Lord's Supper: Farewell Address: Crucifixion and Resurrection

Doctrines and Commandments

47.   *"Verily, verily, I say unto you, He that heareth my word, and believeth on him that sent me, hath everlasting life, and shall not come into condemnation, but is passed from death unto life.*

"Search the scriptures; for in them ye think ye have eternal life: and they are they which testify of me.

"And ye will not come to me, that ye might have life. I receive not honour from men.

"But I know you, that ye have not the love of God in you.

"And this is the will of him that sent me, that everyone which seeth the son, and believeth on him, may have everlasting life: and I will raise him up at the last day.

"Labour not for the meat which perisheth, but for that meat which endureth unto everlasting life, which the Son of man shall give unto you: for him hath God the Father sealed.

"Verily, verily, I say unto you, If a man keep my saying, he shall never see death.

"He that loveth his life shall lose it; and he that hateth his life in this world shall keep it unto life eternal.

"And if I go and prepare a place for you, I will come again, and receive you unto myself; that where I am, there ye may be also.

"All things that the Father hath are mine: therefore said I, that he shall take of mine, and shall shew it unto you.

"As thou hast given him power over all flesh, that he should give eternal life to as many as thou hast given him.

"And this is life eternal, that they might know thee the only true God, and Jesus Christ, whom thou hast sent.

"And as Moses lifted up the serpent in the wilderness, even so must the Son of man be lifted up: That whosoever believeth in him should not perish but have everlasting life.

"And no man hath ascended up to heaven, but he that came down from heaven, even the Son of man which is in heaven."

409.   <u>We may dwell in Christ: Christ may dwell in us.</u> *"Abide in me, and I in you. As the branch cannot bear fruit of itself, except it abide in the vine; no more can ye, except ye abide in me. And I have declared unto them thy name, and will declare it: that the love wherewith thou hast loved me maybe in them, and I in them. At that day ye shall know that I am in my Father, and ye in me, and I in you."*

Part VIII – The Lord's Supper: Farewell Address: Crucifixion and Resurrection

410. <u>How do we come unto Christ?</u> God must draw us to Christ.

"I have manifested thy name unto the men which thou gavest me out of the world: thine they were, and thou gavest them me, and they have kept thy word. I pray for them; I pray not for the world, but for them which thou hast given me; for they are thine."

411. <u>Has any man seen the Father?</u> *"If ye had known me, ye should have known my Father also; and from henceforth ye know him, and have seen him."*

412. <u>Christ's commandments.</u> Are not His but His Father's in heaven, who sent Him. Anyone who does God's will shall know Christ's doctrines. Whether the doctrines be of God or about Christ himself.

"But that the world may know that I love the Father; and as the Father gave me commandments, even so I do.

"A new commandment I give unto you, that ye love one another; as I have loved you, that ye also love one another.

"By this shall all men know that ye are my disciples, if ye have love one to another.

"If ye love me, keep my commandments.

"If ye keep my commandments, ye shall abide in my love; even as I have kept my Father's commandments, and abide in His love.

This is my commandment, that ye love one another, as I have loved you."

252. <u>Christ and I am.</u> *"Believe me that I am in the Father, and the Father in Me: or else believe me for the very works sake.*

"I am the way, the truth, and the life: no man cometh unto the Father, but my me.

"That where I am, there ye may be also: And if I go and prepare a place for you, I will come again, and receive you unto myself:

"At that day ye shall know that I am in my Father, and ye in me, and I in you.

"I am the true vine, and my Father is the husbandman.

"And now I am no more in the world, but these are in the world, and I come to thee. Holy Father, keep through thine own name those whom thou hast given me, that they may be one, as we are."

413. <u>Christ goes to the Father, God.</u> *"Little children, yet a little while I am with you. Ye shall seek me: and as I said unto the Jews, whither I go, ye cannot come; so now I say to you. Ye have heard how I said unto you, I go away, and come again unto you. If ye loved me, ye would rejoice, because I said, I go unto the Father: For my Father is greater than I."*

Part VIII – The Lord's Supper: Farewell Address: Crucifixion and Resurrection

"But now I go my way to Him that sent me; and none of you asketh me, Whither goest thou?

"I came forth from the Father, and am come into the world: again, I leave the world, and go to the Father."

414.   How do we know Chirst: How do we know God?

"If ye had known me, ye should have known my Father also: and from henceforth ye know him, and have seen him. And this is life eternal, that they might know thee the only true God, and Jesus Christ, whom thou hast sent."

241.   We were with Christ in the Beginning. *"But these things have I told you, that when the time shall come, ye may remember that I told you of them. And these things I said not unto you at the beginning, because I was with you.*

"And ye also shall bear witness, because ye have been with me from the beginning.

"As thou hast sent me into the world, even so I also sent them into the world."

268.   Christ Jesus tells us those things that he hears and sees from

his Father, God. *"Henceforth I call you not servants; for the servant knowest not what his lord doeth: but I have called you friends; for all things that I have heard of my Father I have made known unto you.*

"Now they have known that all things whatsoever thou hast given me are of thee.

"For I have given unto them the words which thou gavest me, and they have received them, and have known surely that I came out from thee, and they have believed that thou didst send me."

242.   God is true (Truth) *"Sanctify them through thy truth: thy word is truth."*
"And for their sakes I sanctify myself, that they also might be sanctified through the truth."

415.   Who are Christ's Disciples? How are they chosen?

"By this shall all men know that ye are my disciples, if ye have love for one to another.

"Now ye are clean through the word which I have spoken unto you. I am the vine, ye are the branches: He that abideth in me, and I in him, the same bringeth forth much fruit: for without me ye can do nothing. Herein is my Father glorified, that ye bear much fruit; so shall ye be my disciples.

Part VIII – The Lord's Supper: Farewell Address: Crucifixion and Resurrection

"Ye have not chosen me, but I have chosen you, and ordained you, that ye should go and bring forth fruit, and that your fruit should remain: that whatsoever ye shall ask of the Father in my name, he may give it you."

416. <u>God's commandments</u>: See Doctrines 30 and 419. Our Father's will (412) Christ's commandments.

"But that the world may know that I love the Father; and as the Father gave me commandment, even so I do.

"He that loveth me not, keepeth not my sayings: and the word which ye hear is not mine, but the Father's which sent me.

"If ye keep my commandments, ye shall abide in my love; even as I have kept my Father's commandments, and abide in his love."

417. <u>We may be one with God and Christ</u>. Jesus claims each of us as his own through our belief on Him through our word.

He prays not only for His disciples, *"But for them also,"* meaning each one of us, *"which shall believe on me through their word,"* (John. 17:20) This is what he prays to our Heavenly Father about:

"That they may be one; as thou, Father, art in me, and I in thee, that they also may be one in us: that the world may believe that thou hast sent me." (Jn 17:21)

Jesus also has given us the same "glory" that God the Father has given to him, Jesus. Jesus in his prayer to God says, *"And the glory which thou gavest me I have given them; that they may be one, even as we are one:"* (John.17:22)

"I in them, and thou in me, that they may be made perfect in one: and that the world may know that thou hast sent me and hast loved them, as thou hast loved me."

418. <u>Christ is glorified, and God is glorified in Him</u>.

"Now is the Son of man glorified, and God is glorified in Him. And whatsoever ye shall ask in my name, that will I do, that the Father may be glorified in the Son."

"If God be glorified in him, God shall also glorify Him in Himself, and shall straightway glorify Him. "Father, the hour is come; glorify thy Son, that thy Son also may glorify thee.

"I have glorified thee on the earth: I have finished the work which thou gavest me to do.

"And now, O Father, glorify thou me with thine own self with the glory which I had with thee before the world was."

Part VIII – The Lord's Supper: Farewell Address: Crucifixion and Resurrection

419. <u>Our Father's will</u>: that his Son is sent to the world, that all which He gives to His Son—His Son should lose nothing, but should raise it up again at the last day.

"I have glorified thee on the earth: I have finished the work which thou gavest me to do.

"That everyone that seeth the Son, and believeth on Him, may have everlasting life: and Christ will raise him up at the last day."

Lessons We Should Learn

1.   This chapter holds the keys to the kingdom of God and His Son Christ Jesus. There are forty topics and more than that, many doctrines, commandments, and promises. It is the word of God told by His Son Jesus the Christ. It is the truth and the light and one may comprehend only that which God gives one to see. Pray first for His divine understanding and wisdom and take within yourself His word for it is thebread of life. May this bread of life nourish you unto thetrue manifestation of the child of God—one with Christ and one with our Heavenly Father that glory is unto the Father our God that His word is fulfilled by the prayer from His Son, Jesus the Christ.

2.   *"Father, I will that they also, whom thou hast given me, be with me where I am; that they may behold my glory, which thou hast given me: for thou lovest me before the foundation of the world."*

3.   *"O righteous Father, the world hast not known thee: but I have known thee, and these have known thy name, and will declare it: that the love wherewith thou hast loved me maybe in them, and I in them."* (See doctrine 417)

Part VIII – The Lord's Supper: Farewell Address: Crucifixion and Resurrection

My Thoughts About the Lessons

NOTES

Part VIII – The Lord's Supper: Farewell Address: Crucifixion and Resurrection

40

The Lord Prays to His Father at Gethsemane

After the Lord's Supper and his farewell address ended, they went out into the mount of Olives.

Then saith Jesus unto them, *"All ye shall be offended because of me this night: for it is written, I will smite the shepherd, and the sheep of the flock shall be scattered abroad.*

"But after I am risen again, I will go before you into Galilee."

Peter answered and said unto him, Though all men shall be offended because of thee, yet will I never be offended.

Jesus saith unto him, *"Verily I say unto thee, that this day, even this night, before the cock crow, thou shalt deny me thrice."*

Peter answered and said unto him, Though I should die with thee, yet will I not deny thee in any wise. Likewise also said all the disciples.

Then cometh Jesus with them unto a place called Gethsemane and saith unto the disciples,

"Sit ye here, while I go and pray yonder. Pray that ye enter not into temptation."

And he taketh with him Peter, James and John, and began to be sorrowful, and very heavy.

And saith unto them, *"My soul is exceeding sorrowful, even unto death: tarry ye here, and watch with me."*

Part VIII – The Lord's Supper: Farewell Address: Crucifixion and Resurrection

And he was withdrawn from them about a stone's cast, and kneeled down, and prayed that if it were possible, the hour might pass from him, and fell on his face the ground, and prayed, saying,

"O my Father, Abba, Father, all things are possible unto thee; if it be possible, if thou be willing remove this cup from me: let this cup pass from me; if this cup may not pass away from me except I drink it, thy will be done; nevertheless not what I will, but what thou wilt, be done."

And there appeared an angel unto him from heaven, strengthening him.

And being in an agony he prayed more earnestly: and his sweat was as it were great drops of blood falling down to the ground.

And when he rose up from prayer, and was come to his disciples, he found them sleeping, for sorrow.

And said unto them, *"Why sleep ye? rise and pray, lest ye enter into temptation.*

And saith unto Peter, *"Simon, sleepeth thou? What, could ye not watch with me one hour?*

"Watch and pray, that ye enter not into temptation: the spirit indeed is willing, truly is ready, but the flesh is weak."

He went away again the second time, and prayed, saying,

"O my Father, if this cup may not pass away from me, except I drink it, thy will be done."

And when he returned, he found them asleep again: for their eyes were heavy.

And he left them, and went away again, and prayed the third time, saying the same words.

Then cometh he the third time, and saith unto them,

"Sleep on now, and take your rest: it is enough, behold the hour is come; is at hand. Behold, the Son of man is betrayed into the hands of sinners.

"Rise, let us be going: behold, he is at hand that doth betray me."

Part VIII – The Lord's Supper: Farewell Address: Crucifixion and Resurrection

The Betrayal by Judas

And while he yet spake, lo, Judas, one of the twelve, came, and with him a great multitude with swords and staves, from the chief priests and elders of the people.

Now he that betrayed him gave them a sign saying, Whomsoever I shall kiss, that same is he: hold him fast.

And Judas came to Jesus and said, Hail, master; and kissed him.

And Jesus said unto him, *"Friend wherefore art thou come? Judas betrayest thou the Son of man with a kiss?"*

Jesus therefore, knowing all things that should come upon him, went forth, and said unto them, *"Whom seek ye?"*

They answered him, Jesus of Nazareth.

Jesus saith unto them, *"I am he."*

As soon then as he said unto them, I am he, they went backward, and fell to the ground.

Then asked he them again, *"Whom seek ye?"*

And they said, Jesus of Nazareth. Jesus answered, *"I have told you that I am he: if therefore ye seek me, let these go their way:*

That the saying might be fulfilled, which he spake, *"Of them which thou gavest me I have lost none."*

When they which were about him saw what would follow, they said unto him, Lord, shall we smite with the sword?

Then Simon Peter having a sword drew it, and smote the high priest's servant, and cut off his right ear. The servant's name was Malchus.

And Jesus said, *"Suffer ye thus far."* And he touched his ear, and healed him.

Part VIII – The Lord's Supper: Farewell Address: Crucifixion and Resurrection

Then said Jesus unto Peter, *"Put up again thy sword, into his place, into the sheath: for all they that take the sword shall perish with the sword.*

"Thinkest thou that I cannot now pray to my Father, and he shall presently give me more than twelve legions of angels?

"But how then shall the scriptures be fulfilled, that thus it must be? The cup which my Father hath given me, shall I not drink it?"

In that same hour said Jesus to the multitudes, the chief priests, and captain of the temple, and the elders,

"Are ye come out as against a thief with swords and staves for to take me? I sat daily with you teaching you in the temple, and ye laid no hold on me: and ye took me not, but this is your hour, and the power of darkness.

"But all this was done, that the scriptures of the prophets must be fulfilled."

Then the band and the captain and officers of the Jews took Jesus and bound him.

Then all the disciples forsook him, and fled.

Part VIII – The Lord's Supper: Farewell Address: Crucifixion and Resurrection

NOTES: Scriptures of the Topics	Matt.	Mark	Luke	John
- The Lord prays to His Father at Gethsemane	26:36-46	22:39-46	14:27-42	13:37,38
- The betrayal by Judas	26:50-56	22:47-54	14:43-49	18:4-11

Doctrines and Commandments

420. Christ foretells the future; that we may know.

In these scriptures, Christ tells his disciples that, the sheep of the flock shall be scattered abroad.

"After I am risen again, I will go before you into Galilee."

Jesus tells Peter that before the cock crows, thou shall deny him thrice

421. Pray that you will not enter into temptation.

Christ gives this commandment to his disciples while he went to pray to his Father in heaven.

422. The Lord's prayer to his Father at Gethsemane.

"Father, all things are possible unto thee; take away this cup from me: nevertheless not what I will, but what thou wilt, be done."

"O my Father, if this cup may not pass away from me, except I drink it, thy will be done."

423. The spirit is indeed willing, truly is ready, but the flesh is weak.

The Lord found Peter and the disciples sleeping rather than praying and watching while Christ prayed to his Father.

424. The Son of man is betrayed into the hands of sinners.

All this was done that the scriptures of the prophets must be fulfilled.

425. All they that take the sword shall perish with the sword.

426. Christ's words and works came to pass that the laws and scriptures must be fulfilled.

Part VIII – The Lord's Supper: Farewell Address: Crucifixion and Resurrection

Lessons We Should Learn

1.   With these words of Christ, in this chapter, he told his disciples: that they would be scattered; that he will go to Galilee before them after he is killed and risen; and that Peter will deny him three times before the cock will crow. All of these events did happen exactly as told. Christ Jesus knows these things before they happened and he knows each of us as well as he knows these past events many years ago. Christ really does know our hearts. Several questions we must ask of ourselves: Are we keeping from repenting of our own secrets, that he already knows? Are we being lukewarm in our belief, our trust, and our love for Him?

2.   Daily prayer to our Heavenly Father is the answer to overcome temptation. We may have a weakness of the flesh or something that is tempting us to sin. Go in prayer to God for our help and the answers.

3.   The Lord prayed to our Father, God, at Gethsemane; He prayed not for His life, or His wants, His needs or His desires: He prayed that God's will be done; not his own will. Right to the end Christ Jesus gave his all to his Father in Heaven and the scriptures of the prophets were fulfilled.

4.   They who take the sword shall perish by the sword; the problem is today the sword has advanced to awesome weapons. In today's world, nations are being destroyed by this very law. When will we learn a simple doctrine of truth and apply it to our everyday lives?

5.   Christ Jesus, in his final hours in the world, is betrayed into the hands of sinners who scorned, mocked and tortured him unto death. The very people that Christ came to help; even his beloved disciples betrayed him—except his mother— God bless mothers!

Christ loved his enemies right to the end and forgave them and prayed for them. He fulfilled his words, his doctrines and his commandments. *"Love thy neighbor and thy enemy as thy self."* His Father's will is done and fulfilled!

Part VIII – The Lord's Supper: Farewell Address: Crucifixion and Resurrection

My Thoughts About the Lessons

_____

_____

_____

_____

_____

_____

_____

_____

_____

_____

_____

_____

_____

_____

_____

_____

_____

_____

_____

_____

_____

_____

_____

_____

_____

NOTES

Part VIII – The Lord's Supper: Farewell Address: Crucifixion and Resurrection

41

The Trial of Jesus and His Condemnation

He is Brought before Annas First: Peter's First Denial

The Jews led him away to Annas first; for he was father in law to Caiaphas, which was the high priest that same year.

Now Caiaphas was he, which gave counsel to the Jews, that it was expedient that one man should die for the people.

And Simon Peter followed Jesus, and so did another disciple: that disciple was known unto the high priest, and went in with Jesus into the palace of the high priest.

But Peter stood at the door without. Then went out that other disciple, which was known unto the high priest, and spake unto her that kept the door, and brought in Peter.

Then saith the damsel that kept the door unto Peter, Art not thou also one of this man's disciples? He saith, I am not.

And the servants and officers stood there, who had made a fire of coals; for it was cold: and they warmed themselves: and Peter stood with them, and warmed himself.

The high priest then asked Jesus of his disciples, and of his doctrine.

Jesus answered him, *"I spake openly to the world; I ever taught in the synagogue, and in the temple, whither the Jews always resort; and in secret have I said nothing. "Why asketh thou me? ask them which heard me, what I have said unto them: behold, they know what I said."*

And when he had thus spoken, one of the officers which stood by struck Jesus with the palm of his hand, saying, Answerest thou the high priest so?

Part VIII – The Lord's Supper: Farewell Address: Crucifixion and Resurrection

Jesus answered him, *"If I have spoken evil, bear witness of the evil: but if well, why smitest thou me?"*

Jesus Vows His Messiahship and Godhead

He is Brought Before Caiaphas the High Priest: Peter's second and third denial

Now Annas had sent him bound unto Caiaphas the high priest. And Simon Peter stood and warmed himself. They said therefore unto him, Art not thou also one of his disciples? He denied it, and said, I am not.

One of the servants of the high priest, being his kinsman whose ear Peter cut off, saith, Did not I see thee in the garden with him?

Peter then denied again. And immediately while he yet spake, the cock crew.

And the Lord turned, and looked upon Peter. And Peter remembered the words of the Lord.

And Peter went out and wept bitterly.

And the man that held Jesus mocked him, and smote him. When they had blindfolded him, they struck him on the face, and asked him, saying, Prophesy, who is it that smote thee?

And many other things blasphemously spake they against him. And as soon as it was day he was led before the council, of the chief priests, elders and scribes, and they asked, Art thou the Christ? Tell us.

And he said unto them, *"If I tell you, ye will not believe:*

"And if I also ask you, ye will not answer me, nor let me go.

"Hereafter shall the Son of man sit on the right hand of the power of God."

Part VIII – The Lord's Supper: Farewell Address: Crucifixion and Resurrection

And said they all, Art thou then the Son of God? Art thou the Christ, the Son of the Blessed?

And he said unto them,

"Ye say that I am: Nevertheless I say unto you, I am: Hereafter shall ye see the Son of man sitting on the right hand of power, and coming in the clouds of heaven."

And they said, what need we any further witness? For we ourselves have heard of his own mouth. And they all condemned him to be guilty of death.

Jesus is Brought before Pilate for Sentence of Crucifixion

They led then Jesus from Caiaphas unto the hall of judgment: and it was early; and they themselves went not into the judgment hall lest they should be defiled; but that they might eat the passover.

Pontius Pilate the governor, then went out unto them, and said, What accusation bring ye against this man?

They answered and said unto him, If he were not a malefactor, we would not have delivered him up unto thee.

Then said Pilate unto them, Take ye him, and judge him according to your law. The Jews therefore said unto him, It is not lawful for us to put any man to death:

That the saying of Jesus might be fulfilled, which he spake, signifying what death he should die.

Then Pilate entered into the judgment hall again, and called Jesus, and said unto him, Art thou the king of the Jews?

Jesus answered him, *"Sayest thou this thing of thyself, or did others tell it thee of me?"*

Part VIII – The Lord's Supper: Farewell Address: Crucifixion and Resurrection

Pilate said, Am I a Jew? Thine own nation and chief priests have delivered thee unto me: what hast thou done?

Jesus answered, *"My kingdom is not of this world: if my kingdom were of this world, then would my servants fight, that I should not be delivered to the Jews: but now is my kingdom not from hence."*

And Pilate asked him, Art thou the king of the Jews? Art thou a king then?

Jesus answered, *"Thou sayest it, thou sayest I am a king. To this end was I born, and for this cause came I into the world, that I should bear witness unto the truth. Everyone that is of the truth heareth my voice."*

Pilate saith unto him, What is truth? And when he had said this, he went out again unto the Jews and saith unto them, I find in him no fault at all.

No, nor yet Herod: for I sent you to him; and lo, nothing worthy of death is done unto him but ye have a custom, that I should release unto you one at the Passover: will ye therefore that I release unto you the King of the Jews?

Then cried they all again, saying, Not this man, but Barabbas; Now Barabbas was a robber.

Then Pilate therefore took Jesus and scourged him.

And the soldiers platted a crown of thorns and put it on his head, and they put on him a purple robe.

And said, Hail, King of the Jews! And they smote him with their hands.

Pilate went forth again, saying, Behold, I bring him forth to you, that ye may know that I find no fault in him.

Then came Jesus forth, wearing the crown of thorns, and the purple robe, and Pilate said, Behold the man!

Part VIII – The Lord's Supper: Farewell Address: Crucifixion and Resurrection

When the chief priests therefore and officers saw him, they cried out, saying, Crucify him. Pilate saith unto them, Take ye him, and crucify him, for I find no fault in him.

The Jews answered him, We have a law, and by our law he ought to die, because he made himself the Son of God.

When Pilate therefore heard that saying, he was the more afraid;

And went again into the judgment hall, and saith unto Jesus, Whence art thou? But Jesus gave him no answer.

Then saith Pilate unto him, Speaketh thou not unto me? Knowest thou not that I have power to crucify thee, and power to release thee?

Jesus answered, *"Thou couldest have no power at all against me, except it were given thee from above: therefore he that delivered me unto thee hath the greater sin."*

And from thenceforth Pilate sought to release him. And he said unto them the third time, Why, what evil hath he done? I have found no cause of death in him: I will therefore chastise him, and let him go.

But the Jews cried out saying, If thou let this man go, thou art not Caesar's friend: whosoever maketh himself a king speaketh against Caesar.

When Pilate therefore heard that saying, he brought Jesus forth and sat down in the judgment seat in a place called the Pavement, but in Hebrew, Gabbatha.

And it was the preparation of the Passover, and about the sixth hour: and he saith unto the Jews, Behold your King!

But they cried out, Away with him, away with him, crucify him. Pilate saith, Shall I crucify your King? The chief priests answered, We have no king but Caesar.

Then delivered he him therefore unto them to be crucified. And Pilate gave sentence that it should be as they required. And they took Jesus and led him away.

Part VIII – The Lord's Supper: Farewell Address: Crucifixion and Resurrection

NOTES: Scriptures of the Topics	Mark	Luke	John
- Jesus is brought before Annas			18:20-23
first: Peter's first denial			18:27
- Jesus vows his Messiahship and Godhead. He is brought before Caiaphas the High Priest. Peter's second and third denials.	14:62	22:67-70	18:24,27
- Jesus is brought before Pilate for sentence of crucifixion	15:2		18:34-37
			19:11

Doctrines and Commandments

427. Christ Jesus spoke openly about his doctrines to the world, and in secret he said nothing.

428. Hereafter the Son of man sits on the right hand of the power of God, and coming in the clouds of heaven.

429. Christ's kingdom is not of this world.

"If my kingdom were of this world, then would my servants fight, that I should not be delivered to the Jews."

430. Christ Jesus came into the world that he should bear witness unto the truth, to this end he was born. Jesus says, *"Every one that is of the truth heareth my voice."*

431. One could have no power at all against Christ Jesus, except it were given thee from above.

Part VIII – The Lord's Supper: Farewell Address: Crucifixion and Resurrection

Lessons We Should Learn

1.   Christ Jesus spoke openly to the people about his beliefs and doctrines. Everything that he hears and sees from his Father, he tells us. He had an open communication with his Father in heaven and the people. In this self-giving he received. One must realize that there are greater blessings to give than to receive.

2.   Christ foretells mankind that his kingdom is not of this world and that he will enter into his glory and sit on the right hand of the power of God and coming in the clouds of heaven. He knows that he must fulfill the will of his Father and it must come to pass that the laws and scriptures must be fulfilled; for he knows all things before they happen.

3.   Christ is the manifestation, and the fulfillment of the word of God. All that he hears and sees is from his Heavenly Father. God's words are the truth and Christ Jesus came into the world that he should bear witness unto the truth. To know his words, beliefs, doctrines, and commandments is to know the truth; a true child of God. "Everyone that is of the truth hears his voice."

4.   One could have no power at all against Christ Jesus, except it were given you from above. For it is said in another doctrine that, "All power is given to Christ Jesus in heaven and in earth." Therefore, if one feels that they cannot overcome temptation and evil, your answer is to repent and go unto Christ. "Jesus sends the promise of his Father upon you, and you shall be endued with power from on high."

Part VIII – The Lord's Supper: Farewell Address: Crucifixion and Resurrection

My Thoughts About the Lessons

_____

_____

_____

_____

_____

_____

_____

_____

_____

_____

_____

_____

_____

_____

_____

_____

_____

_____

_____

_____

_____

_____

_____

_____

Part VIII – The Lord's Supper: Farewell Address: Crucifixion and Resurrection

42

The Christ is Crucified

Jesus Bears His Own Cross to the City Gate

And he bearing his cross went forth into a place called the place of a skull, which is called in Hebrew Golgotha.

And they compel one Simon a Cyrenian, who passed by, coming out of country, the father of Alexander and Rufus, to bear his cross.

And there followed him a great company of people, and of women, which also bewailed and lamented him.

But Jesus turning unto them, and said, *"Daughters of Jerusalem, weep not for me, but weep for yourselves, and for your children.*

"For, behold, the days are coming, in the which they shall say, Blessed are the barren, and the wombs that never bare, and paps which never gave suck, then shall they begin to say to the mountains, Fall on us; and to the hills, Cover us."

"For if they do these things in a green tree, what shall be done in the dry?"

And there were also two others, malefactors, led with him, to be put to death, at the place called Calvary.

Part VIII – The Lord's Supper: Farewell Address: Crucifixion and Resurrection

Crucified at Golgotha: Calvary

And they bring him unto the place Golgotha, to be put to death at the place called Calvary, there they crucified him, and the two malefactors, one on the right hand, and the other on the left.

Then said Jesus,

"Father, forgive them; for they know not what they do."

And they gave him to drink wine mingled with myrrh: but he received it not. And it was the third hour, and they crucified him.

And the superscription of his accusation was written over him,

THIS IS THE KING OF THE JEWS

The Pentinent Thief Promised Paradise

And one of the malefactors which was to be hanged railed on him, saying, If thou be Christ, save thyself and us.

But the other answering rebuked him, saying, Dost not thou fear God, seeing thou art in the same condemnation?

And we indeed justly; for we receive the due reward of our deeds: but this man hath done nothing amiss.

And he said unto Jesus, Lord, remember me when thou comest into thy kingdom.

And Jesus said unto him, *"Verily I say unto thee, To day shalt thou be with me in paradise."*

Part VIII – The Lord's Supper: Farewell Address: Crucifixion and Resurrection

His Garments Divided: He Commended His Mother To the Care of John

Then the soldiers, when they had crucified Jesus, took his garments, and made four parts, to every soldier a part; and also his coat: now the coat was without seam, woven from the top throughout.

They said therefore among themselves, Let us not rend it, but cast lots for it, whose shall it be: that the scriptures might be fulfilled, which saith, They parted my raiment among them, and for my vesture they did cast lots. These things therefore the soldiers did.

Now there stood by the cross of Jesus his mother, and his mother's sister, Mary the wife of Cleophas, and Mary Magdalene.

When Jesus therefore saw his mother, and the disciple standing by, whom he loved, he saith unto his mother, *"Woman, behold thy Son."*

Then saith he to the disciple, *"Behold thy mother!"* And from that hour that disciple took her unto his own home.

There Was Darkness Over All the Earth

And it was about the sixth hour, and there was a darkness over all the earth until the ninth hour.

And the sun was darkened, and the veil of the temple was rent in the midst.

Part VIII – The Lord's Supper: Farewell Address: Crucifixion and Resurrection

Christ Commands His Spirit to His Father

And at about the ninth hour Jesus cried with a loud voice, saying, *"Eli, Eli, lama sa-bach-tha-ni?"* which is being interpreted, *"My God, my God, why hast thou forsaken me?"*

And some of them that stood there, when they heard it, said, Behold, he calleth for Elias.

Jesus knowing that all things were now accomplished that the scripture might be fulfilled, saith, *"I thirst."*

And one ran and filled a spunge full of vinegar, and put it on a reed, and gave him to drink, saying, Let alone; let us see whether Elias will come to take him down.

When Jesus therefore had received the vinegar, he said,

"It is finished."

And when Jesus had cried with a loud voice, he said,

> *"Father into thy hands I commend my spirit:"*

and having said thus, and he bowed his head and gave up the ghost.

And behold, the veil of the temple was rent in twain from the top to the bottom; and the earth did quake, and the rocks rent;

And the graves were opened; and many bodies of the saints which slept arose, And came out of the graves after his resurrection, and went into the holy city, and appeared unto many.

Now when the centurion, and they that were with him, saw what was done, they glorified God, saying, Certainly this was a righteous man, truly, the Son of God.

Part VIII – The Lord's Supper: Farewell Address: Crucifixion and Resurrection

NOTES: Scriptures of the Topics	Matt	Mark	Luke	John
- Jesus bears His own cross to the city gate			23:28-31	
- Crucified at Golgotha: Calvary			23:33,34	
- The penitent thief promised paradise			23:43	
- His garments divided: He commended His mother to the care of John				19:26,27
- There was darkness over all the Earth			23:44,45	
- Christ commands His Spirit to His Father	27:46	15:34	23:46	19:28-30

Doctrines and Commandments

420. Christ foretells the future; that we may know.

426. Christ's words and works came to pass that the laws and scriptures might be fulfilled.

432. Jesus loves his mother to the end.

70. Jesus has power on earth to forgive sins.

Lessons We Should Learn

1.   Jesus foretells the future throughout the scriptures, so that we may know and have knowledge of things to come and as warnings. He did this as his sincere love and concern for us right to his death. While carrying His cross to Calvary He gave his last warning to the people of the world.

2.   Christ Jesus has power to forgive sins and if we repent our sins He can forgive them. One must recall that Jesus came not to call the righteous, but sinners to repentance and that our Heavenly Father commits all judgment to Christ Jesus. Also, those who pass from death unto life are those that hear Christ's words and believe God the Father who has sent Christ Jesus to us.

Part VIII – The Lord's Supper: Farewell Address: Crucifixion and Resurrection

3.   Christ Jesus showed the love that one had for their mother by speaking to her and honoring her and concerned about her well being unto his end. She was the last person that He addressed.

4.   Christ Jesus has told the people of the world many times in his words that he can resurrect his body. God the Father has given to the Son to have life in himself, therefore, He commanded his spirit into the hands of his Father from whom He came. By doing so, with His words and works it then came to pass that the laws and scriptures might be fulfilled.

5.   The great hope and promise that Jesus gives to God's children is that we can be with him in paradise and He has atoned for our sins, that we may be one with Him and God with everlasting life.

Part VIII – The Lord's Supper: Farewell Address: Crucifixion and Resurrection

My Thoughts About the Lessons

_____

_____

_____

_____

_____

_____

_____

_____

_____

_____

_____

_____

_____

_____

_____

_____

_____

_____

_____

_____

_____

_____

_____

_____

43

Christ's Resurrection: His Appearances
During Forty Days

Jesus Reveals Himself to Mary Magdalene; She Reports to the Disciples

But Mary stood without at the sepulchre weeping: and as she wept, she stooped down, and looked into the sepulchre,

And seeth two angels in white sitting, the one at the head, and the other at the feet, where the body of Jesus had lain.

And they say unto her, Woman, why weepest thou? She saith unto them, Because they have taken away my Lord, and I know not where they have laid him.

And when she had thus said, she turned herself back, and saw Jesus standing, and knew not that it was Jesus

Jesus saith unto her, *"Woman, why weepest thou? whom seekest thou?"* She, supposing him to be the gardener, saith unto him, Sir, if thou have borne him hence, tell me where thou hast laid him, and I will take him away.

Jesus saith unto her, *"Mary."* She turned herself, and saith unto him, Rabboni; which is to say, Master.

Jesus saith unto her, *"Touch me not; for I am not yet ascended to my Father: but go to my brethren, and say unto them, I ascend unto my Father, and your Father; and to my God, and your God."*

Mary Magdalene came and told the disciples that she had seen the Lord, and that he had spoken these things unto her.

Part VIII – The Lord's Supper: Farewell Address: Crucifixion and Resurrection

Jesus Meets with Mary Magdalene and Mary Mother of James

Mary Magdalene and the other Mary and the others came to see the sepulchre. And the angel answered and said unto the women, fear not ye: for I know that ye seek Jesus, which was crucified.

He is not here: for he is risen, remembering how he spake unto you when he was yet in Galilee, saying *"the Son of man must be delivered into the hands of sinful men, and be crucified, and the third day rise again,"* Come, see the place where the Lord lay.

And go quickly, and tell his disciples, that he is risen from the dead; and, behold, he goeth before you into Galilee; there shall ye see him: lo, I have told you.

And as they went to tell his disciples, behold, Jesus met them, saying, *"All hail."* And they came and held him by the feet, and worshipped him.

Then said Jesus unto them, *"Be not afraid: go tell my brethren that they go into Galilee, and there shall they see me."*

Jesus Appears to the Ten Disciples (Thomas being absent)

Then the same day at evening, being the first day of the week, when the doors were shut where the disciples were assembled for fear of the Jews, came Jesus and stood in the midst, and saith unto them, *"Peace be unto you."*

And when he had so said, he shewed unto them his hands and his side. Then were the disciples glad, when they saw the Lord.

Then said Jesus to them again, *"Peace be unto you: as my Father hath sent me, even so send I you."*

And when he had said this, he breathed on them, and saith unto them, *"Receive ye the Holy Ghost.*

"Whose soever sins ye remit, they are remitted unto them; and whose soever sins ye retain, they are retained."

Part VIII – The Lord's Supper: Farewell Address: Crucifixion and Resurrection

Jesus Converses With Two Disciples and They Don't Recognize Him

It was Mary Magdalene, and Joanna, and Mary the mother of James, and other woman that were with them, which told these things to the apostles.

And their words seemed to them as idle tales, and they believed them no.

Then arose Peter, and ran unto the sepulchre, and he beheld the linen clothes laid by themselves, and departed, wondering in himself at that which was come to pass.

And behold, two of them went that same day to a village called Emmaus, which was from Jerusalem about threescore furlongs.

And they talked together of all these things which had happened.

And it came to pass, that, while they communed together and reasoned, Jesus himself drew near, and went with them. But their eyes were holden that they should not know him.

And he said unto them, *"What manner of communications are these that ye have one to another, as ye walk, and are sad"*

And the one of them, whose name was Cleopas, answering said unto him, Art thou only a stranger in Jerusalem, and hast not known the things which are come to pass there in these days?

And he said unto them, *"What things?"* And they said unto him concerning Jesus of Nazareth, which was a prophet mighty indeed and word before God and all the people:

And how the Jews crucified him; and that certain women had seen a vision of angels, which said that he was alive.

And certain of them which were with us went to the sepulchre and found it even so as the woman had said: but Him they saw not.

Part VIII – The Lord's Supper: Farewell Address: Crucifixion and Resurrection

Then he said unto them, *"O fools, and slow of heart to believe all that the prophets have spoken:*

"Ought not Christ to have suffered these things, and to enter into his glory?"

And beginning with Moses and all the prophets, he expounded unto them in all the scriptures concerning himself.

They constrained him to stay with them: for it was toward evening. And he went into tarry with them.

And it came to pass, as he sat at meat with them, he took bread, and blessed it, and brake, and gave it to them.
And their eyes were opened, and they knew him; and he vanished out of their sight.

Jesus Appears to Eleven Disciples

And they rose up the same hour, and returned to Jerusalem, and found the eleven gathered together, and them that were with them,

Saying, the Lord is risen indeed, and hath appeared to Simon.

And they told what things were done in the way, and how he was known of them in breaking of bread.

And as they spake, Jesus himself stood in the midst of them, and saith unto them, *"Peace be unto you."*

But they were terrified and affrighted, and supposed that they had seen a spirit.
And he said unto them, *"Why are ye troubled? and why do thoughts arise in your hearts.*

"Behold, my hands and my feet, that it is I myself: handle me, and see; for a spirit hath not flesh and bones, as ye see me have."

Part VIII – The Lord's Supper: Farewell Address: Crucifixion and Resurrection

And when he had thus spoken, he shewed them his hands and his feet.

Then saith he to Thomas, *"Reach hither thy finger, and behold my hands; and reach hither thy hand, and thrust it into my side: and be not faithless, but believing."*

And Thomas answered and said unto him, My Lord and my God.

Jesus saith unto him, *"Thomas because thou hast seen me, thou hast believed: blessed are they that have not seen, and yet have believed."*

And while thy yet believed not for joy, and wondered, he said unto them, *"Have ye here any meat?"*

And they gave him a piece of a broiled fish, and an honeycomb.

And he took it, and did eat before them.

And he said unto them, *"These are the words which I spake unto you, while I was yet with you, that all things must be fulfilled, which were written in the law of Moses, and in the prophets, and in the psalms, concerning me."*

Then Jesus opened their understanding, that they might understand the scriptures.

And he said unto them,
"Thus it is written, and thus it behooved Christ to suffer, and to rise from the dead the third day: "And that repentance and remission of sins should be preached in his name among all nations, beginning at Jerusalem. "And ye are witnesses of these things.

"And, behold, I send the promise of my Father upon you: but tarry ye in the city of Jerusalem, until ye be endued with power from on high."

And many other signs truly did Jesus in the presence of his disciples, which are not written in this book:

Part VIII – The Lord's Supper: Farewell Address: Crucifixion and Resurrection

But these are written, that ye might believe that Jesus is the Christ, the Son of God; and that believing ye might have life through his name.

And he led them out as far as to Bethany, and he lifted up his hands, and blessed them.

And it came to pass, while he blessed them, he was parted from them and carried up into heaven.

And they worshipped him, and returned to Jerusalem with great joy:

And were continually in the temple, praising and blessing God. Amen.

Jesus Commands the Eleven to Teach all Nations

Then the eleven disciples went away into Galilee, into a mountain where Jesus had appointed them

And when they saw him, they worshipped him: but some doubted.

And Jesus came and spake unto them, saying, *"All power is given unto me in heaven and in earth.*

"Go ye into all the world, and preach the gospel to every creature.

"He that believeth and is baptized shall be saved; but he that believeth not shall be damned.

"And these signs shall follow them that believe; In my name shall they cast out devils; they shall speak with new tongues;

"They shall take up serpents, and if they drink any deadly thing, it shall not hurt them; they shall lay hands on the sick, and they shall recover.

"Go ye therefore, and teach all nations, baptizing them in the name of the Father, and of the Son, and of the Holy Ghost:

"Teaching them to observe all things whatsoever I have commanded you: and lo, I am with you alway, even unto the end of the world. Amen."

Part VIII – The Lord's Supper: Farewell Address: Crucifixion and Resurrection

So then after the Lord had spoken unto them, He was received up into heaven, and sat on the right hand of God.

And they went forth, and preached everywhere, the Lord working with them and confirming the word with signs following. Amen.

Jesus Charges Peter to Feed His Sheep

After these things Jesus showed himself again to the disciples at the sea of Tiberias; and on this wise shewed himself.

There were together Simon Peter, and Thomas called Didymus, and Nathanael of Cana in Galilee, and the sons of Zebedee, and two other of his disciples.

They fished all day; and that night caught nothing.

But when the morning was now come, Jesus stood on the shore: but the disciples knew not that it was Jesus.

Then Jesus saith unto them, *"Children have ye any meat?"* They answered him, No.

And he said unto them, *"Cast the net on the right side of the ship, and ye shall find."* They cast therefore, and now they were not able to draw it for the multitude of fishes.

Jesus saith unto them, *"Bring of the fish which ye have now caught."*

Simon Peter went up, and drew the net to land full of great fishes, an hundred and fifty and three: and for all there were so many, yet was not the net broken.

Jesus saith unto them, *"Come and dine."* And none of the disciples durst ask him. Who art thou? knowing that it was the Lord.

Jesus then cometh, and taketh bread, and giveth them, and fish likewise.

Part VIII – The Lord's Supper: Farewell Address: Crucifixion and Resurrection

This is now the third time that Jesus shewed himself to his disciples, after that he was risen from the dead.

So when they had dined, Jesus saith to Simon Peter, *"Simon, son of Jonas, lovest thou me more than these?"* He saith unto him, Yea, Lord; thou knowest that I love thee. Jesus saith unto him, *"Feed my lambs."*

He saith unto him again the second time, *"Simon, son of Jonas lovest thou me?"* He saith unto him, Yea, Lord; thou knowest that I love thee. He saith unto him, *"Feed my sheep."*

Jesus saith unto him the third time,

"Simon, son of Jonas lovest thou me?" Peter was grieved because he said unto him the third time, Lovest thou me? And he said unto him, Lord, thou knowest all things; thou knowest that I love thee. Jesus saith unto him, *"Feed my sheep.*

"Verily, verily, I say unto thee, When thou wast young, thou girdedst thyself, and walkedst whither thou wouldest: but when thou shalt be old, thou shalt stretch forth thy hands, and another shall gird thee, and carry thee whither thou wouldest not."

This spake he, signifying by what death he should glorify God. And when he had spoken this, he saith unto him, *"Follow me."*

Then Peter, turning about, seeth the disciples whom Jesus loved following; which also leaned on his breast at supper, and said Lord, which is he that betrayeth thee?

Peter seeing him saith to Jesus, Lord, and what shall this man do?

Jesus saith unto him, *"If I will that he tarry till I come, what is that to thee? follow thou me."*

Then went this saying abroad among the brethren, that that disciple should not die: yet Jesus said not unto him, He shall not die; but,

"If I will that he tarry till I come, what is that to thee?"

This is the disciple which testifieth, of these things and wrote these things: and we know that his testimony is true.

Part VIII – The Lord's Supper: Farewell Address: Crucifixion and Resurrection

NOTES: Scriptures of the Topics	Matt.	Mark	Luke	John
- Jesus reveals himself to Mary Magdalene				20:15-17
- Jesus meets with Mary Magdalene and Mary mother of James	28:9,10		24:7	
- Jesus appears to the ten disciples (Thomas absent)				20:19-23
- Jesus converses with two disciples and they don't recognize him			24:17,19 25,26	
- Jesus appears to the eleven disciples			24:36, 38-49	20:26-31
- Jesus commands the eleven to teach all nations	28:18-20	16:15-18	24:47	
- Jesus charges Peter to feed His sheep				21:15-23

Doctrines and Commandments

433. Jesus reveals Himself to various people before He ascends to His Father.

413. Jesus ascends unto His Father, and your Father, and to His God and your God.

434. Christ Jesus appears and gives commandments, teachings, and directions to His disciples and followers after His resurrection and ascension.

435. God sends Jesus to His disciples and as the Father sends Jesus; even so Jesus the Christ sends you.

436. Receiving the Holy Ghost, Christ gave them authority to remit and retain sin, *"Whosoever sins ye remit, they are remitted unto them; and whosoever sins ye retain, they are retained."*

437. Christ Jesus has His physical body after the resurrection.

He appeared to his disciples in His physical body of flesh, and to get them to believe Him He had them touch Him and He ate a meal with them (See Lk. 24:38-43)

Part VIII – The Lord's Supper: Farewell Address: Crucifixion and Resurrection

438. Christ gives us instructions to go into all the world and preach the gospel to every creature. (See also Doctrine 75:1-27)

439. Repentance and remission of sins should be preached in His name among all nations, beginning at Jerusalem.

440. Signs will follow those who believe: In Christ's name they shall cast out devils; they shall speak with new tongues; They shall take up serpents; and if they drink any deadly thing, it shall not hurt them; they shall lay hands on the sick and they shall recover.

441. Go ye therefore, and teach all nations, baptizing them in the name of the Father, and of the Son, and of the Holy Ghost (see also Doctrine 75:1-27).

442. He that believeth and is baptized shall be saved; but he that believeth not shall be damned.

443. Teaching them to observe all things whatsoever I have commanded you: and lo I am with you alway, even unto the end of the world.

444. Whither I go, thou canst not follow Me now; but thou shalt follow Me afterwards.

445. Christ's words and works came to pass that the laws and scriptures might be fulfilled. *"These are the words which I spake unto you while I was yet with you, that all things must be fulfilled, which were written in the law of Moses, and in the prophets, and in psalms, concerning me."*

446. It behooved Christ to suffer and to rise from the dead the third day thus it is written.

447. All power is given to Christ Jesus in heaven and on earth.

448. Jesus sends the promise of His Father upon you, and you are endued with power from on high.

449. Witness of Christ and you are witness of these things. (See also Doctrine 59)

450. Baptism and receiving the Holy Ghost: Christ Jesus

breathed on His disciples and they received the Holy Ghost.

451. Christ reminds us to believe all that the prophets have spoken; that He was to have suffered these things, and to enter into His glory.

452. Christ Jesus has power from God to resurrect His body:

"Therefore, doth my Father love me." This doctrine was hard for some of the disciples to believe—they had to touch him and see him eat. (See also Doctrine 55)

Part VIII – The Lord's Supper: Farewell Address: Crucifixion and Resurrection

Lessons We Should Learn

1.   Our hearts should be quick to know that Jesus is the Christ of this world and all mankind, and that all power is given to Him in heaven and on earth.

2.   Our knowledge that Christ's words and works came to pass, that the laws and the scriptures might be fulfilled, that He did suffer these things, that He did enter into His glory, and that He did ascend unto His Father brings joy and light to the hearts of man.

3.   Christ Jesus entering into His glory did bring light unto mankind that He did resurrect His body of flesh and bone. He ascended unto our Heavenly Father, our God, thus proving that there is eternal and everlasting life and that we are witnesses to these things in His word.

4.   The fact that Christ Jesus did enter into His power and glory shows that His work was not finished for He appears and gives commandments, teachings, and directions to His disciples and followers after His resurrection and ascension.

5.   Christ Jesus gives His followers, believers and disciples instructions to go into all the world and preach the gospel to every creature. God sends Jesus to His disciples and as the Father sends Jesus, even so Jesus the Christ sends you. An important doctrine is: Teach them to observe all things whatsoever I have commanded. So we are not ready to enter into our glory until we can follow His commandments and complete that which He has for each of us to do.

6.   God prepares us to do His will. Jesus sends the promise of His Father upon you, that you may receive the Holy Ghost, and you be endued with power from on high. Jesus says,

"Go ye therefore, and teach all nations, baptizing them in the name of the Father, and of the Son, and of the Holy Ghost. He that believeth and is baptized shall be saved; but he that believeth not shall be damned."

7.   Christ comforts us while we do His will and receive the Holy Ghost and believe on Him, for He is with us always, even unto the end of the world. He says, *"Lo, I am with you alway, even unto the end of the world."* (Matt. 28:20)

Part VIII – The Lord's Supper: Farewell Address: Crucifixion and Resurrection

My Thoughts About the Lessons

_____

_____

_____

_____

_____

_____

_____

_____

_____

_____

_____

_____

_____

_____

_____

_____

_____

_____

_____

_____

_____

_____

44

Baptism of the Holy Ghost: The Promise of the Father

Knowledge of God's Power

Until the day in which he was taken up, after that he through the Holy Ghost had given commandments unto the apostles whom he had chosen:

To whom also he shewed himself alive after his passion by many infallible proofs, being seen of them forty days and speaking of the things pertaining to the kingdom of God:

And, being assembled together with them, commanded them that they should not depart from Jerusalem, but wait for the promise of the Father, *"which,"* saith he, *"ye have heard of me.*

"For John truly baptized with water; but ye shall be baptized with the Holy Ghost not many days hence."

When they therefore were come together, they asked of him, saying, Lord, wilt thou at this time restore again the kingdom of Israel?

And he said unto them, *"It is not for you to know the times or the seasons, which the Father hath put in his own power."*

Followers of Christ Will Be Given the Power of the Father; After that, the Holy Ghost is Come Upon Them

"But ye shall receive power, after that the Holy Ghost is come upon you."

Part IX – Jesus the Christ Continues His Mission After His Resurrection and Ascension

We Shall be Witnesses unto Christ unto the Uttermost Part of the Earth

"And ye shall be witnesses unto me both in Jerusalem, and in Judaea, and in Samaria, and unto the uttermost part of the earth."

And when he had spoken these things while they beheld, he was taken up; and a cloud received him out of their sight.

And while they looked steadfastly toward heaven as he went up, behold, two men stood by them in white apparel;

Which also said, Ye men of Galilee, why stand ye gazing up into heaven? This same Jesus, which is taken up from you into heaven, shall so come in like manner as ye have seen him go into heaven.

NOTES: Scriptures of the Topics	Acts
- Baptism of the Holy Ghost: The promise of the Father	1:4-8
- Followers of Christ will be given the power of the Father	1:8
- We shall be witnesses unto Christ unto the uttermost part of the earth	1:8

Doctrines and Commandments

453. Baptism of the Holy Ghost is a promise from God the Father.

454. Followers of Christ will be given the power from God and then the Holy Ghost is upon them.

455. Christ Jesus commands His followers to be a witness unto Him unto the uttermost part of the earth. (See also Doctrine 59)

Part IX – Jesus the Christ Continues His Mission After His Resurrection and Ascension

Lessons We Should Learn

1.   If one seeks to be a true disciple and follower of Christ Jesus, then baptism by water and by the Holy Ghost is fulfillment of the promise of our Heavenly Father.

2.   God, our Heavenly Father, gives us his power and sends the Holy Ghost upon us.

3.   What a blessing to be chosen to witness unto Christ Jesus.

How many of us are prepared to go unto the uttermost part of the earth to witness unto him; and to know his teachings (doctrines) and commandments, and to testify to others the Truth and Light therein by living them daily?

Part IX — Jesus the Christ Continues His Mission After His Resurrection and Ascension

My Thoughts About the Lessons

_____

_____

_____

_____

_____

_____

_____

_____

_____

_____

_____

_____

_____

_____

_____

_____

_____

_____

_____

_____

_____

_____

Part IX – Jesus the Christ Continues His Mission After His Resurrection and Ascension

45

The Christed Jesus Speaks to Saul

Christ asks Saul, *"Why persecute me?"*

A nd Saul, yet breathing out threatenings and slaughter against the disciples of the Lord, went unto the high priest,

And desired of him letters to Damascus to the synagogues, that if he found any of this way, whether they were men or women, he might bring them bound unto Jerusalem.

And as he journeyed, he came near Damascus: and suddenly there shined round about him a light from heaven:

And he fell to the earth, and heard a voice saying unto him,

"Saul, Saul, why persecutest thou me?"

And he said, Who art thou, Lord? And the Lord said,

"I am Jesus whom thou persecutest: it is hard for thee to kick against the pricks."

And he trembling and astonished said,

Lord, what wilt thou have me to do?

And the Lord said unto him,
"Arise and go into the city, and it shall be told thee what thou must do."

And the men which journeyed with him stood speechless, hearing a voice, but seeing no man.

Part IX – Jesus the Christ Continues His Mission After His Resurrection and Ascension

And Saul arose from the earth; and when his eyes were opened, he saw no man: but they led him by the hand, and brought him into Damascus.

And he was three days without sight, and neither did he eat or drink.

Jesus Speaks to Disciple Ananias in a Vision

And there was a certain disciple at Damascus, named Ananias; and to him said the Lord in a vision, *"Ananias."* And he said, Behold, I am here, Lord.

And the Lord said unto him,

"Arise, and go into the street which is called Straight, and enquire in the house of Judas for one called Saul, of Tarsus: for, behold he prayeth,

"And hath seen in a vision a man named Ananias coming in, and putting his hand on him, that he might receive his sight."

Then Ananias answered, Lord, I have heard by many of this man, how much evil he hath done to thy saints in Jerusalem: And here he hath authority from the chief priests to bind all that call on thy name.

Christ Chooses Saul to Be a Vessel unto Him

But the Lord said unto him, *"Go thy way: for he is a chosen vessel unto me, to bear my name before the Gentiles, and the kings, and the children of Israel:*

"For I will show him how great things he must suffer for my name's sake."

And Ananias went his way, and entered into the house; and putting his hands on him said, Brother Saul, the Lord, even Jesus, that appeared unto thee in the way as thou camest, hath sent me, that thou mightest receive thy sight and be filled with the Holy Ghost.

And immediately there fell from his eyes as it had been scales: and he received sight forthwith, and arose, and was baptized.

Then was Saul certain days with the disciples which were at Damascus.

And straightway he preached Christ in the synagogues, that he is the Son of God.

Part IX – Jesus the Christ Continues His Mission After His Resurrection and Ascension

NOTES: Scriptures of the Topics   <u>Acts</u>

- Christ asks Saul; *"Why persecute me?"*   9:4-6
- Jesus speaks to Disciple Ananias in a vision   9:10-12
- Christ chooses Saul to be a vessel unto Him   9:15,16

Doctrines and Commandments

456. Christ Jesus appeared and gave commandments, teachings, and directions to His disciples and followers after His resurrection and ascension.

Lessons We Should Learn

1.   Christ Jesus did not end his work on earth with his ascension. He is alive and works with His sheep, His followers, His children.

2.   Christ chooses whom He will; one is blessed to experience a vision or to hear His voice from Him, the Holy Spirit, or His angels.

3.   Others than his remaining eleven disciples had visions and heard his voice and Christ Jesus gave them the gift to experience it.

4.   Those that are chosen go forth and preach and tell of Christ Jesus and His teachings.

5.   Jesus did know of Paul and what he was doing to Christian believers and where he was traveling. So it is, that Jesus knows those very details about each of us each day, where we are and what we are doing. One can look within to see it or he or she would keep doing things not of the Lord until He calls us as He did Paul and say, *"I am Jesus whom thou persecutest: it is hard for thee to kick against the pricks."*

Note: Paul, being not a believer of Jesus Christ, noticed who answered him when he asked, Who art thou Lord?

Part IX – Jesus the Christ Continues His Mission After His Resurrection and Ascension

My Thoughts About the Lessons

Part IX — Jesus the Christ Continues His Mission After His Resurrection and Ascension

46

Jesus Speaks to Paul in a Vision

God Granted to the Gentiles Repentance unto Life

After Christ chose Paul to be a vessel unto him and Paul preached in the synagogues at Damascus that Jesus is the Son of God; then he went to Jerusalem to join with the disciples.

During that time the churches throughout all Judaea and Galilee and Samaria, were edified: and walking in the fear of the Lord, and in the comfort of the Holy Ghost were multiplied.

And it came to pass, as Peter passed throughout all quarters he tarried many days in Joppa with one Simon a tanner. While there, Peter went up upon the housetop to pray, and he fell into a trance.

And saw heaven opened, and a certain vessel descending unto him, as it had been it had been a great sheet knit at the four corners, and let down to the earth:

Wherein were all manner of four footed beasts of the earth, and wild beasts, and creeping things, and fowls of the air.

And there came a voice to him, *"Rise, Peter; kill, and eat."*

But Peter said, Not so, Lord: for I have never eaten anything that is common or unclean.

And the voice spake unto him again the second time from heaven, *"What God hath cleansed, that call not thou common."*

The spirit bade Peter to go with men to Caesarea into a man's house: to tell words whereby all the house shall be saved.

Part IX – Jesus the Christ Continues His Mission After His Resurrection and Ascension

And as I began to speak, the Holy Ghost fell on them, as on us at the beginning.

Then remembered I the word of the Lord, how that he said, *"John indeed baptized with water; but ye shall be baptized with the Holy Ghost."*

When they heard these things, they held their peace, and glorified God saying, Then hath God also to the Gentiles granted repentance unto life.

Be Not Afraid, But Speak and Hold Not Thy Peace

After these things Paul departed from Athens, and came to Corinth: and he reasoned in the synagogue every Sabbath, and persuaded the Jews and the Greeks.

And when Silas and Timotheus were come from Macedonia, Paul was pressed in the Spirit, and testified to the Jews that Jesus was Christ.

And he departed thence, and entered into a certain man's house, named Justus, one that worshipped God, whose house joined hard to the synagogue.

Then spake the Lord to Paul in the night by a vision,

"Be not afraid, but speak, and hold not thy peace:

"For I am with thee, and no man shall set on thee to hurt thee: for I have much people in this city."

And he continued there a year and six months, teaching the word of God among them.

Jesus Reminds Paul; It is More Blessed to Give Than to Receive

Paul was testifying both to the Jews and also to the Greeks, repentance toward God, and faith toward our Lord Jesus Christ. I have showed you all things, how that so labouring ye ought to support the weak, and to remember the words of the Lord Jesus, how he said, *"It is more blessed to give than to receive."*

And when he had thus spoken, Paul kneeled down, and prayed with them all.

Part IX – Jesus the Christ Continues His Mission After His Resurrection and Ascension

Paul Tells the People When He heard Christ's Voice

And it came to pass, that, as I made my journey, and was come nigh unto Damascus about noon, suddenly there shone from heaven a great light round about me.

And I fell unto the ground, and heard a voice saying unto me, *"Saul, Saul, why persecutest thou me?"*

And I answered, Who art thou Lord? And he said unto me, *"I am Jesus of Nazareth, whom thou persecutest."*

And they that were with me saw indeed the light. And were afraid; but they heard not the voice of him that spake to me.

And I said, What shall I do Lord? And the Lord said unto me,

"Arise, and go into Damascus; and there it shall be told thee of all things which are appointed for thee to do."

And when I could not see for the glory of that light, being led by the hand of them that were with me, I came into Damascus.

A certain disciple Ananias, came unto me, and stood, and said unto me, Brother Saul, receive thy sight. And the same hour I looked up upon him.

And he said, The God of our fathers hath chosen thee, that thou shouldest know his will, and see that just one, and shouldest hear the voice of his mouth.

For thou shalt be his witness unto all men of what thou hast seen and heard.

Part IX – Jesus the Christ Continues His Mission After His Resurrection and Ascension

Jesus Speaks to Paul When He Was in a Trance
While He Prayed in the Temple

And it came to pass, that, when I was come again to Jerusalem, even while I prayed in the temple, I was in a trance; And saw him saying unto me,

"Make haste, and get thee quickly out of Jerusalem: for they will not receive thy testimony concerning me."

And I said, Lord, they know that I imprisoned and beat in every Synagogue them that believed on thee:

And when the blood of thy martyr Stephen washed, I also was standing by, and consenting unto his death, and kept the raiment of them that slew him.

And he said unto me, *"Depart: for I will send thee far hence unto the Gentiles."*

And they gave him audience unto this word, and then lifted up their voices, and said, Away with such a fellow from the earth: for it is not fit that he should live.

Jesus Tells Paul to Be of Good Cheer

And Paul, earnestly beholding the council, said, Men and brethren, I have lived in all good conscience before God until this day.

And when he had reported to the council, there arose a dissension between the Pharisees and the Sadducees: and the multitude was divided.

For the Sadducees say that there is no resurrection, neither angel, nor spirit: but the Pharisees confess both.

And when there arose a great dissension, the chief Roman captain, fearing lest Paul should have pulled in pieces of them, commanded the soldiers to go down, and to take him by force from among them, and to bring him into the castle.

Part IX – Jesus the Christ Continues His Mission After His Resurrection and Ascension

And the night following the Lord stood by him, and said, *"Be of good cheer, Paul: for as thou hast testified of me in Jerusalem, so must thou bear witness also at Rome."*

And when it was day, certain of the Jews banded together, and bound themselves under a curse, saying that they would neither eat nor drink till they had killed Paul.

NOTES: Scriptures of the Topics	<u>Acts</u>
- God granted to the Gentiles repentance unto life	10:13-15 11:7-18
- Jesus speaks to Paul in a vision and tells him to be not afraid, but to speak and hold not thy peace	18:9,10
- Jesus reminds Paul that it is more blessed to give than to receive	20:35
- Paul tells the people when he heard Christ's voice	22:7-10
- Jesus speaks to Paul when he was in a trance while he prayed in the temple	22:18-21
- Jesus tells Paul to be of good cheer	23:11

Doctrines and Commandments

457. Christ Jesus appears and gives commandments, teachings and directions to His disciples and followers after His resurrection and ascension. Jesus appears to Paul in a vision.

458. Christ makes his voice and directions known to Peter and to Paul. While in a trance they each can hear the Lord's voice. (See also Doctrine 436)

459. Jesus has power to be present and to protect one from another.

460. It is more blessed to give than receive.

Part IX – Jesus the Christ Continues His Mission After His Resurrection and Ascension

Lessons We Should Learn

1.   Christ's mission for his children and followers and the people of the world did not end with his ascension.

2.   Those who are chosen by Christ—such as Peter and other disciples and followers, and as Paul, who was at the time a sinner—may be blessed to hear and see Christ, or what Christ Jesus wants us to see or hear.

3.   The feeling of giving, such as at Christmas, but in a true spiritual sense instead of the materialistic sense or ritual, is one of the warmest and true blessings one may perceive and experience when it is truly from one's heart.

4.   The Lord tells Paul to be of good cheer; what joy one must have to be handpicked, as Paul was, to testify and witness for Christ. Our daily life is an open book and should be testifying for him in our every action, word, and thought.

Part IX – Jesus the Christ Continues His Mission After His Resurrection and Ascension

My Thoughts About the Lessons

_____

_____

_____

_____

_____

_____

_____

_____

_____

_____

_____

_____

_____

_____

_____

_____

_____

_____

_____

_____

_____

_____

_____

NOTES

Part IX – Jesus the Christ Continues His Mission After His Resurrection and Ascension

47

Paul Reports Christ's Words to Roman King Agrippa and Directs Timothy to Teach Christ's Doctrines

Then said Paul, I stand at Caesar's judgment seat, where I ought to be judged: to the Jews have I done no wrong, as thou very well knowest.

For if I be an offender, or have committed any thing worthy of death, I refuse not to die: but if there be none of these things whereof these accuse me, no man may deliver me unto them. I appeal unto Caesar.

When Paul had appealed to be reserved unto the hearing of Augustus he was commanded to be kept until he might be sent to Caesar.

Then King Agrippa said, I would also hear the man myself. Tomorrow, said he, thou shalt hear him.

At the hearing, King Agrippa said unto Paul, Thou art permitted to speak for thyself. Then Paul stretched forth the hand, and answered for himself.

Whereupon as I went to Damascus with authority and commission from the chief priests, At midday O king, I saw in the way a light from heaven, above the brightness of the sun, shining round about me and them which journeyed with me.

And when we were all fallen to the earth, I heard a voice speaking unto me, and saying in Hebrew tongue, *"Saul, Saul, why persecutest thou me? it is hard for thee to kick against the pricks."*

And I said, Who art thou, Lord? And he said, *"I am Jesus whom thou persecutest.*

"But rise, and stand upon thy feet: for I have appeared unto thee for this purpose, to make thee a minister and a witness both of these things which thou hast seen, and of those things in the which I will appear unto thee;

Part IX – Jesus the Christ Continues His Mission After His Resurrection and Ascension

"Delivering thee from the people, and from the Gentiles, unto whom now I send thee,

"To open their eyes, and to turn them from darkness to light, and from the power of Satan unto God, that they may receive forgiveness of sins, and inheritance among them which are sanctified by faith that is in me."

Whereupon, O king Agrippa, I was not disobedient unto the heavenly vision: But shewed first unto them of Damascus, and at Jerusalem, and throughout all the coasts of Judaea, and then to the Gentiles, that they should repent and turn to God, and do works meet for repentance.

For these causes the Jews caught me in the temple, and went about to kill me.

Having therefore obtained help of God, I continue unto this day, witnessing both to small and great, saying none other things than those which the prophets and Moses did say should come:

That Christ should suffer, and that he should be the first that should rise from the dead, and should shew light unto the people, and to the Gentiles.

Then Agrippa said unto Paul, Almost thou persuadest me to be a Christian.

And Paul said, I would to God, that not only thou, but also all that hear me this day, were both almost, and altogether such as I am, except these bonds.

Then said Agrippa unto Festus, This man might have been set of liberty, if he had not appealed unto Caesar.

Part IX – Jesus the Christ Continues His Mission After His Resurrection and Ascension

Paul Takes Pleasure in Infirmities, in Reproaches, in Necessities, in Persecutions, in Distresses for Christ's Sake

As Paul did minister to the followers of Christ in the churches in Corinth, Macedonia and the regions of Achaia, he wrote that, It is not expedient for me doubtless to glory. I will come to visions and revelations of the Lord.

For though I would desire to glory, I shall not be a fool; for I will say the truth; but now I forbear, lest any man should think of me above that which he seeth me to be, or that he heareth of me.

And lest I should be exalted above measure through the abundance of the revelations, there was given to me a thorn in the flesh, the messenger of Satan to buffet me, lest I should be exalted above measure.

For this thing I besought the Lord thrice, that it might depart from me.

And he said unto me, *"My grace is sufficient for thee: for my strength is made perfect in weakness."* Most gladly therefore will I, Paul, rather glory in my infirmities, that the power of Christ may rest upon me.

Therefore I take pleasure in infirmities, in reproaches, in necessities, in persecutions, in distresses for Christ's sake: for when I am weak, then am I strong.

And lest, when I come again, my God will humble me among you, and that I shall bewail many which have sinned already, and have not repented of the uncleanness and fornication and lasciviousness which they have committed.

Paul Advises Timothy to Labor in the Word and Doctrine of Christ Jesus

In the first epistle of Paul the apostle, to Timothy, Paul teaches Timothy to let the elders, of the early churches, that rule well be counted worthy of double honour, especially they who labour in the word and doctrine.

For the scripture saith, Thou shalt not muzzle the ox that treadeth out the corn. And, *"The labourer is worthy of his reward."*

Part IX – Jesus the Christ Continues His Mission After His Resurrection and Ascension

NOTES: Scriptures of the Topics   Acts

- Saul, Saul, why persecutest thou me?   26:14
- I am Jesus whom thou persecutest   26:15
- Jesus appeared to Paul to make him a   26:16
minister and witness
- Jesus delivers Paul from the people and   26:17
now sends him to them
- Christ sends Paul to the people to: 26:18
1. Open their eyes
2. Turn them unto God
3. Turn them from the darkness and power of Satan
4. That they may receive forgiveness of sins
5. That they will be sanctified by faith that is in   Christ Jesus

	II Cor.	I Tim
- Paul takes pleasure in infirmities, in reproaches, in necessities, in persecutions, in distresses for Christ's sake	12:6-21	
- Paul advises Timothy to labor in the word and doctrine of Christ Jesus		5:17,18

Part IX – Jesus the Christ Continues His Mission After His Resurrection and Ascension

Doctrines and Commandments

461. Christ Jesus chose Paul and opened his eyes and had a special mission for him.

462. Christ Jesus does appear to special people, even sinners as

Paul was, for certain purposes and personal guidance.

Lessons We Should Learn

1.   Jesus the Christ does appear to people then and now and he has special purposes for each one.

2.   Jesus chose his followers, his disciples, his sheep, his children; but one must obey. As Paul became Christ's apostle, he, Paul, chose to follow Christ wherever he was sent and to do whatever Christ wanted him to do.

3.   The purposes that Christ Jesus gave to Paul and those who minister and witness of Jesus the Christ is to: turn them from darkness to light; that they may receive forgiveness of sins; and inheritance among them which are sanctified by faith that is in Jesus Christ.

4.   As we study the words and doctrines of Christ Jesus, we are worthy of our reward. That reward is to know the truth that Jesus teaches in his words about God, about Jesus and about ourselves and about our oneness with them, in life everlasting. All does manifest from God our Heavenly Father and His blessings!

Part IX – Jesus the Christ Continues His Mission After His Resurrection and Ascension

My Thoughts About the Lessons

_____

_____

_____

_____

_____

_____

_____

_____

_____

_____

_____

_____

_____

_____

_____

_____

_____

_____

_____

_____

_____

_____

_____

_____

_____

Part X – The Revelation

48

Christ Jesus Speaks to St. John When John Was in Spirit

"*I am Alpha and Omega, the beginning and the ending,*" saith the Lord, "*which is, and which was, and which is to come, the Almighty.*"

I John, who also am your brother, and companion in tribulation, and in the kingdom and patience of Jesus Christ, was in the isle that is called Patmos, for the word of God, and for the testimony or Jesus Christ.

I was in the Spirit on the Lord's day and heard behind me a great voice, as of a trumpet.

Christ the First and the Last

The great voice saying,

"I am Alpha and Omega, the first and the last: and, What thou seest, write in a book, and send it unto the seven churches which are in Asia: unto Ephesus, and unto Smyrna, and unto Pergamos, and unto Thyatira, and unto Sardis, and unto Philadelphia and unto Laodicea."

And I turned to see the voice that spake with me. And being turned, I saw seven golden candlesticks;

And in the midst of the seven candlesticks one like unto the Son of man, clothed with a garment down to the foot, and girt about the paps with a golden girdle.

His head and his hairs were white like wool, as white as snow; and his eyes were as a flame of fire;

And his feet like unto fine brass, as if they burned in a furnace; and his voice as the sound of many waters.

Part X – The Revelation

And he had in his right hand seven stars: and out of his mouth went a sharp two edged sword: and his countenance was as the sun shineth in his strength. And when I saw him, I fell at his feet as dead. And he laid his right hand upon me, saying unto me, *"Fear not; I am the first and the last:"*

Christ Jesus Is Alive For Evermore
He Has the Keys of Hell and of Death

"I am he that liveth, and was dead; and, behold, I am alive for evermore, Amen; and have the keys of hell and of death."

Jesus Tells John to Write What He Sees In a Book
And Send it to the Seven Churches

"Write the things which thou hast seen, and the things which are, and the things which shall be hereafter;
"

What thou seest, write in a book, and send it unto the seven churches which are in Asia:

"Unto Ephesus, and unto Smyrna, and unto Pergamos, and unto Thyatira, and unto Sardis, and unto Philadelphia and

unto Laodicea."

The Seven Stars and the Seven Candlesticks

"The mystery of the seven stars which thou sawest in my right hand, and the seven golden candle sticks. The seven stars are the angels of the seven churches: and the seven candle sticks which thou sawest are the seven churches."

Part X – The Revelation

NOTES: Scriptures of the Topics   <u>Revelation</u>

- Christ is the first and the last   1:8,11,17
- Christ Jesus is alive for evermore: he has   1:18
the keys of hell and of death
- Jesus tells John to write what he sees in a book   1:11,19
and send it to the seven churches
- The seven stars and the seven candlesticks   1:20

Doctrines and Commandments

463. Christ Jesus is the beginning and the end; the first and the last.

464. Christ Jesus speaks to his disciples when they are in spirit.

465. Christ Jesus is alive for evermore and he has the keys of hell and of death.

466. Jesus the Christ tells his disciple John to write what he sees in a book and send it to the seven churches in Asia.

467. Christ Jesus has an angel for each church of the seven in Asia.

468. Christ Jesus uses symbols, stars, and candlesticks, in what he has John to see. The stars symbolize the angels of the seven churches and the candlesticks symbolize the seven churches.

Lessons We Should Learn

1.   We should learn that Jesus the Christ speaks to his disciples and shows them things and he has specific commandments that he gave for them to write, after his resurrection and ascension. These writings are for us to search and to see the light and the truth in the churches and to see the things in the churches that are wrong and falling short; for Jesus speaks of things in the churches that he is against. He is telling us about them and we should heed his warnings and repent.

2.   Jesus is the Christ, he is alive for evermore and he has the keys of hell and of death for he has ascended.

3.   Jesus the Christ is the true expression, image, and manifestation of God the Father, for he is the beginning and the end, the first and the last. There is not truth and light before or after him and his words.

Part X – The Revelation

My Thoughts About the Lessons

_____

_____

_____

_____

_____

_____

_____

_____

_____

_____

_____

_____

_____

_____

_____

_____

_____

_____

_____

_____

_____

_____

_____

_____

_____

Part X – The Revelation

49

Christ's Messages to the Seven Churches

Unto the Angel of the Church of Ephesus

"*Unto the angel of the church of Ephesus write: These things saith he that holdeth the seven stars in his right hand, who walketh in the midst of the seven golden candlesticks;*

"*I know thy works, and thy labour, and thy patience, and how thou canst not bear them which are evil: and thou hast tried them which say they are apostles, and are not, and hast found them liars:*

"*And hast borne, and hast patience, and for my name's sake hast laboured, and hast not fainted.*

"*Nevertheless I have somewhat against thee, because thou hast left thy first love.*

"*Remember therefore from whence thou art fallen, and repent, and do the first works; or else I will come out unto thee quickly, and will remove thy candlestick out of his place, except thou repent.*

"*But this thou hast, that thou hatest the deeds of the Nicolaitanes, which I also hate.*

"*He that hath an ear, let him hear what the Spirit saith unto the churches; To him that overcometh will I give to eat of the tree of life, which is in the midst of the paradise of God.*"

Part X – The Revelation

Unto the Angel of the Church in Smyrna

"And unto the angel of the church in Smyrna write; These things saith the first and the last, which was dead, and is alive;

"I know thy works, and tribulation, and poverty, (but thou art rich) and I know the blasphemy of them which say they are Jews, and are not, but are the synagogue of Satan.

"Fear none of those things which thou shalt suffer: behold, the devil shall cast some of you into prison, that ye may be tried; and ye shall have tribulation ten days: be thou faithful unto death, and I will give thee a crown of life.

"He that hath an ear, let him hear what the Spirit saith unto the churches: He that overcometh shall not be hurt of the second death."

Unto the Angel of the Church in Pergamos

"And to the angel of the Church in Pergamos write: These things saith he which hath the sharp sword with two edges;

"I know thy works, and where thou dwellest, even where Satan's seat is: and thou holdest fast my name, and hast not denied my faith, even in those days wherein Antipas was my faithful martyr, who was slain among you, where Satan dwelleth.

"But I have a few things against thee, because thou hast there them that hold the doctrine of Balaam, who taught Balac to cast a stumbling block before the children of Israel, to eat things sacrificed unto idols, and to commit fornication.

"So hast thou also them that hold the doctrine of the Nicolaitanes, which thing I hate.

"Repent; or else I will come unto thee quickly, and will fight against them with the sword of my mouth.

"He that hath an ear, let him hear what the Spirit saith unto the churches; To him that overcometh will I give to eat of the hidden manna, and will give him a white stone, and in the stone a new name written, which no man knoweth saving he that receiveth it."

Part X – The Revelation

Unto the Angel of the Church in Thyatira

"And unto the angel of the church in Thyatira write; These things saith the Son of God, who hath his eyes like unto a flame of fire, and his feet are like fine brass;

"I know thy works, and charity, and service, and faith, and thy patience, and thy works; and the last to be more than the first.

"Notwithstanding I have a few things against thee, because thou sufferest that woman Jezebel, which calleth herself a prophetess, to teach and to seduce my servants to commit fornication, and to eat things sacrificed unto idols.

"And I gave her space to repent of her fornication; and she repented not.
"Behold, I will cast her into a bed, and them that commit adultery with her into great tribulation, except they repent of their deeds.

"And I will kill her children with death; and all the churches shall know that I am he which searcheth the reins and hearts: and I will give unto every one of you according to your works.

"But unto you I say, and unto the rest in Thyatira, as many as have not this doctrine, and which have not known the depths of Satan, as they speak; I will put upon you none other burden.

"But that which ye have already hold fast till I come. "And he that overcometh, and keepeth my works unto the end, to him will I give power over the nations:

"And he shall rule them with a rod of iron; as the vessels of a potter shall they be broken to shivers: even as I received of my Father.

"And I will give him the morning star.

"He that hath an ear, let him hear what the Spirit saith unto the churches."

Part X – The Revelation

Unto the Angel of the Church in Sardis

"And unto the angel of the church in Sardis write; These things saith he that hath the seven Spirits of God, and the seven stars; I know thy works, that thou hast a name that thou livest, and art dead.

"Be watchful, and strengthen the things which remain, that are ready to die: for I have not found thy works perfect before God.

"Remember therefore how thou hast received and heard, and hold fast, and repent. If therefore thou shall not watch, I will come on thee as a thief, and thou shall not know what hour I will come upon thee.

"Thou hast a few names even in Sardis which have not defiled their garments; and they shall walk with me in white: for they are worthy.

"He that overcometh, the same shall be clothed in white raiment; and I will not blot out his name out of the book of life, but I will confess his name before my Father, and before his angels.

"He that hath an ear, let him hear what the Spirit saith unto the churches."

Unto the Angel of the Church in Philadelphia

" And to the angel of the church in Philadelphia write; These things saith he that is holy, he that is true, he that hath the key of David, he that openeth, and no man shutteth; and shutteth, and no man openeth;

"I know thy works: behold, I have set before thee an open door, and no man can shut it: for thou hast a little strength, and hast kept my word, and hast not denied my name.

"Behold, I will make them of the synagogue of Satan, which say they are Jews, and are not, but do lie; behold, I will make them to come and worship before thy feet, and to know that I have loved thee.

Part X – The Revelation

"Because thou hast kept the word of my patience, I also will keep thee from the hour of temptation, which shall come upon all the world, to try them that dwell upon the earth.

"Behold, I come quickly: hold that fast which thou hast, that no man take thy crown.

"Him that overcometh will I make a pillar in the temple of my God, and he shall go no more out: and I will write upon him the name of my God, and the name of the city of my God, which is new Jerusalem, which cometh down out of heaven from my God: and I will write upon him my new name.

"He that hath an ear, let him hear what the Spirit saith unto the churches."

Unto the Angel of the Church of the Laodiceans

"And unto the angel of the church of the Laodiceans write; these things saith the Amen, the faithful and true witness, the beginning of the creation of God;

"I know thy works, that thou art neither cold nor hot: I would thou wert cold or hot.

"So then because thou art lukewarm, and neither cold nor hot, I will spue thee out of my mouth.

"Because thou sayest, I am rich, and increased with goods, and have need of nothing; and knowest not that thou art wretched, and miserable, and poor, and blind, and naked:

"I counsel thee to buy of me gold tried in the fire, that thou mayest be rich; and white raiment, that thou mayest be clothed, and that the shame of thy nakedness do not appear; and anoint thine eyes with eyesalve, that thou mayest see.

"As many as I love, I rebuke and chasten: be zealous therefore, and repent.

"Behold, I stand at the door, and knock: if any man hear my voice, and open the door, I will come in to him, and will sup with him, and he with me

"To him that overcometh will I grant to sit with me in my throne, even as I also overcame, and am set down with my Father in his throne.

"He that hath an ear, let him hear what the Spirit saith unto the churches."

Part X – The Revelation

NOTES: Scriptures of the Topics   <u>Rev.</u>

- Unto the Angel of the Church of Ephesus   2:1-7
- Unto the Angel of the Church in Smyrna   2:8-11
- Unto the Angel of the Church in Pergamos   2:12-17
- Unto the Angel of the Church in Thyatira   2:18-29
- Unto the Angel of the Church in Philadelphia   3:7-13
- Unto the Angel of the Church of the Laodiceans   3:14-22
- Unto the Angel of the Church in Sardis   3:1-6

Doctrines and Commandments

469. Churches should write the things that Christ Jesus says.

470. Christ Jesus knows the work being done in each church and he knows the wrongdoing and the areas where the church is falling short.

471. Jesus the Christ set forth specific commandments for the churches to follow. (See Commandments and Promises, and the Commandments and warnings)

472. Christ makes promises to those who overcome and keep his words. (See Commandments and Promises)

473. Christ Jesus warns the churches what will happen if they do not repent and make changes in areas that they have fallen.

474. People should have an ear to hear what the Spirit says unto the church.

475. Some members are of the Church of Satan when they are involved in blasphemy, which say they are Jews and are not.

476. Christ Jesus gives us space to repent our sins.

477. Christ knows our works.

478. Christ Jesus has set before us an open door, and no man can shut it.

479. Because they are lukewarm, Christ would spue them out of his mouth.

480. They are wretched, and miserable, and poor, and blind, and naked who say that they are rich and increased with goods and have need of nothing.

481. As many as I love, I rebuke and chasten: be zealous therefore and repent.

482. Christ Jesus stands at the door and knocks: *"if any man hear my voice, and open the door, I will come in to him, and will sup with him, and he with me."*

483. Christ Jesus has special promises to those who follow his commandments. (There are twelve commandments and promises.)

484. Christ gives warnings to those who have not kept his words, commandments and doctrines, and have fallen and have not repented.

Part X – The Revelation

Commandments and Promises

1.   To him that overcomes, I will grant to sit with me in my throne, even as I also overcame, and am set down with my Father in his throne.

2.   To him that overcame the areas where he has fallen, Christ Jesus will give to eat of the tree of life, which is in the midst of the paradise of God.

3.   Fear none of the things that they shall suffer: for the devil shall cast some of you into prison, that you may be tried and you shall have tribulation ten days: be thou faithful unto death, and I will give thee a crown of life.

4.   He that overcomes shall not be hurt of the second death.

5.   To him that overcomes I will give to eat of the hidden manna, and will give him a white stone, and in the stone a new name written, which no man knoweth saving he that receives it.

6.   He that overcomes, and keeps my works unto the end, to him will I give power over the nations:

And he shall rule them with a rod of iron; as the vessels of a potter shall they be broken to shivers: even as I receive of my Father. And I will give him the morning star.

7.   There are few which have not defiled their garments, and they shall walk with me in white: for they are worthy.

8.   He that overcomes, the same shall be clothed in white raiment; and I will not blot out his name out of the book of life, but I will confess his name before my Father and before His angels.

9.   For those who keep Christ's words and have not denied His name, He will make those of the Church of Satan, which say they are Jews, and are not, but do lie; I will make them come to worship before thy feet, and to know that I have loved thee.

10.   Because you have kept the word of my patience, I also will keep you from the hour of temptation, which shall come upon all the world, to try them that dwell upon the earth.

11.   I come quickly: Hold that fast which you have, that no man take your crown.

12.   Him that overcomes I will make a pillar in the temple of my God, and he shall go no more out: and I will write upon him the name of my God, and the name of the city of my God, which is new Jerusalem, which cometh down out of heaven from my God: and I will write upon him my new name.

Part X – The Revelation

Commandments and Warnings

1.   Remember where you are and have fallen, and to repent, and to do the first works: or else Christ Jesus will come quickly and will remove the church out of his place.

2.   Repent; or else I will come unto thee quickly and will fight against them with the sword of my mouth.

3.   Those that commit fornication and them that commit adultery will be cast into great tribulation, except they repent of their deeds. I will kill their children with death; and all the churches shall know that I am he which searches the reins and hearts: and I will give unto everyone of you according to your works.

4.   Those who have not this doctrine (of fornication and adultery) and which have not known the depth Satan, as they speak; I will put upon you no other burden. But that which you have already hold fast till I come.

5.   Be watchful, and strengthen the things which remain, that are ready to die: for I have not found thy works perfect before God.

6.   Remember therefore how you have received and heard, and hold fast, and repent. If therefore you shall not watch, I will come on you as a thief, and you shall not know what hour I will come upon you.

7.   For those who say they are rich and increased with goods and have need of nothing, I counsel you to buy of me gold tried in fire, that you mayest be rich; and white raiment, that you may be clothed, and that the shame of your nakedness do not appear; and anoint your eyes with eye salve, that you may see.

Part X – The Revelation

Lessons We Should Learn

1.   Churches and their brethren should see that the words and sayings of Christ Jesus are being expressed and fulfilled.

2.   Each church should be sure to repent and remove those things that are not right according to Christ's doctrines and commandments and make every effort to do those things that are within his light and that are pleasing to our Heavenly Father. For Jesus and God know what is going on in each church, right and wrong, and each person in the church and their leaders should know as Christ knows.

3.   Those members who sin and don't repent, as Christ works with them, they bring the Church of Satan within them.

4.   Christ is the Word, the Way, the Power, and the Light.

We should do what He says and repent and overcome our sins and the world. He has promised us many things in the kingdom of God; if we overcome as He overcame. (See Commandments and Promises)

5.   Jesus the Christ knows our works; He gives us space to repent our sins; He sets before us an open door that no man can shut; He loves each of us, but He rebukes and chastens as many as He loves. Each of us, therefore, should be zealous and repent. We must do that daily, maybe hourly, so that we won't join the Church of Satan.

6.   Jesus the Christ sets before each one of us an open door and He stands at the door and knocks: if any man hears His voice and opens the door for Him, He will come into each one of us and will sup with each one who does this. The sad lesson is that very few of us even know that He is there; then if we do know and have faith that He is there we don't have ears to hear His voice and to open the door for Him. Most feel He is far off in the distant heavens, and don't believe that He is here waiting for any one to hear His voice and open the door.

Part X – The Revelation

My Thoughts About the Lessons

Part X – The Revelation

50

Messages to Each of Us from Jesus the Christ

<u>Behold I Come Quickly</u>

And he said unto me, These sayings are faithful and true: and the Lord God of the holy prophets sent his angel to show unto his servants the things which must shortly be done.

"Behold I come quickly: blessed is he that keepeth the sayings of the prophecy of this book."

<u>My Reward to Give Every Man According as His Work Shall Be</u>

And he saith unto me, Seal not the sayings of the prophecy of this book: for the time is at hand.

He that is unjust, let him be unjust still: and he which is filthy, let him be filthy still: and he that is righteous, let him be righteous still: and he that is holy, let him be holy still.

"And behold, I come quickly; and my reward is with me, to give every man according to his work shall be.

"I am Alpha and Omega, the beginning and the end, the first and the last."

<u>Jesus Has Sent His Angel to Testify These Things in the Churches</u>

Blessed are they that do his commandments, that they may have right to the tree of life, and may enter in through the gates into the city.

For without are dogs, and sorcerers and whoremongers, and murderers, and idolaters, and whosoever loveth and maketh a lie.

"I Jesus have sent mine angel to testify unto you these things in the churches."

Part X – The Revelation

Christ Jesus the Offspring of David and the Bright and Morning Star

"I am the root and the offspring of David, and the bright and morning star."
He which testifieth these things saith,

"Surely I come quickly." Amen. Even so, come, Lord Jesus.

The grace of our Lord Jesus Christ be with you all.

Amen.

NOTES: Scriptures of the Topics	Revelation
- Behold I come quickly	22:7,12,20
- My reward to give every man according as his work shall be	22:12,13
- Jesus has sent His angel to testify these things in the churches	22:16
- Christ Jesus is the offspring of David and the bright and morning star	22:16

Doctrines and Commandments

485. Christ Jesus shall come quickly.

486. Christ Jesus has a reward for each of us; to give to every man according to what his work has been.

487. Christ Jesus is the beginning and the end; the first and the last.

488. Christ Jesus has sent his angel to testify to us the things in the churches.

489. Christ Jesus is the root and offspring of David, and the bright and morning star.

Part X – The Revelation

Lessons We Should Learn

1.   We should realize that Jesus the Christ has special promises, messages, doctrines and commandments for each of us.

2.   Jesus the Christ has the power from God the Father to give each of us rewards according to what one's work has been. Therefore, one should strive to continually do the will of God the Father.

3.   Jesus the Christ is the true expression, image, and manifestation of God the Father, for He is the beginning and the end, the first and the last. There is no truth and light before or after Him and His words.

4.   Christ Jesus has authority over an angel to send to us to testify the things in the churches.

5.   Jesus the Christ is the light of mankind, of heaven and earth from the beginning of man's early beliefs of God.

Part X – The Revelation

My Thoughts About the Lessons

_____

_____

_____

_____

_____

_____

_____

_____

_____

_____

_____

_____

_____

_____

_____

_____

_____

_____

_____

_____

_____

_____

_____

www.ingramcontent.com/pod-product-compliance
Lightning Source LLC
Chambersburg PA
CBHW081226090426
42738CB00016B/3201